Small States in World Markets

Cornell Studies in
Political Economy

EDITED BY
PETER J. KATZENSTEIN

Small States in World Markets

INDUSTRIAL POLICY IN EUROPE

PETER J. KATZENSTEIN

CORNELL UNIVERSITY PRESS

Ithaca and London

First published 1985 by Cornell University Press.

International Standard Book Number (cloth) 0-8014-1729-5
International Standard Book Number (paper) 0-8014-9326-9
Library of Congress Catalog Card Number 84-45796
Printed in the United States of America
Librarians: Library of Congress cataloging information
appears on the last page of the book.

The paper in this book is acid-free and meets the guidelines
for permanence and durability of the Committee on Production
Guidelines for Book Longevity of the Council on Library Resources.

FOR MARY

Contents

Tables

Preface

The small democracies of Western Europe pose an interesting puzzle to the social sciences. Political scientists return from their travels recording the stability that these states have discovered in their corporatist arrangements. Yet economists typically view the same countries as models of economic flexibility and market competition. Across the last five years I have been attempting to develop an argument that will resolve that conundrum. The argument I advance is conditional. It applies primarily to the small corporatist states in Europe that, because of their open economies, have been vulnerable to shifts in the world economy during the twentieth century. Political stability and economic flexibility, I argue, are not contradictory but mutually contingent.

Large industrial countries are beginning to experience an increasing economic openness and vulnerability, conditions novel to them but familiar to their small neighbors throughout modern history. In the small European states this economic openness and vulnerability have made possible corporatist arrangements that are less common among larger countries. Small states thus provide something of a model by which to judge developments in large ones.

This is one of two volumes exploring the political economy of the smaller European democracies. *Small States in World Markets* develops the argument in general terms for Scandinavia, the Low Countries, and Central Europe. *Corporatism and Change* applies it to Austria and Switzerland in particular. These two volumes show how economic openness and democratic corporatism shape the politics and policy of industrial adjustment in the small European states.

Small States in World Markets argues that the interlocking crises of the 1930s and 1940s—Depression, fascism, and World War II—fundamentally reorganized the politics of the small European states.

9

The democratic corporatism that emerged has been reinforced since the 1950s by the pressures of a liberal international economy. Flexible economic adjustment and a stable politics have been the result. History explains why the potential for reaching a political compromise between business and labor in the 1930s and 1940s was greater in the small than in the large industrial states. The politics of agriculture and religion before the Industrial Revolution explain why, in contrast to large countries, the small European states experienced a divided political Right and a reformist political Left in the nineteenth and twentieth centuries. In the last two centuries, furthermore, the small European states adopted a strategy of specialization for exports that has tended to narrow the gap between different sectors of their societies. And with the adoption of universal suffrage these states opted for systems of proportional representation rather than majority rule, thus showing an early willingness to share power among disparate political actors.

Although the small European states resemble each other in their corporatist arrangements and in the substance of their strategies of industrial adjustment, they show marked differences in the form of their politics and in the style of their policies. Today there exist two varieties of corporatism, one "liberal" and the other "social." The timing of industrialization, their experience in times of war, and the patterns of divisions in society help in explaining these differences among the small European states. In some of these states adjustment has global scope and is organized privately; in others, adjustment is national and public. The small European states thus choose different ways of combining economic flexibility and political stability, of making the requirements of international politics compatible with the requirements of domestic politics.

Among the small European states, I argue, the difference between these two variants of corporatism is greatest in Austria and Switzerland. I wrote *Corporatism and Change* hoping that strangers can paint good family portraits. Sketching the characteristic features of Austria and Switzerland yields a picture of two distant cousins, with predictable differences and unanticipated similarities. Austrian Social Democrats point proudly to the extension of their welfare state in the 1970s, while Swiss businessmen cherish their liberal market economy. Yet in both countries the search for consensus is a national passion. I have attempted to resist the temptation to contrast presumed characteristic traits, for example Swiss industriousness with Austrian indolence, and to build an argument around those presumptions. Rather, the systematic description I have chosen yields insights into the political incentives and structures that make the search for consensus in different settings so compelling. Such insight is central for understanding how the small European states cope in the international economy. It is also a modest step toward an interpretation of the substance and style of Central European politics.

Small States in World Markets states the argument in general terms. In comparing small and large industrial states, it emphasizes how historically shaped structures make possible a particular strategy of industrial adjustment. Since this argument risks overgeneralization, *Corporatism and Change* adds a detailed analysis of Austria and Switzerland. For a better understanding of Austrian and Swiss politics, I have followed the very recent history of four industries in trouble: watches in Switzerland, steel in Austria, and textiles in both. These industries differ along a number of dimensions, including the source of economic change, the process of internal differentiation, the typical economic actor, the political organization of the industry, and its political ties to other sectors. If viewed as four different settings for the politics of industry, this recent history varies in ways that help identify some of the enduring patterns of policy and politics.

These two books show how structure and process interact in politics. I have chosen to think through the implications of this interaction with varying degrees of abstraction. Doing this cuts against some established conventions in political science. Area specialty achieves intellectual clarity by exploring in great depth a political reality that is complex. Broad comparative studies typically seek to impose intellectual order by viewing reality from vantage points often deliberately chosen to contradict the core assumptions of a national culture. Since both methods serve their purpose, the canons of social science research have in recent years expressed the hope that, in the long run, both methods should be combined. At the end of my own marathon, I heartily agree.

I have tried to learn how to link the specific to the general. Familiarity with detail is necessary for drawing the connections between different parts of Austria's and Switzerland's political life, for discerning how these parts yield a distinctive structure, and for understanding how that structure regenerates itself in daily politics. The affinity in the subtitles of the two books thus attempts to convey my interests in linking macro- and microlevels of analysis. The industrial policies of the small European states result from distinctive structural constraints and opportunities. The politics of industry in Austria and Switzerland reconfirm on a daily basis the logic that informs particular choices. Thus both books argue that in tightly linking policy with politics, the small European states have made economic flexibility compatible with political stability.

In working on this project, I have relied on methods that are well tried in political science. Comparisons between small and large states, between Austria and Switzerland, and among different industries have been essential for developing my argument. Because I wanted to understand the constraints and opportunities provided by the corporatist structures of the small European states, I have spent a good deal of time tracing the policy process in Austria and Switzerland. I have read widely, visited Austria and Switzerland repeatedly, and interviewed more than eighty policy makers, businessmen, trade-union officials, journalists, and academics over a period of five years. I have used interviews not so much as a source for data as a way of learning from others, checking out my own ideas, and trying out new ones. But when I could not find a crucial piece of evidence in the written record, interviewing has helped me fill the gap. I have found newspaper clipping archives in Austria, Switzerland, and West Germany to be of great help in providing me with the postwar history of different industries. Using newspapers is not without risk. Schopenhauer once said that newspapers are nothing but the second hands of history— they always tell the wrong time. But newspapers provide information that is sufficiently good to hurry the researcher to the stage of probing the political significance of economic life.

This project has benefited enormously from the help of a large number of colleagues and friends. Over a period of five years they have kept talking and listening, and they have commented on what I knew were too many drafts. I have often exploited them shamelessly, used their ideas, and taxed their patience. Even when we disagreed, their reactions to my work have sharpened my ideas. Their intellectual presence has given meaning to the inevitable drudgeries of scholarship. My greatest intellectual debt is to those who actually sat down and read one or two drafts of a manuscript that originally encompassed the two volumes now published separately: Francis Castles, William Diebold, Gösta Esping-Andersen, Peter Gourevitch, Jeffrey Hart, Thomas Ilgen, Mary Katzenstein, Robert Keohane, Stephen Krasner, David Laitin, Peter Lange, Gerhard Lehmbruch, Arend Lijphart, Bernd Marin, T. J. Pempel, Richard Rosecrance, Charles Sabel, Martin Shefter, Margret Sieber, Sidney Tarrow, and John Zysman. I have also received helpful comments from colleagues who read papers developing the general argument of the two books: Ronald Brickman, David Cameron, Miriam Golden, Peter Hall, Steven Jackson, Jeanne Laux, Martin Lipset, Charles Lipson, Theodore Lowi, Henrik Madsen, Peter McClelland, Sandra Peterson, Ronald Rogowski, Michael Shalev, Gabriel Sheffer, Charles Tilly, and Harold Wilensky; from a group of European scholars whom I met in a series of colloquia convened by John Ruggie: Barry Buzan, Helge Hveem, Gerd Junne, and Alberto Martinelli; and from my colleagues at the Center for Advanced Study: Alfred Kahn, Natalie Ramsøy, and William Wilson.

This project has been supported financially by fellowships from the German Marshall Fund of the United States (Grant no. 3-51025) and from the Rockefeller Foundation (Grant no. RF 77020-87). A first draft of both volumes was prepared while I spent a year at the Center for Advanced Study in the Behavioral Sciences, Stanford, California, in 1981–82. I am grateful for the financial support provided by a National Science Foundation Grant (no. BNS76-22943).

Over the last five years, a group of Cornell students has helped me in my research. I would like to thank in particular Mark Hansen, Gretchen Ritter, and Rhonda Wassermann. Dorothy Hong, Bruce Levine, and Diane Sousa have also assisted me.

At the Center for Advanced Study, Deanna Dejan, Barbara Homestead, and Anna Tower typed a first draft of the manuscript from which these two books eventually emerged. The staff of Cornell University's Government Department, beyond all reasonable expectations, kept on speaking terms with me while retyping several subsequent versions.

Walter Lippincott showed an early interest in this project. In its later stages he suggested a publication format that I have found congenial: two separate books, two similar subtitles, and one preface. John Ackerman read drafts of the introduction and conclusion to both volumes and gave me useful editorial advice. But my greatest debt of gratitude goes to Roger Haydon. In editing these two volumes without complaining, he learned more than he ever wanted to know about little countries. He had superb judgment on how the material of one large manuscript should be organized into two books. His tenacity pushed me to clarify my thinking; his pencil uncluttered my prose; his diplomacy left my feathers unruffled; and his humor made much of the hard work fun.

Some of the material in this book has previously appeared in two edited volumes. Portions of chapters 2 and 3 have been published in "Political Compensation for Economic Openness: Incomes Policy and Public Spending in Austria and Other Small European States," in Kurt Steiner, ed., *Tradition and Innovation in Contemporary Austria,*

13

pp. 99–108, copyright © 1982 by SPOSS Inc., and are reproduced with permission, part of chapter 3 appeared in "The Small European States in the International Economy: Economic Dependence and Corporatist Politics," in John G. Ruggie, ed., *The Antinomies of Interdependence: National Welfare and the International Division of Labor* (New York: Columbia University Press, 1983), pp. 91–130 and is used here with permission.

I have had all the support I could reasonably expect at home. Tai and Suzanne, I suspect, enjoyed this project. When I went to Europe, their consumption of pizza increased, and when I returned they could look forward to Austrian dirndls or Swiss chocolates. I dedicate the second of these books to Mary, part of a dynamic intergenerational duo that has transformed my life.

PETER J. KATZENSTEIN

Ithaca, New York

Small States in World Markets

CHAPTER ONE

Introduction

Like many other industrial countries, the United States is experiencing far-reaching structural changes of its economy. Like many others, it is responding with the cure that has worked best in the past: liberal policies and unfettered market competition. By the middle of the 1980s, however, Americans remained divided in their assessments of both the character of the crisis and the adequacy of the cure.

The signs of crisis have become unmistakable. In the early 1980s an ever-growing list of books employed the language of statistics to demonstrate that rampant inflation and high unemployment—either separately or in combination—had shifted the American economy from growth to stagnation. An impressive array of statistical measures, moreover, productivity, capital formation, and the international balance of trade among them, indicated that the U.S. economy was lagging behind those of a growing number of other industrial states. Even as the share of American products in world markets continued its gradual decline, it dropped sharply in certain key domestic markets. At the same time the strength of the economic recovery in 1983–84, the dramatic lowering of the inflation rate, and decreases in unemployment which, compared to those in several European countries, could only be called impressive, all pointed to America's inherent economic strength. Its markets continue to be large and dynamic. In the 1970s America accepted while Europe rejected large numbers of migrant workers. The American economy nevertheless generated 20 million new jobs across the decade; Europe produced none. In several high-technology industries, moreover, the American lead over Europe was increasing.

Because the evidence supports both pessimistic and optimistic assessments of the American economy, analysts differ in their policy prescriptions. They agree, however, that America's economic performance lacks international competitiveness. In June 1980 *Business Week* titled one of its special issues "The Reindustrialization of America." Barry Bluestone and Bennett Harrison's widely noted study of plant closings bears the same title with one slight but all-important change—*The Deindustrialization of America.*[1] Whatever the diagnosis and whatever the cure, no one knew whether the world economy, and with it the American economy, had in the mid-1970s started a prolonged period of economic stagnation or a transition prior to renewed economic vitality.

By 1982 five European states had surpassed the United States in per capita gross domestic product (GDP), among them Switzerland, Sweden, Norway, and Denmark.[2] The average Norwegian or Danish family today enjoys a standard of living higher than its American counterpart. If they are aware of it, this fact disturbs Americans accustomed by a generation of prosperity and international leadership to thinking of themselves as number one. Their concern suggests that the small European states' experience with industrial policy deserves more attention than it has received in American public discourse.

THE NEW GLOBAL CONTEXT

During the last 25 years the American economy has opened itself up to global competition to a degree that is unique in this century.[3] More than one-fifth of America's industrial output is now exported. Forty percent of American farmland produces for foreign markets, as does one of every six jobs in manufacturing industries. Exports and foreign investments account for almost one-third of the profits of U.S. corporations, and for many of America's largest and most successful firms that proportion exceeds 50 percent. Imports meet more than half of U.S. demand for 24 of the 42 raw materials most important to industry, and the cost of oil imports alone increased from $3 billion to $80 billion in the course of the 1970s. The weakening of the dollar in 1977–78 helped push America into double-digit inflation. Between 1978 and 1980, 60 percent of the modest increase in gross national product (GNP) could be credited to a sharp improvement in the U.S. trade balance: America's exports grew twice as fast as world trade in each of these years. Similarly, the deep recession of 1981–83 was accentuated by the appreciation of the dollar in international markets. In short, international factors now influence America's domestic economy in an unprecedented fashion.

The increasing dependence of the American economy on global markets has been coupled since the mid-1970s with the success of Japan's export offensive on the American market. Japan's achievements have convinced a growing number of Americans that a nation's competitiveness depends on more than its endowment with natural resources and the workings of the market. But America's national debate on industrial policy betrays the strength of a liberal ideology. We conceive of the political alternatives that confront us as polar opposites: market or plan. The biases of our ideology are reinforced by a veritable national obsession with Japan, a country that American businessmen in particular view as a statist antidote to America's ideological celebration of market competition.

Our political debate typically pits the proponents of government action against the advocates of market competition. Fundamentally, the debate concerns the character of state involvement in the economy. Is the state smart or stupid? Should it be generous or frugal? The successes and failures of Japan often become important reference points in the discussion of American priorities and choices. One influential group, whose members became known as "Atari Democrats," relies on a sophisticated interpretation of what Chalmers Johnson has called Japan's "developmental state."[4] This view suggests competition rather than collusion as the organizing concept for industrial policy. Government action is informed by long-term market developments. It assists individual firms, segments of industry, or whole industrial sectors to prepare for international competition. (This interpretation of Japan draws on both the notion of Japan Incorporated that informs the views of many businessmen and on those liberal economists who stress the intense competition in Japan's domestic market.)

This "smart-state" view of industrial policy is, however, open to criticism.[5] Japan's developmental state has failed in areas as different as textiles and commercial aircraft. America's system of government, moreover, has institutional limitations that inhibit the implementation of a smart-state strategy. Such criticism serves as a useful corrective to the mixture of artistic and athletic imagery used by those who emphasize the suppleness and swiftness of Japan's industrial policy. At the same time, however, these criticisms risk conceding the debate by default to those who base their case against industrial policy on the mythical notion of unfettered market competition.

A second set of arguments addresses the question whether the state should be generous or frugal. AFL-CIO officials drawing on the experience of several European states and Robert Kuttner among other writers give pride of place to human capital and the impact of industrial policy on labor markets and social welfare.[6] A "generous-state" strategy views welfare and efficiency as complementary rather than conflicting goals. A well-trained labor force whose representatives are involved in shaping fundamental economic choices is, it holds, an essential ingredient in maintaining a competitive position in global markets. Critics of this argument point to a lack of competitiveness that, they argue, stems directly from the excesses of the welfare state both in Europe and in the United States.[7] Social fat must be cut to stop the atrophy of economic muscle. In emphasizing the long-term benefits of efficiency and competition, these critics accept that the transition from an uncompetitive welfare state that impoverishes to a competitive market economy that enriches will carry unavoidable costs. It is primarily the politically weak and the economically poor who must foot the bill. Perhaps the hardest of all the lessons in the education of David Stockman was the fact that the Reagan administration was more successful in cutting the strong claims of weak clients than it was in curtailing the weak claims of strong clients.[8]

One important voice in the debate, Robert Reich, has argued that today we face a choice "between evading the new global context or engaging it—between protecting the American economy from the international market while generating paper profits, or adapting it to meet international competition."[9] But what are the ingredients of successful adaptation? The debate about industrial policy is of little help in analyzing those ingredients because it is organized around misplaced polarities of state action: smart vs. stupid, generous vs. frugal. Americans are beginning to perceive foreign threat in terms not only of revolutionary Communism but also of competitive capitalism. It is therefore unwise to lump together, as Reich does, Europe and Japan or all of Europe. In celebrating or criticizing foreign capitalism, generalization stresses how much of an exception America is. Comparative analysis is a useful antidote to this subtle form of ethnocentrism.

Today we can discern three dominant political forms of contemporary capitalism: liberalism in the United States and Britain; statism in Japan and France; and corporatism in the small European states and, to a lesser extent, in West Germany. The high-tech shoot-out between liberal America and statist Japan, cowboy and samurai, has so captured the imagination of the American public as to exclude serious consideration of other political possibilities within contemporary capitalism.

This book analyzes the industrial adjustment strategy of small, corporatist European states: Sweden, Norway, Denmark, the Netherlands, Belgium, Austria, and Switzerland. It compares them with one another as well as with the large industrial countries: the United States, Britain, Germany, France and Japan.[10] I focus on this particular group of small states, excluding Ireland, Finland, and some of the Mediterranean countries, for reasons both practical and historical. This group of seven states is close to the apex of the international pyramid of success, yet we lack good comparative studies of how they manage their relations with the global economy. The group is large enough to allow some plausible inferences about the effects of structural constraints and opportunities, yet not so large as to defy intellectual mastery. Moreover, since these seven small states industrialized earlier than did other small states on the European periphery, they have related to the international economy in a distinctive manner. Finally, in these seven states a decisive realignment of their domestic economies with world markets occurred no later than around the turn of the century, a generation or two earlier than in the European periphery.

Although I use numbers in this book where relevant, I deliberately differ from statistically inclined investigations that seek to enhance our understanding by correlating small size with a broad range of economic, social, and political outcomes. In method of analysis I accord pride of place to historically informed comparisons rather than to statistical investigations. Granting the specifics of national settings, the historical evolution of these seven small European states justifies our particular attention.

The experience of the small European states in the international economy illustrates a traditional paradox in international relations concerning the strength of the weak. That experience is instructive in studying the problems of large, advanced industrial states, including America, for three different reasons. First, the large states are shrinking. This proposition is patently true in terms of territory: in the course of the last generation the large industrial states completed their withdrawal from their traditional empires, and no new formal empires are likely to emerge in the foreseeable future. Second, the diminution of the large states is reflected in the growing openness of their economies and their weakening control over the international system. Throughout the 1970s, for example, the economies of large industrial states opened up faster than those of small European states.[11] The large states are gradually relinquishing their traditional prerogative of imposing political solutions on others and are adjusting like small states to changes imposed from abroad. For America and the large states, "rule taking" rather than "rule making" is becoming increasingly important.[12] Finally, the production of goods for profitable niches in international markets has long been an economic reality for the small European states—a reality that the large industrial states, not accustomed to being squeezed, have acknowledged only rhetorically. But for the large industrial states, rhetoric is quickly becoming reality. They too must learn how to tap-dance rather than trample.

THREE POLITICAL RESPONSES TO ECONOMIC CHANGE

The 1970s and 1980s have been years of rapid change in the global economy. One way to suggest the rapidity with which change has occurred is to list the major issues that have affected the international economy since the early 1970s: global inflation, explosion in energy prices, prolonged recession, increases in trade rivalries and protectionism, volatile foreign-exchange markets, skyrocketing interest rates and debts, and structural readjustment. Alternatively, one could simply observe the behavior of economists who are in the business of making predictions. In the 1950s and 1960s their models generated impressively accurate results. Today an economic prediction often involves little more than averaging everyone else's guesses about future trends—and even that method often does not work. Among energy specialists, for example, few economists predicted with any degree of accuracy the glut in international oil markets in 1981–82, much less the glut that accompanied a major war in the Gulf in 1984, and still fewer were willing to hazard a guess about its probable duration.

The sources of these changes in the global economy are diverse. They include political realignments in the international state system as well as major changes in the supply conditions and production structures of many countries. At no time since the end of World War II have questions of economic competitiveness and economic security so riveted attention throughout the industrialized world.

None of the major competing schools of thought in economics have offered a plausible diagnosis of accelerating change, let alone a workable means of dealing with it. Yet the deepening problems of the advanced industrial world have prompted substantial changes in the policies of several industrial states. Examples illustrating the point are easy to come by. In the hope of overcoming stagflation through invigorating market institutions, Britain under Prime Minister Thatcher and the United States under President Reagan made sharp breaks with the past, pursuing deflationary policies and deregulation. In sharp contrast, in the first year of President Mitterrand's administration France was looking to more government intervention and an inflationary growth policy as the most promising cure for economic problems—an approach that Mitterrand was later compelled to abandon. In ways unanticipated a decade ago, moreover, and without any policy worth the name, northern Italy is witnessing the emergence of an embryonic but highly competitive, decentralized economy, one that challenges the long-presumed superiority of industrial mass production. As these policies suggest national elites are attempting to meet structural change in the world economy in different ways.

In the interest of systematic analysis we need categories to group diverging policies. This book relies on a threefold scheme that corresponds to the dominant political forms of contemporary capitalism.[13] Liberal countries such as the United States rely on macroeconomic policies and market solutions. Lacking the means to intervene selectively in the economy, the United States, in those extraordinary situations where the traditional market approach appears to fail, tends to export the costs of change to other countries through the adoption of a variety of limited, ad hoc protectionist policies. Such policies often create a temporary "breathing space" for producers hard pressed by international competition, but they rarely address long-term structural shifts in international competitiveness. Conversely, statist countries such as Japan are endowed with the means and the institutions to preempt the costs of change through policies that pursue the structural transformation of their economies. Because they seek to meet structural changes in the world economy head on, their strategy often requires systematically protectionist policies, at least in the short and medium term. Exporting or preempting the costs of economic change in times of adversity are political options for those large industrial states whose power is sufficient to exercise effective control either over parts of their international environment or over parts of their own societies.

This book is about a different kind of response. It is a response that does not fit easily into the categories of analysis (competition or intervention, market or state) suggested by the experience of the large industrial states. The small European states lack the power demanded by the strategies with which the United States and Japan typically deal with adverse economic change. For the small European states, economic change is a fact of life. They have not chosen it; it is thrust upon them. These states, because of their small size, are very dependent on world markets, and protectionism is therefore not a viable option for them. Similarly, their economic openness and domestic politics do not permit them the luxury of long-term plans for sectoral transformation. Instead, elites in the small European states, while letting international markets force economic adjustments, choose a variety of economic and social policies that prevent the costs of change from causing political eruptions. They live with change by compensating for it. In doing so, the small European states have cultivated a strategy that both responds to and reinforces their domestic structures. Their strategy differs profoundly from the liberal and statist principles that inform the political choices and structures of the large industrial states.

Exporting, preempting, or living with the costs of change are convenient short-hand summaries for the broad political choices that distinguish different industrial states.[14] In analyzing these choices I do not include the element of conscious intention that scholars normally assume to be an essential part of the concept of strategy. In talking with businessmen, union leaders, and especially government officials in the United States, Europe, and Japan about problems of industrial adjustment, I have been struck by the different levels of abstraction in their thinking about these problems. Most of the people I interviewed were interested in discussing individual decisions; few of them thought of bundles of decisions as "policy"; and only a handful grouped bundles of policies together as "industrial strategy." My tentative conclusion, based on this collage of individual impressions, is that the level of abstraction increases as one travels from the United States to Europe and from Europe to Japan.

For the range of political experiences that this book seeks to illuminate, I have found it useful to describe the industrial adjustment strategies of the small European states under two broad headings. What do these states seek to accomplish (international liberalization and domestic compensation)? Where and how do they accomplish it (national adaptation and public compensation vs. global adaptation and private compensation)? In terms of the semantic smorgasbord from which the current debate on U.S. "industrial policy" picks and chooses, the use of these categories implies a broad definition of that term. Industrial policy is concerned with the structure of the economy, that is the patterns of production in different sectors. It includes both adjustment-promoting and adjustment-retarding measures that operate directly or indirectly at both the macro- and the microlevel. Its purpose is to influence industrial competitiveness and through it achieve objectives such as employment, investment, growth, or an improved balance of payments.

Confronted with economic change, the U.S. government and U.S. firms prefer adjustment in global markets to reliance on government action. Free trade and foreign investment by firms rather than industrial policy coordinated by the government is the option they favor. This market orientation is expressed in America's preference for lower tariffs in the postwar world. To be sure, there exist important exceptions to America's liberal approach. Since 1945, for example, the federal government has spurred high-technology industries, including electronics and aerospace, through vast military expenditures. Not only large-scale preparation for war but also economic adversity has forced the government to act. When confronted with large-scale unemployment or massive bankruptcies, the U.S. government tends to favor policies that are defensive, seeking to reduce the rate of adverse economic change through protectionism.

For the American textile industry, because of political strength in Congress, protection came as early as the mid-1950s, at the dawn of the liberalization of the postwar international economy. American policy makers forced on Japan a "voluntary" control of their exports to the American market. The far-reaching liberalization of international trade negotiated under the auspices of the Kennedy Round in the 1960s rested on a political compromise between President Kennedy and the textile lobby in the U.S. Congress. The domestic agreement led to an internationalization of American protectionist practice in the Long Term Arrangement on Cotton Textiles, which in modified form eventually covered virtually all of the international trade in textiles. Between 1969 and 1974 the American steel industry also benefited from voluntary export controls negotiated with Japan. Since the oil shock of 1973 a growing list of industries, including footwear, consumer electronics, steel, and automobiles have benefited from the adoption of protectionist policies by the federal government. In footwear protection was granted only temporarily; steel experienced what looks like a more permanent change in American trade policy. In consumer electronics protection was largely ineffective in revitalizing the industry; in autos it may well facilitate adjustment. But in all instances the government chose protection when, lacking alternative policy instruments, it was pressured by strong coalitions to ameliorate sectoral crises. Indeed, in industrial policy broadly defined America's distinctive innovations are policies of

25

voluntary export restraints, orderly marketing agreements, and administrative interventions such as the Trigger Price Mechanism, which has protected the steel industry since 1977. This contrasts with the policy innovations elsewhere, for example, sectoral or incomes policies as practiced respectively by Japan or the small European states.

Japan favors confronting economic change with a process of domestic industrial adjustment in which the government assists firms in a variety of ways to exploit long-term market developments, both at home and abroad. In essence the state helps industry prepare for international competition. Because foreign investment by Japanese corporations was typically low throughout the 1960s, the government's industrial policy (including protection) provided the preferred mode of adjusting to economic change. In contrast to the defensive adjustment strategy of the United States, Japan's policy is geared to anticipating structural changes in markets; it aims to assist firms to become competitive in particular industry segments or product lines. Comparative advantage is conceived of not only as a result of market forces but also of political action that affects competitiveness.

Several Japanese industries, among them steel and computers, reveal this pattern of policy. The emergence of Japan's steel industry as the most efficient producer in the world depended on a variety of innovative policies, including administrative guidance, recession and rationalization cartels, and the socialization of risk through assorted financial arrangements. Armed with these policies and favored by the international climate, Japan succeeded in creating an industry that within two decades had outgrown the protection and assistance it had received in earlier days. Japan's computer industry became a similarly important target of government attention in the 1960s and 1970s. Policies helped either to narrow significantly or to close the gap between it and leading American firms in important segments of the industry. By the late 1970s the industry has become largely independent of the need for protection. In these and several other cases Japan's innovative industrial policy focused on long-term market developments, relied on protection while establishing international competitiveness, and relinquished that protection, often under intense foreign pressure, when international competitiveness had been achieved.

Both the utter indifference of the United States and the ambitious initiatives of Japan offer a notable contrast to the flexible measures of industrial policy pursued by the small European states. In all industrial states, of course, be they large or small, one can find a substantial

26

array of policies seeking to modify market conditions through such instruments as subsidies, tax policies, regional development, concentration, and nationalization. Countries that adhere to a basically liberal stance on economic policy, such as the United States, often adopt these policies in the hope of slowing the political impact of economic change, if not economic change itself. The small European states may at times try to do the former but have no illusions about accomplishing the latter. The openness of their economies has resulted in a fully developed awareness of the inescapability of economic change. In Japan these policies are often employed, at least in part, in the ambitious attempt to preempt adverse economic change through timely transformation of industrial structures. In contrast, the small European states, even those which, like Austria or Norway, feature a large public-sector economy and a strong Left, apparently lack the political capacity to employ the full range of policy instruments in a far-reaching policy of structural transformation.

Instead, Austria and Norway, like all of the small European states, have a preference for a reactive and flexible policy of industrial adjustment. Since the late 1950s they have proceeded by small steps, relying heavily on indirect policy instruments such as taxation rather than broad-gauged political efforts to transform the structures of their economies. The 1970s saw the beginnings of convergence between small and large: the policies of most of the large industrial countries became more specific, moving either from traditional indifference to a new interest in industrial policy or from a focus on sectors and firms toward greater attention on products and production processes. At the same time the policies of some of the small European states were becoming less specific. At least some countries confronted for the first time the possibility that large-scale political interventions might be necessary. By and large, though, political indifference or policies of structural transformation typical of the United States and Japan still differ notably from the reactive, flexible, and incremental pursuit of industrial adjustment by the small European states.

Characterizing the industrial adjustment strategy that typifies the small European states is one thing. Thinking about the criteria by which one judges its success or failure is another. Economists of diverse persuasions found the variations in the economic performance of small industrial states in the 1970s increasingly difficult to explain. Why, for example, did Austria and Switzerland both have a low inflation rate in the 1970s even though Austria experienced high economic growth while Switzerland experienced low growth? Why is unemployment in Belgium much greater than in Sweden despite

roughly comparable growth rates? Economists have no simple answers to such questions. But if simple explanation is difficult for
economists, it is even more difficult for political scientists. Political
choices have an effect on economic outcomes without determining
them. A political analysis that, like the one offered in this book, draws
on variables that change relatively slowly will have difficulty ac-
counting for the rapidly changing economic performance of the small
European states between 1960 and 1980. Furthermore, an analysis
that emphasizes both similarities and differences in political structures and processes in different societies is hard pressed to yield a
systematic and parsimonious explanation of economic performance.
Economic performance, then, is not a yardstick by which we can directly measure the successes and failures of the small European states.

Can we use a political criterion to gauge success or failure?
Through their policies, political leaders in the small European states
have maintained the legitimacy of the political arrangements governing their societies. In neither Switzerland nor Austria has widespread
popular disenchantment challenged the main political institutions.
Political parties retain a tight hold on mass participation, and electoral
changes in both countries have been very small. In Scandinavia
groups representing the interests of business and workers continue to
operate with the consent, in the main, of the myriad small firms and
the union rank and file. In the Low Countries government agencies
and the courts administer and adjudicate without large-scale public
protests. Single-issue movements and citizen-initiative groups, which
have grown in political importance in other European countries, have
been incorporated in their political regimes. In short, by the criterion
of political performance the small European states look like exemplary success stories.

The problem with this second yardstick for gauging success and
failure is the inverse of the first. The measure is not easy to disaggre-
gate into different dimensions, and it is not easily disconfirmed.
Legitimacy is a broad construct; it covers a wide array of political
experiences across the last three decades. Widespread loss of legitimacy occurs only very rarely—even Britain and Italy could be interpreted by this standard as political success stories. Despite the crude
and misleading terminology of the news media, Britain has refused to
"go down the drain" and Italy has not submitted to "political chaos."
Considering the magnitude of the economic and political problems
that these two societies confronted in the 1970s, they might be judged
even greater political successes than, for example, the small European
states or Germany and Japan. Indeed, from this vantage point it

would be difficult to find any evidence short of total political collapse and social disintegration that would not lend credence to the argument that virtually all industrial states, the small European nations included, have succeeded politically.

Common sense approves our measuring success or failure in adjusting to economic change by economic or political yardsticks. But both procedures generate problems for analysis, and I have therefore chosen a third yardstick. It measures the extent to which social coalitions, political institutions, and public policies facilitate or impede shifts in the factors of production that increase economic efficiency with due regard to the requirements of political legitimacy.[15] The small European states, like the United States and other large advanced industrial states, have had to confront the problem of adjusting the production profiles of their economies to rapid changes in technology and global competition. This book argues that the small countries have largely succeeded in this task, and they have done so by taking into account both the economic and the political requirements of rapid change. Economists understand the problem of adjustment in terms of economic incentives that shape politics to fit the logic of the market; what matters is the elimination of distortions to competition. Political scientists see the problem in terms of power calculations that shape market outcomes; of central importance is the imposition of state preferences on markets at the level of the industrial sector or sector segment. The successful strategy of adjustment practiced by the small European states bridges the divergent requirements of international competitiveness and political preference. These states adjust to economic change through a carefully calibrated balance of economic flexibility and political stability.

Compensating for the costs of change, I hasten to admit, can be simply another way of failing to adjust. The possibility is illustrated by the growing list of ailing industries and firms that live off state subsidies around the industrial world. But this form of compensation is not characteristic of most small European states. For example, Switzerland and the Netherlands, in the name of efficiency, rely primarily on market-driven adjustment. But their reliance is tempered by the awareness that compensatory political gestures are essential for maintaining consensus on how to adjust. Austria and Norway, in the name of equity, are inclined to rely on political efforts to slow down the rate of economic change. But their inclination is held in check by the knowledge that the state lacks the economic resources to offset adverse market changes for prolonged periods. Characteristic of both policies is the close link between the political and the economic re-

quirements of flexible adjustment. Compensating too little for adverse economic changes can be detrimental to the political consensus
on coping with change; compensating too much can impair economic
efficiency. In assessing the success or the failure of adjustment, we
need to take into account both its economic and its political costs and
benefits.

Measuring success and failure by this third yardstick—the political
facilitation or retardation of shifting factors of production—is related
indirectly to the commonsensical but problematic measures I mentioned earlier: success or failure in terms of economic performance or
political legitimacy. Flexibility in shifting factors of production pre-
sumably strengthens economic performance. Compensating for these
shifts by political means rather than ignoring them should reaffirm
political legitimacy. Precise examination of these links is beyond the
scope of this book, but establishing them on grounds of plausibility
will, I hope, suffice for those readers who wonder whether in their
successes and failures the small European states have been smart or
stupid, lucky or unlucky.

DEMOCRATIC CORPORATISM

Similarities in what I shall call their corporatist arrangements set
the small European states apart from the large industrial states. Yet
different variants of corporatist arrangements, liberal and social, can
be found among the small European states. Two sets of comparisons,
between large and small and among the small, offer a map of the
relations between the different components of corporatist structures
as these European countries confront economic change. But a map
simply traces the contours of the terrain the traveler will encounter; it
does not explain them. The corporatist arrangements that distinguish
the small European states, I shall argue, have their origin in the
catastrophic changes of the 1930s and 1940s. In those two decades
business and unions, as well as conservative and progressive political
parties, became convinced that they should impose strict limits on
domestic quarrels, which they viewed as a luxury in a hostile and
dangerous world. Since the mid-1950s the requirements of international competition have helped to maintain that conviction.

Corporatism is an ambiguous and evocative concept.[16] Broadly
speaking, it has three different meanings. First, it refers to the political arrangements of several European states in the 1930s that had a
close affinity to political authoritarianism and fascism. Mussolini's

Italy, Salazar's Portugal, and the Austria of Dollfuss were all profoundly antidemocratic in their repression of unions and leftist parties and antiliberal in their pursuit of relative economic autarchy. Contemporary interpretations of corporatist tendencies in southern Europe and Latin America often have this authoritarian variant as their implicit benchmark.

Second, the concept of corporatism refers to the economic and political organization of modern capitalism, as expressed in contemporary discussions of "corporate capitalism" or "state capitalism." The view of Japan as a big business firm (Japan Inc.) or of the United States as run by Wall Street emphasizes both the dominance of the giant corporation in economic life and the integration of business into the decision making of governments and state bureaucracies. This second variant differs from the first in two ways. It fosters the relative political exclusion (rather than the repression) of unions and leftist parties from the centers of power. It also emphasizes the liberal pursuit of international interdependence through trade and investment.

Finally, there is the democratic corporatism of the postwar period. Its essence can be grasped by looking at changing interpretations of German politics. The "organized capitalism" of twentieth-century Germany makes plausible those historical interpretations which draw on either of the first two meanings of corporatism.[17] But such interpretations do not capture the main political currents in West Germany since 1945. West Germany's political economy is founded on the political inclusion of business and unions as well as conservative and progressive political parties. The Federal Republic favors the principles of market competition and international trade. The country's postwar experience, moreover, illustrates why democratic corporatism need not necessarily be considered anathema by Social Democrats who associate all corporatism with the repression or exclusion of labor. West Germany comes closer than any other large industrial state to the logic by which political life in the small European states is organized. How this democratic corporatism deals with economic change is the subject of this book.

Scholarly interest in democratic corporatism has surfaced twice in the postwar period.[18] Throughout the 1950s and into the early 1960s buoyant economic growth prompted American political scientists to focus on the political question of recreating a moderate democratic politics in Europe by freeing unions from Communist parties on the Left and the Catholic church on the Right. The mid-1970s saw a resurgence of interest in corporatism, this time prompted by the slowing of economic growth and the prospect of prolonged economic crisis in the 1980s. Recent studies of advanced industrial states have coined various terms for a phenomenon on whose existence most observers agree: the voluntary, cooperative regulation of conflicts over economic and social issues through highly structured and interpenetrating political relationships between business, trade unions, and the state, augmented by political parties. As Peter Lange has observed, however, corporatism has been viewed in different ways. Some scholars understand it as a transformation (either in progress or completed) of interest-group participation (from pluralism to corporatism), others as a transformation of the mode of economic production (from capitalism to corporatism) or of the form of the state (from parliamentary to corporatist).[19] These differences in theoretical and political orientations have led to different characterizations and interpretations of corporatism.

Democratic corporatism is distinguished by three traits: an ideology of social partnership expressed at the national level; a relatively centralized and concentrated system of interest groups; and voluntary and informal coordination of conflicting objectives through continuous political bargaining between interest groups, state bureaucracies, and political parties. These traits make for a low-voltage politics.

The first trait, an ideology of social partnership on questions of economic and social policy, permeates everyday politics in corporatist societies. This ideology mitigates class conflict between business and unions; it integrates differing conceptions of group interest with vaguely but firmly held notions of the public interest. Even to the casual visitor the self-dramatization of smallness is evident, ritually invoked in any interview or sustained discussion by the words, "You must understand that this is a very small country." References to the ideological cohesion that emanates from smallness convey the mistaken impression that in corporatist societies all important political conflicts have been resolved. Political elites in these systems, in their world view and in their daily behavior, do express satisfaction with the status quo, it is true. They regard redistribution as less important than an equitable sharing in economic gains and losses. Yet the prominence of the notion of public interest in this ideology of social partnership does not mean that individual attributes are unusually skewed toward valuing compromise. Individual predispositions, attitudes, or beliefs are not the roots of ideological cohesion. Rather, the "culture of compromise" that pervades democratic corporatism reflects political arrangements that manage to couple narrowly conceived group interests with shared interpretations of the collective good.

Second, democratic corporatism is distinguished by relatively centralized and concentrated interest groups. Centralization is a measure of the degree of hierarchical control. Interest groups in corporatist systems are aptly called "peak associations" because power is exercised at the summit over a relatively compliant base. Concentration is a measure of the degree of inclusiveness. Peak associations in corporatist systems are broadly based and organize a very large proportion of producers and workers. High degrees of centralization and concentration give a misleadingly orderly appearance to political life. Politics is of great importance, but it is important within interest groups, determining which issues get on the public agenda and setting the parameters of political choice. Political struggles fought and decided within interest groups prevent the crowding of public agendas with the political infighting of different segments of business or labor.

The importance of centralized and concentrated institutions lies in their shielding a particular style of political bargaining, the third defining characteristic of democratic corporatism. Bargaining is voluntary, informal, and continuous. It achieves a coordination of conflicting objectives among political actors. Political preferences in different sectors of policy are traded off one against another. Victory or defeat on any given issue does not lead to an escalating spiral of conflict because a continuous sequence of political bargains makes all actors aware that victory today can easily turn into defeat tomorrow. The predictability of the process enhances the flexibility of the actors.

Democratic corporatism is tied in each of its three distinctive features to political parties and electoral politics, but it avoids being dominated by them. Electoral competition between political parties limits the degree to which an ideology of social partnership can become a threat to democratic politics. Furthermore, the close relation between political parties and interest groups contributes to the centralization of domestic structures, especially on the Left. Finally, political parties and the perception of electoral losses or gains influence the degree to which groups coordinate diverging objectives. Democratic corporatism, as Stein Rokkan has argued, operates on two tiers: the democratic tier and the corporatist tier.[20] Political leaders of parties, interest groups, government agencies, the legislature, and the cabinet always operate on both levels. The cumulation of roles by the same political elite—so distinctive of the small European states—strengthens a complex web of political relations between the two tiers. For the past four decades that web has been sufficiently strong to make the political arrangements of the small European states simultaneously corporatist and democratic.

In sum, corporatist politics has three distinguishing characteristics.

33

All states share in some of these characteristics, but none exhibits all of them fully—in this sense democratic corporatism can be found everywhere and nowhere in the industrialized countries. But different countries exhibit democratic corporatism to different degrees. We can therefore distinguish between "strong" and "weak" systems of democratic corporatism in the advanced industrial states. The small European states, with their open and vulnerable economies, exemplify a democratic corporatism that among the large industrial states only West Germany approaches.

A taxonomy by which one can distinguish the strong corporatism of the small European states from the weak corporatism of the large industrial states is not the same thing as an explanation of why strong corporatist structures came into being and why they have lasted. The explanation this book proposes is, in a word, historical. The democratic corporatism of the small European states was born in the 1930s and 1940s amidst the Great Depression, fascism, and World War II. In many ways the domestic structures and political strategies that emerged in these two decades set guidelines for the generation of leaders charged until the 1960s with economic reconstruction and expansion. Economic openness and dependence established a compelling need for consensus, which through complex and delicate political arrangements has transformed conflict among the main social forces in small European states. Truces between business community and labor movement were expressed in Norway's "Basic Agreement" of 1935, Switzerland's "Peace Agreement" of 1937, Sweden's "Saltsjöbaden Agreement" of 1938, the Netherlands' fifth, corporatist chapter of the new Constitution of 1938, and Belgium's "Social Solidarity Pact" of 1945. Those truces have since been translated into durable peace. Austria's memories of the civil war of 1934 and Denmark's postwar settlement have encouraged a similar development.

Reflecting on the importance of international events for a consensual domestic politics, Arend Lijphart concluded that "in all of the consociational democracies the cartel of elites was either initiated or greatly strengthened during periods of international crisis, especially the First and Second World Wars."[21] In all cases external threat impressed on the elites the need for internal unity and cooperation. Johan Olsen similarly argues that "during wars, depressions, or other national crises, as well as during crises in specific sectors of society, integrated organizational participation by peak associations becomes more frequent."[22] The political manifestations of what he calls "integrated organizational participation" can be found in corporatist political practices and institutions. In the small European states, moreover, political metaphors reinforce the historical memories of the 1930s and 1940s. They emphasize that all members of society are in the same small boat, that the waves are high, and that everyone must help pull the oars. Domestic quarrels are a luxury that prudent persons will not tolerate in such adverse circumstances.

But why did the crises of the 1930s and 1940s establish in the small European states political regimes that met the requirements of international competitiveness as well as the objectives of prosperity and legitimacy? Not every serious crisis is met successfully. When faced with far-reaching changes, for example, Britain in the 1960s and Poland in the 1970s failed to recast their political strategies or reshape their domestic structures. In the small European states, however, a tradition of accommodative politics dating back beyond the nineteenth century facilitated the political reorientation that took place in the 1930s and 1940s.

Some of the small European states—Belgium, the Netherlands, and Switzerland—societies politically divided into different ethnic, linguistic, and religious camps, found corporatist patterns compatible with political accommodation that had emerged generations earlier.[23] "Consociationalism" and "Amicable Agreement" are terms that observers have used to capture the distinctive political structures and practices of these small European states, where groups are held together by pragmatic bargains struck by a handful of political leaders.[24] Though for different historical reasons, I shall argue, Austria's "Proporz Democracy" achieves similar results. Compromise across the main social cleavages assures political quiescence and, equally important, reinforces political control within each camp. The greater the segmentation of these continental societies, the more pronounced, typically, are elite coalescence and consociational arrangements that diffuse conflict.[25] In the Scandinavian countries, on the other hand, what mattered was an independent peasantry and a deep division between city and countryside. Political alliances between urban and rural sectors were the result in societies less troubled by social segmentation. As Arend Lijphart writes, "The coalescent style of decision-making has become quite pervasive . . . probably more so than elsewhere in the Western World," at least with respect to economic and social policy.[26]

The "historical compromise" that business and labor negotiated in the crisis-ridden 1930s and 1940s broadened narrow conceptions of class interest to include an acute awareness of the fragility of the small European states in a hostile world. An increasingly liberal interna-

35

tional economy in the postwar years offered daily confirmation of that awareness. International competition intensified, underlining the enormous benefits of limiting domestic conflicts over economic issues. For example, strikes in the small European states are so costly for everyone—business, unions, governments, and consumers—that they occur very rarely. Political negotiations over prices and wages (what is usually called an "incomes policy"), on the other hand, are prevalent. In short, because the small European states have very open economies, political actors rarely lose the sense of being exposed to an international economy beyond their control.

This argument, which links the historical experience of the 1930s and 1940s to the creation of democratic corporatism and attributes its maintenance and adaptation to the effects of a liberal international economy since the mid-1950s, draws supporting evidence from post-war Germany and Japan. The experience of the Depression, fascism, defeat in war, and occupation remade political life in Germany and modified it in Japan. Comparative studies of corporatism, though sometimes uneasy about Japan, concur that both states approximate more closely than any other large industrial nations the kind of demo-cratic corporatism distinctive to the small European states.[27] West Ger-many features both an ideology of social partnership and peak associations. It falls short of strong corporatism, however, because political parties play a greater role in the handling of conflicting ob-jectives across different sectors of policy. Japan has both peak associa-tions of business and a strong ideology of social partnership at the level of the firm. But because of the strength of the Japanese state and the exclusion of labor unions at the national level, Japan manages diverging objectives in ways utterly alien to the logic of democratic corporatism.[28] The comparison with Switzerland is instructive. Like Japan and unlike Austria, Norway, or Sweden, Switzerland has a rela-tively decentralized system of collective bargaining that rests on a shared ideology at the level of the firm. In sharp contrast to their counterparts in Japan, however, Swiss unions are important actors in the national policy process, the Left is included in the cabinet, an ideology of social partnership exists at the national level, and the state bureaucracy is not dominant.

In the global economy the odds are stacked against small and de-pendent states. Yet somehow the small European states defy the odds. As early as 1931 Richard Behrendt was noting that the small Euro-pean states were an embarrassing exception to virtually all explana-tions of the political economies of larger countries.[29] In the 1960s Harry Eckstein observed that "the small European countries are strangely overlooked by American political scientists who seem to know more about Uganda or the Ivory Coast than about Denmark or Holland. Comparative politics has, after all, always had something of a great-power fixation, particularly in regard to Europe."[30] Twenty years later Eckstein's appraisal of our familiarity with the African political scene may be optimistic, but his assessment of our ignorance of the small European states remains valid. Since we know so little about the small European states, their success in the postwar world either remains baffling or is glibly credited to two factors: "One is that they exported all their economists to America and Britain. . . . The other is that it is always easier to keep a small house in order."[31]

Students of international politics have also shown little interest in understanding the coincidence of economic strategies that favor flexibility with political structures that produce so much order. As one reviewer concluded, "a common feature of the studies on economic problems of small states [in the 1970s] . . . is that they concentrate on the external conditions. . . . Small states have, however, reacted in different ways to similar external conditions and one reason for this could be the internal structure of the small states themselves, a factor wholly neglected in the studies."[32] The small European states do illustrate that periods of great crisis can profoundly affect the way domestic politics is organized; periods of relative normality can, moreover, reinforce that pattern of organization. But international factors affect political strategies and outcomes only indirectly: they are funneled through domestic structures that are shaped by different histories and embody different political possibilities. Because of their greater vulnerability and openness, the small European states have felt a greater impact of international factors on domestic structures than have the large industrial states. But, as this book illustrates, international factors have not determined political strategies and domestic structures. Rather, while external events induced convergence, internal events drive countries to different responses. The result is to create among the small European states two distinct variants of democratic corporatism.

In the next chapter I detail both how small European states differ from large industrial countries in their political response to economic change and how they differ among themselves. Chapter 3 explains these similarities and differences in terms of the domestic structures of the small European states. Their economic openness and the structure of their party systems are conducive to corporatist political arrangements, which distinguish small from large industrial countries.

But the small European states differ in the form of their corporatism, liberal or social. Chapter 4 gives a historical analysis of both the conditions that permitted the emergence of democratic corporatism and the conditions that account for its taking a liberal or a social form. Chapter 5 draws out some of the broader implications of this analysis.

Corporatism was born out of political chaos and economic competition, but the authoritarian version of the 1930s was not the only possible political response to a period of crisis. A second, democratic form of corporatism also emerged in reaction to the antiliberal currents of the 1930s and 1940s. Nourished by the strong effect of a liberal United States on the postwar global economy, democratic corporatism is a way of organizing politics that differs from the liberal and statist models typical of the United States and Japan. It accommodates the logic of the market by compensating for it, and it tolerates the power of the state by circumscribing it. Democratic corporatism merits study for its response to economic change. Exposed to global markets that they cannot control, the small European states have accommodated themselves to a situation that Americans are now beginning to experience as crisis. How the small European states made a political virtue of economic necessity is the subject of this book.

CHAPTER TWO

Flexible Adjustment in the Small European States

The small European states differ from larger ones in how they respond to economic change. Avoiding policies of protection and of structural transformation equally, they combine international liberalization with domestic compensation. The result is flexible policies of adjustment that, on questions of industrial policy, avoid both the indifference of some large states and the ambition of others. Despite their similarities, however, the small European states do differ from one another in the specific type of industrial policy they adopt. Industrial policy is relatively passive in some small states and relatively active in others.

This chapter describes the response of small European states to economic change. The first three sections compare a strategy of international liberalization, domestic compensation, and flexible industrial adjustment to that of the large states. These sections establish that the small European states do indeed follow a distinctive strategy. The final section, by contrast, emphasizes the difference among small European states by examining two extremes of economic strategy: the relatively passive industrial policy of Switzerland and the more active approach of Austria.

INTERNATIONAL LIBERALIZATION

Political and economic elites in the small European states mention three principal reasons why free trade is a policy to which they see no alternative. First, protection raises the price of intermediate goods and thus undermines the competitiveness of exports in world mar-

39

kets. Second, the adoption of protectionist policies sets a bad precedent in domestic politics. What is granted as an exception might become the political rule. Finally, the fear of economic retaliation by larger and less vulnerable states inhibits protectionist instincts.

The securing of a liberal international economy has been an overriding objective for the small European states. Since the position of small states is intrinsically weak, this group of states has a strong interest in lowering tariffs, in preventing the formation of economic blocs, and in strengthening the principle of multilateralism.[1] When in 1954 the United Kingdom attempted, unsuccessfully as it turned out, to amend the General Agreement on Tariffs and Trade (GATT) by adding a new article permitting preferential trade links between a metropolitan country and its colonies—provided such links contributed substantially to the exclusive benefit of the dependent territory—the small European states were counted among the proposal's most vigorous opponents.[2] The small European states, for a variety of reasons, were also highly critical of the European Coal and Steel Community (ECSC).

The small European states have not shied away from forming their own regional trading arrangements: Benelux, the Nordic Union, and in the late 1950s the European Free Trade Area (EFTA). But these arrangements were always constructed so as not to inhibit trade with the rest of the world. Moreover, when the Benelux countries joined the European Economic Community (EEC), the Netherlands and Belgium strongly opposed all political developments that might have led to a Western European trading bloc; instead, they pressed hard for British entry and the enlargement of the community.[3] For them, as for the other small European states, the reasons for favoring global trade were plain. The open economy of the Netherlands, for example, depends critically on access to raw materials, semimanufactures, and capital goods. In Sweden and Denmark import competition is viewed as a useful check on domestic inflation and on monopolistic tendencies in small domestic markets. In Norway industrial development since 1945 has been based on a conviction of the government which Alice Bourneuf expresses thus: "the solution is not to develop such industries and protect them from more efficient foreign competitors."[4]

In 1958 these states welcomed the advent of free convertibility. By 1962 they had dropped all trade restrictions designed to strengthen their balance of payments. While Canada (1962), the United Kingdom (1964 and 1968), France (1968), and the United States (1971) invoked the GATT's balance-of-payments safeguard provision, Denmark was alone among the seven small European states in levying a temporary import surcharge (in 1971) for balance-of-payments reasons.[5] The picture is similar when one looks at other measures of trade restriction. In the late 1950s, for example, quotas on industrial products were less common among the small European states than among the large countries.[6] By the early 1970s GATT member states had invoked provisions promising relief from injurious imports on 61 occasions: the United States, France, Germany, Italy, and the EEC did so 24 times. Austria, on the other hand, was the only small European state to use this escape clause, on four occasions.[7]

The use of quantitative import restrictions in the trade of nonagricultural commodities also illustrates commitment to the principle of free trade. In the late 1960s the five large industrial countries—the United States, Japan, Britain, West Germany, and France—had imposed a total of 77 quantitative restrictions; the seven small European states together imposed only eleven.[8] Between 1 July 1969 and 1 July 1977 there was a total of 294 antidumping cases pending in the United States, Britain, and the EEC as compared to a total of only six in Denmark, Norway, and Austria, the three most protectionist of the seven small European states.[9]

These small states have been active and enthusiastic supporters of successive rounds of tariff reductions culminating in the Tokyo Round Agreements of 1979. In the words of Andrew Shonfield, they "exercised a distinct influence on the tone of postwar international economic relations."[10] Although methodological and statistical difficulties demand caution, a comparison of nominal tariff levels provides us with one rough indicator of the degree of economic liberalism or protection in different countries. Generally speaking, during the last thirty years tariff rates in the small European states have been substantially lower than rates in the large advanced industrial countries. Two different studies reported their tariff levels as below those of the large countries in 1952, by margins of 15 and 45 percent.[11] By the end of the 1950s the situation had changed little.[12] During the Kennedy Round the weighted average tariff reductions by Switzerland, Sweden, and Austria exceeded those of the United States, the European Communities, Britain, and Japan.[13] By the conclusion of the round the weighted average of tariff levels stood at 13.1 percent for large countries, 9.9 percent for the small European states.[14] When one makes distinctions among product categories at different stages of processing, one finds that in 1970 the average tariffs of the small European states were above those of the large industrial countries in only six of 15 finished products, in only four of

28 semimanufactured goods, and in only three of 22 raw materials.[15] Because of already low tariffs the small European states reduced their average rates in the Tokyo Round of tariff negotiations slightly less than the large countries did—but the estimated welfare benefit was higher.[16] In sum, low tariff rates reflect a political preference for a liberal international economy.

Although small states may have influenced the tone, they did not determine the substance of tariff negotiations. Multilateral commercial diplomacy still focuses primarily on the big states, and small states often find their special needs and interests disregarded. In the Kennedy Round of negotiations, for instance, the disparities in the tariff schedules of the United States and the EEC were very large. One possible solution, which for a while appeared to gain favor with the main protagonists, would have shifted the costs of compromise largely onto Switzerland. Ten percent of Swiss exports fell into selected import categories that the EEC was partially to exempt from large tariff cuts in order to balance American tariffs on other items. Together with the Scandinavian countries, Switzerland let it be known that it would stall negotiations by refusing to submit a list of exceptions if full reciprocity were not granted. That decision was tactical: the small European states calculated, correctly as an eventual compromise proved, that their insufficient political leverage would be improved if they kept the large states in doubt as to their ultimate contribution to the overall tariff package. Needless to say, the Swiss were well prepared to deal with the disparity question in the Tokyo Round. A special "Swiss formula" was adopted; it established a workable compromise between the American preference for linear reductions and the EEC proposal for tariff harmonization.[17]

But nominal tariff figures give only an incomplete picture of the "new protectionism." Various forms of invisible trade restrictions, including export support schemes and a variety of nontariff barriers, impede imports and are also less easy to measure. Available evidence suggests that here as well, the small European states are much more liberal in their trade policies than the large industrial countries. A United Nations study concluded in the late 1950s that the most fully developed export credit guarantee schemes could be found in the large countries.[18] Twenty years later, in April 1978, risk coverage and financial conditions for medium-term credits were again more advantageous in the large countries than in the small European states.[19] An analysis of expenditures for export promotion in 1972 yields similar results: West Germany, France, and Britain spent a total of $102.1 million on trade promotion as compared to $37.7 million for six of the seven small European states.[20] In that same year the small states had 29.6 percent of the population and 31.1 percent of the total export trade of the large states, but they were spending a disproportionately low 18.5 percent for export promotion.[21] The evidence on export cartels is at best spotty, but what we have also suggests that the large states favor cartels more than the small states do, even though cartel legislation is typically less restrictive in the small European states than in the large countries.[22]

The small European states have lower nontariff barriers than the large countries. In their government procurement policy, for example—and in contrast to the large industrial states—there exists little evidence of Dutch or Belgian government discrimination against foreign producers.[23] Although selective tenders limiting the number of suppliers are the rule and although the requirements for public disclosure of bids vary widely, the small European states are apparently less discriminatory than the large countries.[24] Compared to an estimated 42 percent tariff equivalent imposed by American procurement policies in 1958 and a 43 percent figure for France in 1965, even Norway with its formal price preference rule of up to 15 percent looks like a free trader.[25] The multilateral liberalization of government procurement policies, a result of the Tokyo Round agreements, is estimated to free about six times as much international trade from the discriminatory practices of the large countries as from those of the small European states.[26]

These findings are supported by other studies of a variety of nontariff barriers in world trade during the 1960s and 1970s. Several studies have concluded that in the late 1960s the proportion of imports subject to nontariff restrictions was twice as large in the large industrial states as in the small European states.[27] As protectionist forces gained strength in the mid-1970s, the difference between these two groups of countries most probably became greater still.[28] While the GATT found that at the dawn of liberalization, in 1959–60, all of the small European states had taken restrictive action against what they regarded as disruptive imports, in the 1970s they showed considerable hesitation about introducing new nontariff barriers.[29]

With different forms of trade restrictions, both visible and invisible, spreading in the 1970s, the small European states could be counted among the persistent champions of a liberal international trade regime. The initiatives for a reordering of the international monetary system after 1971 and the implementation of sector-specific trade regimes in declining industries have without fail emanated from the large countries. On every conceivable occasion the small European states have pressed hard for a reaffirmation of the principle of free trade. Their pursuit of economic liberalism is not based on disinterested notions of aggregated welfare but is rooted firmly in the awareness that their political autonomy and economic welfare are best served by diffusing dependence in a wider market rather than concentrating it on particular states. This preference of the small European states has a long tradition to draw on. As Andrew Shonfield notes, "there was nothing novel about these attitudes . . . they were a continuation in strengthened form of general lines of policy pursued before World War II. The additional strength can be reasonably explained by the marked improvement in the international economic environment in the postwar world."[30] It is overstating the point only a little to argue that for the small European states international liberalization is ersatz patriotism.

For the small European states, with their open economies and fear of retaliation by other governments, exporting the costs of change through protectionist policies is not a viable political strategy. Protectionism would not only invite retaliation but also increase the costs of the intermediate inputs of products manufactured for export, thus undermining the international competitiveness of these small, open economies. Whatever their political persuasions or economic interests, on this point all of the elites and mass publics in the small European states agree strongly. Only a total collapse of the international economy and a basic reorganization of their domestic politics will dislodge this encompassing consensus. Since the end of World War II processes of economic growth and decline as well as of industrial obsolescence and rejuvenation have occurred faster in the small industrial states than in the large ones. Political leaders in the open economies of the small states are thus accustomed to accept as normal rates of economic change and dislocation that elites in large countries regard as intolerably high.[31]

A strategy of international liberalization can be very conducive to international cooperation. In their research and development policies, for example, the small European states have chosen a cooperative, international response to the constraints that the smallness of their exposed domestic markets imposes on autonomous R and D. Since 1945 scientific research has been shaped decisively by the concerted efforts of large industrial countries to develop big programs in military, nuclear, space, and aeronautics technology. The greatest difference between the large industrial countries and the small European states (with the exceptions of Japan and Sweden) exists in these new areas of science and technology.[32] Only two of the

seven small states, Sweden and the Netherlands, have an indigenous
aircraft industry; and in the 1970s the intense Swedish debate over a
fifth-generation fighter plane illustrated how heavily even the largest
of the small European states was burdened by sustaining an independent effort. Several statistical studies also support the conclusion that
size of country is a major determinant of R and D spending in industrial states.[33] Today research and development requires vast resources
and entails numerous risks and uncertainties that are simply too great
for the small and open economies of these European states to bear.[34]

The small states' response has been a deliberate attempt to involve
themselves in cooperative research projects in areas from which they
would otherwise be excluded for lack of resources. In space research,
for example, the small European states rely solely on international
cooperative ventures such as ELDO and ENDO.[35] In the nuclear field
the same is largely true. The small European states view their involvement not from the vantage point of national security but from an
economic perspective. Four of them—the Netherlands, Belgium,
Switzerland, and Norway—have succeeded in attracting at least one
major international research center to their territory.[36] All seven states
rely disproportionately on international research cooperation to compensate for the lack of domestic capacities, to gain access to knowledge and technologies developed elsewhere, and to facilitate the
process of technology transfer.[37] In 1973 participation in international
organizations or multinational research ventures accounted for 15 to
20 percent of national R and D expenditures in Switzerland and
Sweden, 30 percent in Norway and the Netherlands, and about 50
percent in Belgium.[38]

This dependence on foreign sources of technology is a mixed bless-
ing. In relative terms the small European states lead the large countries in fundamental research and in the development of abstract
science. But they lag behind the large countries in experimental development and in the application of science to the development of
new technologies, patents, and products. The closer scientific and
technological development comes to commercial application, in sum,
the more disadvantageous is the position of the small European
states.[39] Yet whatever its advantages or disadvantages, this interpene-
tration with foreign research systems is the core of the R and D strategy of most small European states.

These states have a strong interest in the smooth functioning of
international economic organizations that facilitate policy coordination between states. With the encouragement of the large industrial
countries, nationals of this group of states have taken positions of

leadership in organizations such as the GATT, the IMF, and the OECD. Indeed citizens of the small European states have occupied the leading positions in those three organizations for more than half the time since the end of World War II.[40] In the debate about a New International Economic Order, which the less developed countries pressed on the advanced industrial states in the 1970s, the small European states tended to be more accommodative than the large industrial states. Their attitude was also reflected in economic aid much more generous than that granted by the large industrial states. In the United Nations Common Development Fund (UNCDF), for example, the small European states have played a leading role. Between 1973 and 1979 the Netherlands, Sweden, Norway, and Denmark accounted for 80 percent of total contributions of $92 million, as compared to only 4 percent for the United States.[41] This generosity betokens the unwillingness of the small European states to see the basic structure of the international economy disrupted by fundamental conflict between poor and rich states.[42]

A preference for a harmonious, liberal international economy goes hand in hand with enthusiastic support for detente between the major powers. In both instances self-interest rather than altruism dictates a political strategy through which the small European states seek to spread dependence and vulnerability among a larger number of actors. In the mid-1960s, for instance, members of the "Group of Nine," drawn from both Eastern and Western Europe, hoped to increase the scope of national action by opposing strictly defined power blocks and favoring international pluralism.[43] This preference for detente is hardly surprising; with the exception of Sweden the small European states typically spend relatively less on military security than do middle-sized powers or large states. Per capita defense expenditures of one group of small European states amount to less than one-half of per capita expenditures in large advanced industrial states, and the difference increases greatly in some defense-related industries, such as civil aerospace.[44] But interest in a reduction of international tensions stems also from the awareness that the security of the small states is best served by a general orientation toward war avoidance. Small states, in the language of strategic analysis, rely on political deterrence rather than military defense.[45]

In their pursuit of detente the small European states rely heavily on international organizations, because these organizations offer a forum where small states can hope to be more successful than in bilateral dealings.[46] Well-organized caucusing among groups of small states—the Scandinavian countries, the Benelux countries, the Group

of Nine—enhances not only the probability of blocking disadvantageous initiatives from bigger states but also a chance for small states to
seize the initiative themselves.[47] The emphasis of small European
states on international organizations in security issues is illustrated
both by the three decades when their citizens held the position of
secretary general of the United Nations and by their prominent role
in UN peace-keeping missions. These political contributions are not
acts of magnanimity. They are instead dictated by the enlightened
self-interest that all small states have in well-functioning international
organizations.[48]

Since 1945 the small European states have tended to make fewer
demands on the international state system and have been more interested in the process of detente than is true of other groups of states.[49]
They differ from both the less developed countries and the large
advanced industrial states in their conservative orientation. They
have tended to favor a "pragmatic" over an "ideological" orientation,
emphasizing universal conciliation rather than exclusionary activism
and avoiding "talking big" and "acting small."[50] Even those small
European states which joined alliances after 1945 have opted cautiously for multilateral alliances rather than the riskier options of
bilateralism or "mixed multilateralism."[51] And those following a policy
of neutrality have emphasized a low-risk defensive posture, in contrast to the nonalignment of Third World countries (which has been
compatible with a higher-risk, offensive stance).[52] In short, the small
European states, compared to the less developed countries and the
large advanced industrial states, have chosen strategies for security
that match their strategies in economic matters; both express their
satisfaction with the status quo.

DOMESTIC COMPENSATION

The small European states complement their pursuit of liberalism
in the international economy with a strategy of domestic compensation. Since their leverage over developments in international markets
is insignificant, the small European states seek to exert some degree of
control over their destiny through a variety of domestic policies.
These policies are carried by the conviction that it is important to
counter some of the harmful effects of international liberalization.
Political laissez-faire is a luxury of large industrial countries, a luxury
in which the small European states cannot indulge. Even liberal theo-
rists of international trade now widely agree that "the link between

47

the case for free trade and the case for laissez-faire has been broken."[53] Marxist scholars are similarly impressed by the distinctive capacity of the small European states for domestic compensation.[54]

Policies designed to provide compensation for instabilities in investment and employment are common among all of the small European states. The most celebrated of all stabilization policies is Sweden's investment reserve, which is designed to smooth out fluctuations in the business cycle.[55] Created in the mid-1950s under legislation dating back to 1938, this reserve fund compensates for the decreasing usefulness of such direct controls as licenses and regulations and adds strength to more traditional instruments of indirect influence on the economy. Firms enjoying high profits in good times can avoid taxation by freezing some of their profits in a special reserve fund; on the downward swing of the business cycle these funds are released for specific, approved projects. By the early 1970s the Swedish investment fund accounted for about 12 percent of total annual investment.[56] Sweden's experience is not unique. In the mid-1960s, for example, Norwegian firms could deposit up to 20 percent of taxable profits in a special account of the Central Bank, to be invested (at a considerable tax saving) at some future time of slack demand. Denmark had a comparable policy.[57] Switzerland's government procurement policy also responds to fluctuations in the business cycle, permitting firms to defer investment until periods of underemployment.[58]

The small European states differ further from the large industrial countries in both the extent and the explicitness with which they support employment, either directly through a variety of manpower policies or indirectly through the sheer size of public subsidies to individual firms. In the 1960s and 1970s all of the small European states, and in particular Switzerland, deliberately used foreign workers as a buffer with which to protect the employment of the indigenous work force. In the 1970s most small European states encouraged growth in public-sector employment. The Netherlands and Norway, among others, have taken a considerable interest in vocational training programs as well as temporary employment measures, including temporary wage subsidies.[59] But in the sheer size and sophistication of such programs no small European state rivals Sweden.[60] Concentrated heavily in the construction industry, Swedish programs have had very sizable employment effects. Since 1972 grants have been extended to firms in temporary difficulties to prevent layoffs. In 1972–73, for example, unemployment would have doubled without an active employment policy funded by the investment reserve fund. Instead, the number of workers in retraining increased, from 100,000 in 1972 to 142,000 in 1973.[61] Between 1972 and 1976 the minimum number of people in retraining per annual quarter was 1,350; the highest was 19,600; and the largest quarterly variation exceeded 10,000.[62] In 1973 vocational training and retraining in Sweden could have been matched proportionately if the United States had trained 3.9 million workers or if West Germany and Britain had trained 1 million workers each.[63] By the early 1980s financial support for these programs weighed heavily on a Sweden struggling to regain its international competitiveness.

Most prominent among policies of domestic compensation are the restraints on wage and price increases imposed or agreed upon in the name of a national "incomes policy." Reliance on political rhetoric and "neutral" experts are politically costless forms of incomes policy, and they can be found in industrial countries large and small. What is distinctive of the small European states is wage control through centralized bargaining and even more far-reaching stabilization agreements, with or without quasi-government- or government-imposed price controls, legal sanctions, and direct restraints on the public sector.[64]

The most celebrated example of incomes policy occurred in a country with an extremely open economy. The Dutch policy of deliberate wage restraint and price control throughout the 1950s and 1960s, as Murray Edelman and R. W. Fleming note, came close to the "displacement of collective bargaining by public and semi-public agencies."[65] Even though government involvement in collective bargaining was far more important than any legal sanction in making the system work, Dutch incomes policy was distinguished from that of the large industrial countries by its great formalism. Bram Peper summarizes: "Underlying the entire system is the principle that the government has a responsibility for involving itself in the state of industrial relations."[66] Dedicated to the principles of free trade and operating in an international economy with fixed-exchange rates, the Netherlands faced a "mercantilist dilemma."[67] It could not hope to accelerate its industrialization in the 1950s and 1960s through the traditional instruments of protection, high tariffs, and devaluation. Thus the infant-industry argument amounted in Dutch terms to relatively low wages and prices achieved through incomes policy. Direct price controls were indispensable, especially in the 1950s, to the success of the policy, because price controls hardened the opposition of employers to wage increases. Moreover, many prices were specified in the country's elaborate economic plans.

Developments in the 1960s and 1970s changed the basis for this centrally guided system of incomes policy. Between 1950 and 1960 Dutch wage and salary earners covered by collective bargaining agreements increased from 34 to 57 percent of the working population while those covered by binding regulations declined from 48 to 26 percent.[68] The absence of any serious balance-of-payments crisis in the 1960s and changes in union structure and policies further eroded the formal mechanisms of incomes policy, until the whole system finally collapsed in 1968. Although a substantial amount of informal control and centralization survived, cooperation in Dutch industrial relations declined sharply in the 1970s as the centrally guided system was increasingly replaced by industry-level—and even company-level—negotiations and contracts. Free collective bargaining, with occasional statutory controls, marked the 1970s. But even in this new system of wage and price determination bargaining still exhibited a vague consensus derived from the openness of the Dutch economy to international markets: the new militancy of the unions, for example, did not translate into a larger number of strikes. In detailing the changes of the 1960s and 1970s Steven Wolinetz concludes that both business and unions, their public protestations to the contrary notwithstanding, still quietly welcomed government intervention. If so, then what the Dutch have, he concludes, is "responsible unionism in disguise."[69]

In contrast to the Netherlands, in Sweden the central wage bargain has since 1956 included a legally sanctioned "peace clause" without direct state interference but with state collaboration. It serves purposes essentially similar to those of the more formalized, government-supervised Dutch incomes policy.[70] Sweden's informal incomes policy is based on the sanctity of free collective bargaining; it works directly from inside the industrial relations system rather than indirectly through pressure from outside. Since the mid-1960s price and wage increases in Sweden's dual-sector economy have been determined by the effect of international markets on the high-productivity "competitive" sector and the effect of the unions' determination to spread wage gains to the lower-productivity "sheltered" sectors. Minimizing wage differentials between workers in different sectors is thus the result of deliberate policy. Swedish officials tolerate this narrowing of wage differentials in the interest of social justice and industrial rejuvenation. Sweden has only rarely, as in 1970, had recourse to a formal freezing of prices in order to narrow its trade deficit and slow the outflow of capital. In general Sweden has sought to achieve the same objectives by informal means through controlling investment in the construction industry and, at times, through attempting to restrict consumption. Developments in the late 1960s and early 1970s, such as the revolt of the rank and file against centralized wage bargains and the assertiveness of white-collar unions, pointed to a dilution of union centralization and the growth of wage determination in labor markets without government interference. These changes became more marked after a conservative coalition government was voted into office in 1976. Yet wage increases were still determined largely in accordance with government policy. As Sergio Lugaresi says, "From 1977 to 1982 the real wages of industrial workers fell by almost 10 percent, a datum which finds no equal in other European industrial countries."[71] In 1984 the unions and employers decided to abandon Sweden's system of centralized wage negotiations. The result, the government charged, was to turn wage negotiations into a free-for-all, impeding the government's efforts to lower Sweden's annual inflation rate from 9 percent in 1983 to 4 percent in 1984. In April 1984 the government imposed a freeze on prices and was discussing in public a variety of measures to contain what it regarded as excessive wage increases.[72]

The Netherlands and Sweden provide the two versions of formal incomes policy and centralized wage bargain that also inform the strategies of Denmark and Norway. Denmark's strong interest in an incomes policy came only after three successive balance-of-payments deficits in the early 1960s. Unlike their opposite numbers in Sweden and Norway, Danish officials have not accepted the idea of a "dual-sector economy." Like policy makers in the Netherlands in the 1950s and 1960s, they have relied on a legislative approach to incomes policy, supplemented by a collective bargaining system less centralized than those in neighboring Scandinavian countries. As was the case in the Netherlands in the 1960s and 1970s, incomes policy in Denmark has had a spotty record; the institutional basis of incomes policy weakened across the 1970s, as illustrated by the strikes of 1973. But incomes policy, especially statutory wage freezes, was of sufficient political appeal to provide, as in Norway, the country's main response to the prolonged economic recession of the 1970s.

Because Denmark and Norway both had recourse to an incomes policy, in the early 1960s as well as in the late 1970s, they have more seeming similarities in their attempts to achieve wage restraint than is in fact the case.[73] Norway's policy more closely resembles the Swedish model of a "private" incomes policy than the Dutch "public" version. At the heart of the Norwegian approach lies, as in Sweden, a system of free collective bargaining, fully centralized since 1963, and a union policy of wage solidarity. Only three times since World War II—in 1956, 1961, and 1974—has a central wage bargain been negotiated. It is true that the Norwegian use of direct planning and price controls resembled Dutch policies until 1978, when the government introduced a short-lived wage and price freeze. But it is important to note that these controls were never extended to wage determination. As in Sweden, wage levels are fixed in consultation with the government; since 1975 they have frequently been coordinated with the government's negotiations with agricultural organizations over prices and subsidies and with public-sector employees over wages. Free collective bargaining persists nonetheless.

Economic openness has made the adoption of incomes policies an opportunity with which most of the small European states have experimented in the last two decades. As this discussion has shown, the small European states have evolved a broad range of institutional solutions to address their common predicament. But in most instances the international pressure for a cooperative solution has been intense. Balance-of-payments problems offer a danger signal particularly obvious in small, open economies. As Lloyd Ullman and Robert Flanagan argue, that signal "probably remains the most effective incentive to union cooperation with incomes policy. . . ."[74]

For the large industrial states, incomes policies have been a relatively unimportant element of domestic compensation.[75] The United States, for example, has never instituted a successful incomes policy. True, a variety of proposals for "tax-based incomes policies" were discussed in the 1970s. The basic idea was to reward workers with tax credits for accepting low wage increases or to penalize employers with higher taxes for conceding high wage increases. Such proposals, if enacted, would have left the determination of wage levels to individual actors in labor markets rather than to centralized peak associations. Compared to the mixture of statutory control and political bargaining that distinguishes the small European states, tax-based incomes policies would have relied heavily on the market for control. In any event, the strong political support enjoyed by monetarist doctrines in the early 1980s makes the adoption by the United States of any kind of incomes policy highly unlikely.

Britain has had some experience with incomes policies. But weak peak organizations of labor and business and a highly decentralized system of collective bargaining have condemned British efforts to no more than intermittent success. Across the Channel, because of the importance of corporatist traditions in French social thought and the existence of institutions with strong corporatist features (such as the

Conseil Economique et Social and the tripartite Commissions de Modernisation), France might be thought fertile ground for a successful incomes policy. But the failure of the *économie concertée* in the 1960s was due largely to the absence of a national incomes policy in the French system of economic planning. Labor and business strongly opposed the idea, and the weakness of French unions and the decentralization of collective bargaining would have made effective cooperation among peak associations impossible. The same reasoning applies to Japan, which has never experimented with an incomes policy.

West Germany has some corporatist structures similar to those of the small European states. As a result, West Germany's experience with incomes policy in the 1960s and 1970s resembles that of small states more than that of any other large industrial state. However, the establishment of a voluntary "Concerted Action" *(Konzertierte Aktion)* in 1967 centered around exchange of information rather than bargaining among peak associations, the federal government, and the Bundesbank. The foundation of that exchange, a consensus on macroeconomic policy and scientific expertise, was not sufficiently strong to withstand the distributional struggles that broke out in the harsher political and economic climate of the mid-1970s. In short, the failure of West Germany's "weak" incomes policy illustrates that incomes policy has been a less important and durable element of domestic compensation for all of the large industrial states than it has been for the small European states.

In the eyes of Lane Kirkland, head of America's AFL-CIO, a policy of wage restraint is a "detour into routes carved out by other tighter little societies."[76] With the exception of Switzerland, the small European states rather than the large industrial countries lead the movement from separate to parallel collective bargaining for blue- and white-collar employees (as in Belgium, the Netherlands, and Sweden) and from bilateral to trilateral or multipartite negotiations in which the wage bargain (as in the Netherlands, Austria, and Norway) is only one element in a much broader set of politically negotiated issues including profits, dividends, prices, pensions, and taxes.[77] In short, the small European states are at the forefront of developments where, Efén Córdova writes, "negotiations may be said to be moving from the distributive to the integrative model or at least to a halfway house between the two."[78] The small European states have taken to a variety of incomes policies in coping with the economic changes of the 1970s, and so frequently as to make it quite evident that, in the words of Christopher Saunders, "incomes policy cannot be regarded simply as an instrument of economic management, short-term or long-term, on the same plane as monetary policy. It is political in the widest sense."[79]

The small European states also rely on their public sector as a critically important component in domestic compensation. John Stephens puts it well: "Governments in nations with open economies have sought to counter the effects of external dependence by expanding their control over the domestic economy through the nationalization of a large portion of the national income."[80] The size and rate of increase of the public economy have been unusually large in the small European states. Numerous studies suggest that governments of the Right, Center, and Left in these states have increased spending more rapidly than in the large industrial states. One OECD analysis of public expenditure trends shows, for example, that in the small European states "the share of public expenditure in GDP has increased by two-thirds in the last twenty years, notably on account of a well-above-average growth in 'welfare' outlays."[81] The increase in total government expenditure between 1960–63 and 1977–79 in the small European states was also uniformly greater than in any of the five large industrial countries.[82]

This growth in the public economy is due primarily to a substantial increase in transfer payments, largely from government to households but also to producers, rather than to growth in government consumption itself. In the early and mid-1970s the proportion of Gross National Income (GNI) devoted to nonmilitary public-sector spending was substantially greater in the small European states (41%) than in the large industrial states (32%).[83] Public social welfare efforts in the small European states (excepting Switzerland) have been active and progressive in countries as divergent as the Netherlands, Sweden, and Denmark. Increases in pensions, which account for about two-thirds of all income-maintenance programs, brought expenditure elasticities for income-maintenance programs close to the OECD's maximum of two in the Netherlands, Sweden, Denmark, and Norway.[84] Changes in the demographic composition of the population and an extension of eligibility to a higher proportion of older people have pushed pension costs upward in all countries, irrespective of their size; but all of the small European states made concerted political efforts between 1962 and 1972 to increase benefits substantially.

This generosity characterizes the social welfare efforts of the small European states more generally. As a percentage of GDP in current prices, these states spent 5.4 as compared to 3.7 percent for the large states on education, 5.3 as compared to 4.3 on health, and 12.9 as compared to 8.6 on income maintenance programs. In the area of defense, by way of contrast, in the mid-1970s the small European states spent on the average only 2.5 as compared to 3.7 percent for the large states.[85]

It was only in the 1950s and 1960s—that is, during the time of international liberalization—that the public sector assumed such a prominent role in the small European states. OECD data show that in the 1950s the total public expenditures (as a percentage of GDP) of the large industrial countries slightly exceeded those of the small European states. From the mid-1960s on, however, an increasingly rapid divergence occurred, and by the mid-1970s the average for the small European states was 45 percent of GDP as compared to 38 percent for the large industrial countries.[86] In 1956–57 the share of social security expenditures in national income was identical, 13 percent in both the small European and the large industrial states; but by 1971 the small European states were on the average spending 20.9 percent of their GNP on social security as compared to 14.3 percent for the large industrial states.[87] "The largest governments—size being measured by government expeditures as a percentage of national income—were to be found in the Federal Republic of Germany, France, and the United Kingdom in the 1950s but in Denmark, the Netherlands, and Norway in the 1970s," writes one analyst.[88] Between 1950 and the early 1970s the average annual increase in government expenditures as a percentage of national income varied for the small European states between a high of 1.84 percent for Sweden and a low of 0.62 percent for Switzerland as compared, among the large industrial countries, to a high of 0.55 percent for the United Kingdom and a low of 0.44 percent for France. Put slightly differently, the growth of public spending during the postwar years in "conservative" Switzerland exceeded the growth of spending in "socialist" Britain.[89] It still remains true, though, that Switzerland defies the rule among the small European states of a large public economy. Nevertheless, Switzerland's public economy grew fast between 1967 and 1976 and in fact experienced the highest relative growth rate among all OECD member states.[90]

Large and rapidly growing public expenditures in the small European states were, of course, accompanied by increasing tax burdens, which are now greater than in any other part of the Western world. In 1955–57 the average tax burden in the five large industrial countries exceeded by one percentage point the 26 percent in the small European states. But with the early 1960s taxation began to rise sharply in the small European states. By the mid-1960s their levels of taxation exceeded those of the five large countries, and by the mid-1970s the relative share of total taxes in GDP was 41 percent in the small European states, 32 percent in the large countries; the greatest difference occurred in the incidence of direct taxation.[91]

This heavy tax burden is a major reason why growth in public-sector spending has met active resistance. Denmark provides the most frequently cited example of "welfare backlash."[92] Between 1953 and 1973 public consumption, rather than transfer payments as in the Netherlands, grew more sharply in Denmark than in any other small European state. Since most of the revenues were raised through direct taxes, Danish citizens could not help noting that they had become the most heavily taxed population in the OECD.[93] In 1970 the share of the Danish work force in the public sector exceeded the work force in manufacturing industry (19% versus 17%),[94] and by the late 1970s the deleterious consequences for Denmark's international competitiveness were obvious. The backlash against the welfare state shattered the foundations of Denmark's party system. But despite high inflation, an unemployment rate of about 10 percent, and pressing balance-of-payments deficits in the 1980s, the rebellion of the Danish voters does not appear to signify that any sizable segment of either the general public or the political elite wants to discard the Danish welfare state. Sounding a common theme, one study concludes that the welfare state has not been dismantled, only pruned. "The basic programs of the welfare state have not been cut; adjustments have been made on the margin, and future promises are more modest. . . . There is greatly increased awareness of their sensitivity and vulnerability to regional and international economic developments. Neither in Denmark nor Sweden has this dependence and interdependence been received passively, but it has taken trial and error to find appropriate policies."[95]

The imperatives of domestic compensation set the boundaries over a wide range of issues for the public policies that the small European states pursue. These countries have tried to restrain their wages and, occasionally, prices through a government-coordinated incomes policy (as in the Netherlands and Denmark), or through a centralized system of collective bargaining (as in Sweden and Norway), or though some combination of the two (as in Austria). Wage restraint has been linked to generous public spending. In the era of economic growth wage restraint typically coincided with a sizable expansion of publicly funded, rapidly increasing, income-supplementing payments. In the era of stagflation Sweden tried to create the conditions for wage restraint by coordinating tax cuts to increase disposable income, while in the Netherlands the government occasionally facilitated collective bargaining by reducing social welfare premia, thereby providing employers with an inducement to settle for wages higher than they might otherwise have agreed to. Whether by increased spending or reduced taxes or social security contributions, the distributional struggle in most of the small European states has been shifted away, Douglas Hibbs argues, "from the private marketplace, where allocation takes place through collective bargaining and industrial conflict, to the public arena, where labor and capital compete through political negotiation and electoral mobilization."[96]

FLEXIBLE INDUSTRIAL ADJUSTMENT

The small European states share a political strategy of industrial adjustment that combines international liberalization and domestic compensation. The commitment of the small European states to the principle of international liberalization is not mere rhetoric. These states have been more hesitant than their larger counterparts to protect declining industrial sectors from inexpensive imports. Throughout the postwar years, moreover, the small European states have consistently welcomed the inflow of foreign capital, which they see as an ingredient essential rather than detrimental to their economic and political aspirations. International liberalization is balanced against domestic compensation. While each of the small European states has developed a distinctive capacity, a particular set of policies, these countries as a group are distinguished by the range and innovativeness of their policies of domestic compensation. These instruments include incomes policy, a large public sector, and generous social welfare expenditures.

The small European states are clear exceptions to the generalization that liberalism in the international economy and interventionism in the domestic economy are incompatible.[97] The experience of the small European states suggests instead that political intervention in the domestic economy in the interest of domestic compensation does not constrain international liberalization, it is its necessary concomitant. In the 1970s conspicuous deviations from the principle of free trade occurred not so much in small states as in those large industrial states which lacked well-designed, broad-ranging policies of domestic compensation.

In linking international liberalization with domestic compensation, the small European states respond to economic change with flexible policies of industrial adjustment. They neither export the costs of change through protection nor preempt the costs of change through structural transformation. Instead, they deal with the problems of change rather than wishing them away. And they do not expect to solve problems with strong-arm methods and a few decisive blows. Instead, there are many small hands, many small blows, many mistakes, and many corrections. This sort of response looks confused and disorderly. In an increasingly uncertain economic environment where rates of economic change are accelerating, however, the response is the small European states' important contribution to the repertoire of modern capitalism.

In all countries, be they large or small, the textile and apparel industries suffer from competitive pressures, overcapacity, and the need to confront more efficient producers in low-wage countries. In this context even "the smaller industrialized countries of Europe . . . appear to be caught up in the protectionist vogue"[98] to some extent. But even in this hardest-pressed of industrial sectors several small European states have shown a willingness and a capacity to conduct continuous and incremental adjustment. The Netherlands, for example, consciously tried to reduce the size of the Dutch textile and apparel industry by moving a large part of production to low-wage countries in Eastern Europe and Northern Africa.[99] The apparel industry, in particular, responded to this policy of open borders by increasing productivity and concentration first and shifting production abroad later. By 1978, 20 percent of total imports of apparel were Dutch products manufactured abroad. As a result of government policy and corporate response, the total number of jobs in textiles and apparel in the Netherlands declined from 60,000 to 20,000 between 1968 and 1978.

Belgian industry, just across the border, was very much affected by these changes. Between 1960 and 1977 Belgium's textile and apparel industry shrank by more than 9,000 jobs; more than half of these jobs were in Dutch-owned firms, which moved in growing numbers to North Africa when Belgian production costs became too high. The foreign firms that Belgium had courted so avidly in the 1960s were thus contributing to the country's economic problems in the 1970s through their policy of divestment. Like the Netherlands, Sweden has through free-trade policy encouraged a drastic reduction in the size of its textile industry.[100] In 1977 the import of textiles accounted for 72 percent of domestic consumption, as compared to 36 percent in the EEC and 12 percent in the United States.[101] A variety of specific policies in vocational training, export incentives, mergers, and investment aids attempted to strengthen competitive producers.

These different experiences in small European states share a willingness to bear the costs of change. It would be difficult to argue that in the case of textiles the policy of the small European states has been more "successful" by some objective, economic standard. But the reactive and flexible process of industrial adjustment shows that the motivation for policy does not lie solely in "succeeding." Problems not only have to be solved, they have to be lived with. Reactive, flexible adjustment, which proceeds by way of many small steps to acknowledge the continuous change in the world economy, seems well suited both to adjusting to unforeseen developments and to holding together domestic societies continuously threatened by external instabilities.

Distinctive differences also exist between the large industrial countries and the small European states in public policies that seek to modify market conditions abroad. Large industrial states tend to export the costs of change while the small European states tend to live with them. It was the large countries, not the small ones, that were at the forefront in developing various policies—voluntary export restrictions, other forms of invisible protection, and sector-specific trade regimes within the GATT framework—to accomplish that objective within the liberal postwar economy. The United States, for example, has done so in textiles since the 1950s, steel since the 1960s, and a growing number of industrial sectors, including automobiles, that have faced serious problems in the 1970s and early 1980s. The same was increasingly true of the European Communities in the 1970s. In its trade policies only Japan has apparently withstood the protectionist trend of the 1970s, perhaps because it never permitted full-blown liberalization.

Their adherence to international liberalization has, by and large, made the small European states prefer a different course. This does not mean that the small European states never imitate the political innovations through which the large industrial countries export the costs of change. Additionally, some of the small European states, notably Switzerland, have equipped their societies with a foreign work force whose manipulation makes it possible to absorb virtually all of the costs of change in the international trade system. Other small states, Austria for instance, have a lower capacity to absorb rapid change in international commerce; they more frequently try to export the costs of change to others through selective sector- or product-specific trade restraints. On balance, though, large and small countries differ considerably in their capacity and willingness to live with the costs of change.

Different industries lend themselves to different forms of political intervention in international markets. In textiles and steel, in particular, the small states have had to live with the rules set by the large industrial countries. In the 1950s Austria and the Scandinavian countries were very critical of the European Coal and Steel Community (ECSC) and worried over their supplies of coke, scrap iron, and iron ore, especially in times of shortage. Such exporters of high-quality steel as Austria and Sweden were also concerned over the ECSC's tariff harmonization and pricing policy, and questions of market access. In the end these fears proved to be unfounded. The community's tariffs on steel declined, in part because of the insistent prodding of its small members.[102]

The resurgence of protectionism in the 1970s organized in sector-specific trade regimes, especially in declining industries, also emanated from the large industrial countries. In the late 1960s the five large industrial countries had imposed a total of twenty quantitative import restrictions on textile products; the seven small European states had imposed none.[103] Since 1975 small and large countries alike have introduced import surveillance systems on textile products, but only Britain, France, and Italy insist on cumbersome administrative methods designed to impair imports.[104] The growing pressure of low-cost exports from the less developed countries in a time of declining economic growth has forced the small European states to a more restrictive course. But the amount of liberalization that small countries can offer in exposed sectors is severely circumscribed by the policy of the European Community. Every tightening of the protectionist screw in Brussels displaces low-cost exports from the developing countries to adjacent markets, which, because of their small size, threaten to be swamped unless some protectionist measures are instituted. Nonetheless, in these sectors and more generally, the small European states have resisted to an astonishing degree the temptations of the "new nationalism."[105]

The industrial policy dilemmas confronting the small European states in the late 1970s were not unique—they had faced similar dilemmas in economic planning in the late 1950s. In the first postwar decade the small European states had relied heavily on planned methods of large-scale economic reconstruction or deliberate modernization.[106] The planning policies of the small European states, designed to make changes in the national economy more predictable and less costly, differed from those in the large industrial states. The United States, Britain, and West Germany, with their commitment to liberalism, rapidly dismantled the machinery of economic control in the late 1940s and early 1950s; Japan and France, meanwhile, embarked on policies of state-initiated and supervised sectoral transformation. The small European states carved a path between liberalism and statism; it led them toward indirect forms of economic control. In an assessment that captures the distinctiveness of economic planning in all of the small European states, one analyst noted that "Swedish planning is a type of indicative planning midway between the French system of highly centralized detailed planning and the 'mild' form of economic coordination used in the U.S."[107] What unites the political experience of the small European states and sets them apart from the large industrial countries is the *premise* of their planning efforts, adaptation to external market forces.[108]

In the 1950s and 1960s the Netherlands and Norway made the greatest advances in the development and application of planning methods suited to the structural constraints that the small European states faced. Indeed, the theory of economic planning had been developed most systematically by Dutch and Norwegian economists, men like Jan Tinbergen and Ragnar Frisch who, in 1969, were jointly awarded the Nobel Prize in economics.

The elaborate economic plans of the Netherlands in particular rested on technical sophistication.[109] Planning methods relied after 1950 on econometric methods, and economists have been highly influential, both as officeholders and as advisers. As James Abert describes the situation, "Although the Central Planning Bureau (CPB) and the Central Statistics Bureau do not have the formal power to make policy themselves, their work as staff to policy makers, both in the cabinet and in the extra-Parliamentary advisory bodies, strongly influences the range, rationality, and direction of the economic decision-making process."[110] The systematic application of economic science to the problems of the Dutch economy was in striking contrast to the more liberal inclinations of the United States, Britain, or West Germany on the one hand and the statist planning that emerged in France and Japan on the other. Dutch planning was not indicative in the French sense of concerted action *(économie concertée);* but it offered more of a guiding idea *(économie orientée)* to policy makers than was true in, say, West Germany.[111] The Dutch approach was not to attempt real planning but to make contingency forecasts.

Norwegian planning also differed in kind from the planning efforts of the large advanced industrial states. In contrast to France, with which it was frequently compared, technical advances in input-output analysis in the 1960s were not translated into a politically ambitious attempt at indicative planning on the sectoral level.[112]

Norwegian forecasts, furthermore, stressed aggregate rather than detailed figures and hoped to provide a broad framework for the annual budget rather than to maximize economic growth or efficiency. Although the control of investment capital by the government and the nationalized banks was one of the key ingredients in what throughout the 1970s remained one of the highest investment ratios in Europe, Norway's industry is not tied closely to the public sector. The Norwegian government thus lacks the kinds of credit controls typical of France or Japan.[113] The Norwegian planning authorities also lacked a tripartite body representing labor, business, and the government that could have strengthened the hand of the planners. An economic planning council established in 1945 stopped functioning in the 1950s when the business community withdrew its support. Throughout the 1960s Norway's nationalized sector was relatively small; instead of public ownership or the control of investment capital, the Norwegian government exercised its influence directly on big or strategically located sectors or enterprises.[114] In sum, the Norwegian government had fewer policy instruments than France or Japan by which it could shape developments in different sectors of the economy. Indeed, one could argue that Norwegian planning more nearly resembles Dutch efforts, in making its central contribution in the 1960s not in the form of a planned modernization program but through strengthening Norway's incomes policy. One year before Norway instituted its incomes policy in 1963, for example, 70 percent of all prices in Norway's cost-of-living index were controlled by the government.

The planning experience of the small European states has been marked by one distinctive feature: estimates for the development of exports and imports have, because of the openness of their economies, normally been way off the mark. This has been especially true of the Netherlands, Norway, and Sweden.[115] The gradual elimination of direct import controls during the 1950s took an important instrument out of the hands of the planners and left them in their medium- and long-term planning unable to defend their national economies against the effects of changes in international markets. Indeed, Belgium, in contrast to France, avoided the term "planning" altogether in the 1960s and preferred instead to talk about "program"; its ad hoc and pragmatic economic planning focused primarily on the competitive role of the Belgian economy in international markets.[116] This lack of defenses makes more intelligible why the Dutch do not really plan but produce contingency forecasts; why Austria, with the largest nationalized sector in the OECD, has no more than rudimentary planning instruments; and why Norway shifted to medium-term sectoral policies in the 1960s (on the premise that economic openness was forcing all planning to be little more than short-run policy).[117] For this reason, perhaps, "Swedish planning is unaccompanied by sanctions except the sanction imposed by the force of economic intelligence and what Rehn once called 'the dictatorship of circumstances.'"[118] The small European states generally found comprehensive or sectoral planning efforts increasingly inapplicable, simply because of their economic openness. They needed, in Raymond Vernon's words, "to remain upright and watertight in a heaving international sea; for them, therefore, the problem was one of selecting the devices of stabilization that were in harmony with their social objectives."[119] But economic openness also inhibited the small European states from relinquishing planning altogether.

On questions of R and D policy that are closely connected to the international competitiveness of industrial economies, the small and the large industrial states differ markedly in the domestic influence they seek to exercise. Generally speaking, the large industrial states concentrate their R and D funds in modern, science-based sectors of the economy with substantial risks while the small European states tend to spend their funds, with the exception of pharmaceuticals, in more traditional industries facing less uncertainty and lower growth rates.[120] But the small European states have created good conditions for innovative firms in more traditional sectors of their economy. In the 1960s and 1970s they allocated a large portion of their total R and D budget to stimulate industrial innovation, a substantially larger portion than any large industrial country except West Germany.[121] The small European states, furthermore, emphasize the absorption and dissemination of scientific and technological information rather than an interventionist science policy. Their distinguished technical universities play a central role in bridging the gap that often separates pure from applied science and inhibits industrial applications of science and technology. The large industrial countries set up specialized research institutes, for example the French CNRS or the German Max-Planck institute, to fulfill a similar purpose in the name of a government-directed R and D policy, frequently concentrating in areas of big science.[122] The small states' emphasis on dissemination and absorption is also illustrated by the importance that they attach to vocational training programs, which are on average about twice as large as those in the large industrial countries.[123]

R and D policies in the small European states are economically oriented partly because of the absence of large-scale government-funded research for national security and partly because of the prominence of business in the financing of the total R and D budget. In the 1960s and 1970s the relative share of R and D expenditures in GDP increased in the small European states while, on average, it declined in the large industrial states.[124] In the 1970s, one OECD study of the R and D policies in five small European states could conclude, "today the feeling prevails . . . that the distance which separates them from other countries is shrinking."[125] The particular competence of these seven states lies in their adaptation to changing demand patterns in international markets.[126] Their approach is less expensive, more flexible, more oriented toward the needs of industry, and less influenced by political pressures than is typically true of the large industrial states. They tend to favor, in other words, a route that at least one major study has identified as the most likely avenue to success.[127]

According to the OECD, in sum, "traditions, institutions and structures form a context and impose policies which bear no resemblance to those of the larger European countries."[128] Growing international liberalization in the 1950s and 1960s devalued direct controls and the tariff as instruments of policy.[129] Unlike large liberal industrial states, the United States and West Germany among them, the small European states paid more attention to industrial policy as one possible instrument for pacing the structural changes in their domestic economies. But the small European states shunned the kind of systematic, large-scale reordering of specific industrial sectors that became the hallmark of the statist strategies of Japan and France.

An analysis of Swedish developments in the 1970s supports this argument. An American firm, the Boston Consulting Group, was commissioned to develop a framework for Swedish industrial policy.[130] It reported that Sweden lacked what might be called a coherent and selective industrial policy. The report usefully illustrates that a "Japanese" or "French" approach to structural transformation is utterly misplaced in the small European states. The firm recommended to the government that it was time to turn away from Keynesian aggregate-demand policies supplemented by a very active labor-market policy and turn instead toward a seriously considered and sustained industrial policy, targeted in particular on growth industries. The Swedish prime minister appointed a committee to evaluate the report, and this special economic delegation criticized the report severely. The committee's "main message . . . is that the future development of the Swedish economy depends on the general economic and social situation, rather than the specific economy policy measures." Despite vehement debate over the two contrasting analyses, neither report "led to any tangible changes in Swedish industrial policy. Sweden continues to depend primarily on the traditional, well-known economic policy methods."[131] Yet compared to the scope of these policies, the improvisations of Sweden's reactive industrial policy are striking.

What was true of Sweden characterized the situation of the small European states more generally: "The main function of policy is therefore to help industry adapt to the changing competitive order as opposed to protecting industry from this competition."[132] In particular, small European states have provided generous assistance for individual firms coping with the adverse consequences of economic change.[133] The small European states have lagged somewhat behind the large countries in statistical measures of general government intervention in industry including nationalization. But they have been more active in specific interventions.[134] In both 1960 and 1976 the small European states granted, in relative terms, about twice as much in public subsidies to enterprises as did the large industrial countries.[135] These subsidies included both temporary assistance in times of difficulties and support for attempts to regain competitiveness. Some case studies of individual firms in trouble suggest that small countries seek to defend firms, especially well-established, large ones, in danger of being eliminated by adverse market developments.[136] Since structural change is perceived to occur within rather than between industrial sectors. Individual enterprises are to be preserved if at all possible. To establish large firms in the small, open markets of these countries is an extremely costly task, especially since these firms are social institutions of considerable importance which are sacrificed only with great reluctance. What distinguishes the approach of the small European states is the political attention they pay to questions of industrial policy and the continuity in their responses to particular problems in the 1960s and 1970s, not some systematic and overarching strategy of industrial redevelopment.[137]

During the postwar era, for example, the Netherlands moved from nationally planned industrialization in the 1940s and 1950s to reactive industrial policy in the 1960s and 1970s.[138] Since 1970 about thirty sectoral studies have been concluded, but one can detect no clear, overarching policy of industrial adjustment to changes imposed by shifts in international markets.[139] Ad hoc measures and improvisation in such declining industrial sectors as shipbuilding, textiles, or mining are the rule rather than the exception. To the extent that there is a clear policy, it reinforces rather than restrains market developments, as the internationalization of the Dutch clothing industry in the 1970s shows[140]—a firm Dutch belief in the efficacy of the international divi-

65

sion of labor has meant that declining domestic textiles have received little assistance. Dutch industrial policy appears to be more systematic in high-technology sectors, where a deliberate attempt has been made to join international production ventures (for example, in aircraft or satellites) or to rely heavily on Dutch multinational corporations (for example, in electronics).[141] In other instances, however, the Dutch have failed to strengthen competitive firms or industry segments. On balance, the Dutch experience in the 1970s offers no unambiguous record.

Sweden, like the Netherlands, developed an industrialization policy in the 1950s, targeted to individual firms, in the hope of achieving full employment and price stability. "In general Sweden's policies are similar to those of other small countries, like Belgium and the Netherlands," the Boston Consulting Group concluded, but they "are less comprehensive than those of the larger countries who are Sweden's major competitors."[142] An active industrial policy, one might have thought, could have been legitimized by the sharp reduction in tariffs in the postwar years coupled with Swedish unwillingness to tolerate wide wage differentials between internationally exposed and sheltered sectors of the economy. But Sweden's industrial policy has remained reactive.[143]

Since the early 1960s Sweden's pension fund has given the government a potent financial instrument. Economic problems appearing in the mid-1960s prompted the government to create several new agencies to deal with problems of industry: a ministry of industry, a council for industrial policy, a technological development board, the Swedish Development Corporation, a corporation founded to acquire or start up industries in economically depressed regions, and a holding company for state enterprises.[144] Yet Sweden's industrial policy lacks an overall institutional focus.[145] A public investment bank was indeed established in 1967 with the intent of channeling pension funds into medium- and long-term financing of promising but risky industrial investments; it has restricted itself instead to relatively conservative lending policies, increasingly centered around the defense of existing jobs.[146] Initially a large share of these pension funds went into a conventional financing of Sweden's paper and pulp industry as well as some bail-out operations of endangered firms.

Over the years investment policies have come to favor the engineering industries as well as an improvement in Sweden's export financing system. Between 1970 and 1976 government assistance to industry measured as a percentage of gross capital formation increased from 8 to 24 percent, before jumping to over 50 percent in

1977. During the same years government assistance favored declining over growth sectors by a sizable margin. In the late 1970s, in particular, a very substantial amount of resources—relief work, wage subsidies, and government procurement—were provided to firms and sectors suffering severe economic distress.[147] Emergency interventions and bail-out operations for firms in severe difficulties prevailed. No broader strategy of industrial adjustment developed, among other reasons because of the suspicions of the Swedish business community that it might lead to a form of state socialism.[148]

Although selective programs occasionally have shown ingenuity crowned by success, Sweden, generally speaking, lacks a coherent and selective industrial policy.[149] The Boston Consulting Group advised the government to move away from its traditional reliance on Keynesian aggregate-demand policies supplemented by an active labor-market policy and to return, as it had done briefly in the late 1960s, to industrial policy as a more promising and appropriate instrument for adapting to economic change. The report explicitly criticized the defensive use of investment funds and the lack of a long-term planning perspective on problems of structural adjustment, concluding that various "programs have eased the problems of declining industries, but no coherent strategy has been developed for growth industries. . . . Sweden's policy has been defensive, reacting to crises rather than carefully planning necessary assistance with a long-term perspective."[150]

The experiences of the other small European states in trying to develop policies of industrial adjustment, though less noteworthy, bear some resemblance to the Dutch and Swedish cases. With virtually no public ownership of industry, in the 1960s Denmark was in the process of developing a long-term framework for Danish industry; yet throughout the 1970s Danish policy relied primarily on the creation of a good investment climate and frequent ad hoc consultations between government, business, and the unions.[151] In Norway a report issued by the Lied Committee in 1980 also recommended a form of long-term industrial adjustment policy that was relatively passive: "The committee positions itself much closer to the special economic policy delegation in Sweden" than to the report of the Boston Consulting Group.[152]

Since passing the Economic Expansion Law of 1970, Belgium has relied on great selectivity in government intervention and conscious strategy, especially with regard to high-technology sectors. One indicator of this recent turn in policy is sharp increases in official loans for industrial research.[153] The National Investment Corporation, which was set up in 1962, has become an important instrument of policy.[154] Acting as an industrial development bank, it permits public authorities to acquire temporary minority holdings in firms and thus to become directly involved in industrial reconversion. In 1972 the Agency for Industrial Development was set up, to strengthen the hand of public authorities.

All in all, public involvement has substantially influenced investment in Belgium. Between 1959 and 1969 about one-half of total investment in industry and mining benefited from low-cost loans or state guarantees. And the proportion is still higher if other benefits (e.g., capital goods, interest-free advances for R and D, and special tax incentives) are included in the computation. Yet despite Belgium's shift toward a more selective, focused policy of industrial adjustment, most of the instruments provided by the 1970 legislation for an active policy have not been used—quite possibly because of the ethnic and regional conflict that dominates Belgian politics.[155] Furthermore, the prolonged crisis in international markets has put enormous pressure on the government. While Belgian subsidies per ton of steel produced far exceed those in any other Western European country, 400,000 Belgian workers were nevertheless out of work in 1981, about 10 percent of the country's work force. Unemployment compensation is among the highest in Western Europe and absorbs about 10 percent of the national budget.[156] In times of acute crisis industrial redeployment has virtually no room for maneuver, for massive subsidies consume the available resources.

If there exists anywhere among the large industrial states an incomplete analogue to the adjustment strategy of the small European states, it is to be found in West Germany.[157] The secret of West Germany's industrial policy is its invisibility; there exists a division of labor between the public and the private sector understood and appreciated by almost everyone. Throughout the postwar years the West German government has followed liberal policies of nonintervention in the economy, policies that have been compatible with political interventions in particular sectors. As far back as the mid-1950s, for example, the West German government decided to develop a nuclear industry with a significant export capacity. Two decades later that decision would result in a severe economic and political challenge to America. In the 1960s the federal government orchestrated a sharp but orderly reduction in the size of West Germany's coal industry; on the threshold of the 1980s the government was in a position to shape the future of that critical industry. The aircraft and computer industries offer similar instances of targeted government intervention.

The government's intervention is supported by the important role that West Germany's banks play in industrial policy. Industrial reorganization in the 1970s relied heavily on the coordination and supervision that the banks provided. The transformation of West Germany's moribund textile industry in the late 1960s, the defense of Daimler against foreign acquisition in the mid-1970s, and the refinancing and reorganization of such industrial giants as AEG and Klöckner in the late 1970s, all are episodes illustrating, for better or for worse, the banks' deep enmeshment in West German industry. Equally important, the banks in their joint roles as guardians of stockholder interests and owners of capital closely monitor and influence the strategic decisions taken inside corporate boardrooms. These private institutional links between industry and finance are effective, and they free the government from the need to be more deeply involved in the affairs of West German industry.

The limited range of direct government involvement in West German industry has been both cause and consequence of a liberal foreign trade policy that has resembled and converged with American policies (with the notable exception of agriculture). West Germany's "private" industrial policy anticipated and corrected for economic change in international markets, thus weakening protectionist pressures. But the apparent lack of protectionist forces in Bonn is deceiving. West Germany's trade policy could afford to be so liberal because Brussels, not Bonn, offered the institutional arena for striking covert protectionist bargains with other European partners across national boundaries.

A recent OECD survey of industrial policy revealed no systematic differences in the objectives or instruments of industrial policies in small and large countries. Norway and Austria, which by most accounts come closest to the statist approach of France or Japan, still lacked many instruments for industrial adaptation in the 1960s and 1970s and instead relied heavily, as liberal states do, on taxation policy.[158] It is perhaps for this reason that the industrial policies of the small European states do not express a new form of "economic nationalism" or "diffused protection."[159] Despite the large and active public sector in Sweden, Norway, and Austria, the formulation and the implementation of trade and industrial policy are assigned to different ministries.[160] Small, open economies have only one overriding political interest: a liberal international economy. And they have always backed their words with deeds. During the past two decades the tariff levels of the small European states have been well below those of the large industrial countries, including the United States.

On the other hand, small states' openness to the influences of the internationl economy forbids indifference to questions of industrial adaptation. Openness also enforces those changes in industrial structures which a France or a Japan tries to impose through broader political strategies of sectoral transformation.

INDUSTRIAL ADJUSTMENT IN SWITZERLAND AND AUSTRIA

Although the small European states all adjust flexibly to economic change, they differ in how actively they pursue their adjustment policies. Switzerland and Austria illustrate the breadth of difference involved. The Swiss government pursues a passive industrial policy, lacks the control over investment capital so essential to state intervention in markets, has little direct impact on firm strategies, absorbs the costs of economic change primarily through a reliance on the market, and celebrates the economic invigoration that derives from rapidly changing industrial structures. In contrast, the Austrian government follows a more active industrial policy, has greater control over the allocation of investment capital thus assuring itself of the capacity to intervene in markets, has direct effects on firm strategies, seeks to absorb some of the costs of economic dislocation through the government's selective intervention in market processes, and prides itself on maintaining social consensus in times of rapid structural change. In Switzerland industrial change is often described in medical terminology as a process of slimming down *(gesundschrumpfen)*. The Austrian government, by way of contrast, prides itself on having achieved a fundamental transformation of Austrian industry without major surgery. These different policies of industrial adjustment are part and parcel of different political strategies and responses to economic change.

Switzerland

Switzerland's industrial policy can be described only as passive. By all accounts the involvement of political elites in planned restructuring of Switzerland's industrial base is negligible. When, for example, a government commission proposed a sharp reduction in subsidies in the mid-1960s, not a single cut could be made in the area of industrial policy—for the simple reason that no outright government financial subsidies had been granted to any industrial sectors or firms.[161] The one instance of organized capacity reduction of uncompetitive segments in Switzerland's textile industry in the last three decades occurred in 1967; it was privately organized. A survey of different aspects of Switzerland's economic policy in the 1970s thus lacks a chapter on industrial policy.[162] Apart from commissioning three sectoral studies of the machinery, textile, and watch industries in the mid-1970s, the federal government has deliberately chosen to treat problems of industrial adjustment at arm's length. The term sectoral policy *(Strukturpolitik)*, to the extent it is used at all by policy makers, refers primarily to Switzerland's embryonic regional policy. So far, at least, the Swiss have not focused their attention on the relation between foreign investment abroad and industrial redeployment at home. Indeed, it would take catastrophic economic changes to bring the issue to the fore. The Swiss government would not dream either of engaging in a systematic industrial reorganization with the help of foreign firms or of practicing costly policies designed to protect employment, options that Austria pursued actively in the 1970s.

This is not to argue that the Swiss government would never intervene directly in support of its industry. Since the mid-1970s, for example, the federal government has made modest, selective efforts to reinforce the R and D efforts of Switzerland's medium-sized and small firms. By the political standards prevailing in Austria and in many other countries, however, conditions must be extreme to justify intervention. Half-jokingly, one high-ranking official in the federal government defined those conditions: "We will support ailing industries only when the next-to-last firm in the industry has gone bankrupt."[163] It remains true in the eyes of the Swiss that "the state cannot decide which economic structures should be weakened and which should be strengthened."[164]

The greatest impediments to the Swiss government's pursuit of an active industrial policy are its lack of full control over the instruments of fiscal policy, its lack of a government procurement policy, and, most important, its lack of control over capital markets and a public investment bank. The debate about the budget cuts in 1975, for example, revealed once again what the Swiss have always suspected: that political leaders (and the public sector more generally) lack even a rudimentary conceptual basis for clarifying options and specifying criteria by which different industrial policy choices could be justified. Even if it wanted to intervene, the government simply does not have the instruments for an active industrial policy.

Indirectly, of course, public policy does affect Switzerland's industrial structure. In the 1960s, for example, the undervaluation of the franc, the unprecedented influx of foreign workers, and the docility of Switzerland's unions all contributed to an overexpansion of industry and a relative delay in the adjustment of firms to changing production structures in the world economy. Similarly, throughout the postwar years the investment rate of Swiss firms has been increased by their involvement in the country's extensive stockpiling of supplies for national emergencies; participation entitles firms to substantially subsidized interest rates, which help finance inventories. The restrictions placed on the influx of additional foreign workers also had an immediate, differential effect on various sectors.[165] Yet federal and cantonal governments have been both unable and unwilling to use the potentially powerful tool of manpower policy to influence Switzerland's industrial structure. Instead, responding to the appreciation of the franc and the economic crisis on the 1970s, it was Swiss firms that, recognizing fundamental changes in market conditions, refused to continue to employ a quarter of a million foreign workers after their work permits expired. A serious political issue was, for the Swiss, solved through market institutions.

This aversion to selective, direct intervention agrees with a frequent interpretation of low import tariffs—that they form part of a structural policy impartial in its effect because it conforms to market principles. Export risk insurance is similarly thought of as "liberal" because it is allegedly neutral in its impact on Switzerland's industrial structure. Furthermore, the appreciation of the Swiss franc in the 1970s, it is often argued, "impartially" forced an adaptation that, in light of the traditional undervaluation of the franc, was particularly harsh for those sectors of Swiss industry, textiles and watches among them, which relied on domestic production and foreign sales. In response to the numerous indirect effects of Switzerland's strategy, industries suffering from a structural decline in their international competitiveness have moved to redeploy their production facilities abroad, thus imitating the much earlier move of other sectors of industry.[166]

Since the large Swiss corporations typically meet their investment needs through retained earnings, the government would in any event have a difficult time directly influencing investment decisions. Reliance on national or international capital markets is relatively unimportant. The Basel chemical company Hoffmann-LaRoche, for example, went to the capital markets for the last time in 1920. That company holds the unique distinction among the world's large corporations of having literally paid back all outstanding stock issues. In the mid-1970s a single company share, had it been available for sale by a member of the family owning the company, would have cost in the neighborhood of a quarter-million francs.[167] Although Hoffmann-LaRoche is extreme, it suggests the autonomy that Switzerland's large firms derive from their sound financial basis. Even if one allows for the uncertainties of aggregate statistical estimates, Swiss industry's 83 percent investment rate through retained earnings is among the highest, if not the highest, in the world.[168]

The industrial adjustment currently under way in Switzerland occurs within established industrial structures. In the 1970s the dramatic appreciation of the franc illustrated the enormous rates of change to which Swiss industry must adjust. The innovation and adaptation required today of some of Switzerland's traditional export industries are very great; and so is the economic and social dislocation involved.[169] Recognizing the limits that the scarcity of Swiss labor, foreign protection, and the dangers of environmental pollution impose on the future expansion of industry, Switzerland's dynamic firms are moving beyond the production of industrial hardware. They are establishing consulting firms that sell industrial software which solves problems and is tailored to the individual needs of the customer. Since Switzerland is short on facilities specializing in industrial mass production, its firms are in an excellent position to exploit these profitable market niches. In the 1970s the federal government tried to reinforce strength in this area through the establishment of a school for the development of industrial software. In Switzerland, then, adjustment to economic change is defined largely as a strategic problem at the level of the firm.[170] Emphasis has been placed on the production of high-value-added goods (such as luxury consumer goods or investment goods), on the deliberate search for goods with low price elasticities occupying special market niches, and, most recently, on the transformation of an artisanal form of production (e.g., in embroidery or watches) to technical expertise and service (e.g., in machinery). The flexibility of many of Switzerland's small and medium-sized firms is an essential precondition to the adaptability of the entire economy.

Larger firms, by way of contrast, and in particular Switzerland's giant multinational corporations, rely in their adjustments on exceptionally high retained earnings, a very sound capital base, and their far-flung international operations. But Switzerland's multinationals do not form a monolithic whole; there are several distinct types of firms following different strategies of adjustment.[171] Vertically integrated companies, Nestlé and Alusuisse for example, are like America's oil companies truly global in their need for access to raw materials. Hoffmann-LaRoche and Ciba-Geigy resemble IBM or

Xerox; they are multinational due to their technological lead in several product lines. Unlike Nestlé, Ciba-Geigy often internationalizes production because of such nontariff barriers as the American Selling Price; it still exports from Switzerland on a significant scale. Brown Boveri and other Swiss multinationals in the machinery industry, such as Sulzer, are horizontally integrated, resembling automobile corporations such as General Motors; they are distinguished not only by their technological lead but by their control over market shares and sheer size. Finally, Switzerland also has its conglomorates. Bührle, for example, like Litton Industries, is integrated by financial strategies mixing profitability and risk dispersion through diversification.

These differences in corporate structure and strategy are substantial and make it difficult for Switzerland's large corporations to unite behind a privately orchestrated, coherent strategy of industrial adjustment. Instead, these firms feel better served by an exclusive reliance on corporate strategies of adjustment. Broadly speaking, industrial adjustment in all firms, be they large or small, depends greatly on maintaining key features of Switzerland's institutional economy: an entrepreneurial drive in industry strengthened by bank credits at favorable terms, dealing with cooperative labor leaders, and unencumbered by government intervention.[172]

Austria

In comparison with Switzerland Austria has an industrial policy that is both ambitious and expensive.[173] Government involvement dates back to the early years of the Second Republic. Marshall Plan aid required full-blown planning, which vested state agencies with responsibility for the reconstruction and rejuvenation of Austria's industrial structure. By the end of the aid program, in the Raab-Kamitz era of the 1950s, striking economic gains had provided a political climate in which the Austrians could adopt the West German social market economy.[174] Fear of European integration and Austria's diminishing economic growth rates in the mid-1960s renewed public debate. It resulted in the programmatic commitment of both major parties in 1968 to modernize the structure of Austria's economy through political efforts. Legislation passed in 1969 gave financial incentives for mergers, and concentration was undertaken in Austria's nationalized industries in the hope of increasing both economic efficiency and international competitiveness.[175]

In the 1970s Austria's industrial policy was carried by a broad consensus about the need for a competitive and efficient manufacturing industry.[176] Austria's industrial policy had two main objectives. On the one hand, it attempted to slow the process of deindustrialization and to smooth adjustment in declining industrial sectors; on the other hand, industrial policy also attempted to create new jobs, typically in high-technology sectors. The main preoccupation throughout the latter 1970s was to preserve jobs by slowing the rate of change—questions of employment affecting more than one hundred workers were typically discussed and dealt with by the national cabinet, often in an atmosphere of crisis. With more than 50,000 industrial jobs lost permanently in the 1970s, political concern over the structure and future growth of Austrian industry reached the very highest political levels.

Supplementing the defense of existing jobs was the creation of new jobs. Austria did not simply rely on market changes; the government became actively and increasingly involved in the effort to modernize Austria's industrial structure through consolidation, increasing efficiency and, at times, reducing the size of particular sectors or sector segments, frequently with the help of large foreign corporations.[177] The government concentrated its efforts on six or seven major projects in industries such as paper and pulp, automobiles, chemicals, and textiles. Motivated by diverse objectives—imbalance of trade in automobiles, unemployment in textiles, rationalization and modernization in paper and chemicals—these state-initiated efforts were a deliberate attempt to introduce major changes in Austria's industrial structure. In an address to the nation former chancellor Bruno Kreisky reiterated in 1980 that his government would increasingly direct its "attention and promotion to the restructuring of Austria's industry and small business."[178] Former finance minister Androsch had made the improvement of Austria's industrial structure one of his leading concerns in the late 1970s.[179] The government's declared objective for the 1980s is to develop a structural policy organized around the task of increasing industrial adjustment through greater energy efficiency.[180] Such explicit, programmatic commitments by the federal government would be unthinkable in Switzerland.

These commitments require substantial financial resources controlled by the government. While Switzerland has no outright subsidies for industry, direct subsidies in Austria amounted to more than a half-billion dollars a year in the later 1970s. The relief granted to business through a variety of tax measures favoring investment was about eight times greater.[181] "As compared with other member countries," one OECD report concluded, "the financial inducements offered to the individual industrialist in Austria are among the highest available."[182] In the words of Chancellor Kreisky, "in Austria unlike West Germany we do not have to talk about investment controls; for that task we have the public funds."[183]

The government's financial leverage is illustrated by the prominent role played by a large number of public investment funds, which provide the government with direct access to capital markets and give it considerable control over investment decisions in the private and public sectors. Not counting various regional and municipal development funds that disburse substantial amounts of aid, different funds granting preferential loans spent more than $180 million in 1974 alone. At the federal level in 1980 there were thirty different funds; the various provinces maintained an additional 95 funds operating at a much smaller scale. Between 1963 and 1979 industry was granted investment subsidies, totaling 16 percent of all industrial investment, by Austria's most important investment fund, the Counterpart Funds of the European Recovery Program.[184] In the late 1970s, 40 percent of the total volume of credits and loans extended to firms and individuals were subsidized.[185]

The government's massive involvement in the allocation of capital had served both to further a high-growth strategy and to defend or create jobs. Austria's gross investment in the 1970s increased substantially over the rate in the 1960s. Between 1970 and 1978 Austria experienced a 4.4 percent annual investment growth, far exceeding West Germany's rate of 1.6 percent and the 1.3 percent average of the EEC.[186] Among the OECD countries in the 1970s only Japan and, under the impact of its oil boom, Norway allocated a higher proportion of GNP to investment than did Austria. According to one recent study, moreover, the business community in Austria, because of these investment incentives, enjoys a more favorable tax system than its counterparts in Switzerland, West Germany, and Sweden.[187]

The investment decisions taken in Austria's nationalized firms reinforce the government's objective of adjusting to changing economic conditions through a steady and high investment rate. In the 1970s investment intensity increased much faster in Austria's capital-intensive basic industries, which are largely nationalized, than it did in the consumer and investment goods industries dominated by private firms.[188] The investment programs of the nationalized industries, moreover, have tended to be countercyclical. These industries invest heavily in times of recessions and defer their investments in times of high growth. Because they carried out their investment programs in the interest of long-term profitability, Austria's nationalized firms increased their share of total industrial investment from one-quarter to about one-third in the severe recession of the mid-1970s.[189]

Austria's nationalized banks also play an important role, although it is difficult to pinpoint precisely. In the 1950s Austria's public sector was reported not to have enjoyed a privileged position in the lending policies of these banks.[190] But the policy of job protection in the 1970s changed that. The chairman and director general of Austria's largest bank, the Creditanstalt, acknowledged with some discomfort in 1979 that "our role is now almost to run the industries, especially if they are in trouble. That is an additional risk that one should not take. Not only do we have the risk of the shareholder and the risk of the creditor, we also have the risk of the manager, and in the long run that is intolerable."[191] In 1981 an accumulation of bad debts almost proved to be the undoing of Austria's second-largest bank, the Öster-reichische Länderbank. A massive $180 million infusion of capital by the government was necessary for the bank to survive the collapse of two major companies that, in the name of a "socially responsible" policy, had saddled it with large potential loan losses.[192]

Government policies designed to achieve both full employment and industrial modernization also have important effects on Austria's industrial structure. Informed by Scandinavian experiments, Austria invested heavily in the 1970s to develop a manpower policy that can cope with increasing rates of economic change and is at the same time responsive to the requirements of Austria's evolving industrial structures. The cumulative impact of such policies on Austria's industry, subject to the government's political calculus, is far from negligible. Unlike their Swiss opposite numbers, Austrian officials do not value the impartiality of the indirect effects of their various policy measures. Rather, they evaluate these indirect effects from the perspective of maintaining existing jobs and generating new ones within an economy that can compete in international markets. International competitiveness is explicitly linked to national well-being.

One Swissair advertisement asserts that Switzerland's success is easily comprehended: the Swiss add so many improvements to the raw materials they import that they can export these raw materials in the form of new products.[193] While admitting that Austria's economic successes cannot be quickly copied by the large industrial states, a recent assessment of Austria's political economy similarly concludes that "there are lessons for other governments, and not only socialist ones, in this flexibility."[194] Geographical proximity and political differences explain why Switzerland's and Austria's experiences are frequently viewed as mutually instructive. Switzerland's highly specialized industrial structure is often held up as a model for Austria's industrial future. The OECD, for example, noted in 1967 that "Austria should change the structure of its industry towards the pattern of Switzerland."[195] A more recent analysis echoes the same theme: "This is how the recent discussions on structural policies in Austria must be viewed, i.e., as an ambitious attempt to create an industrial and economic structure capable of meeting the most vigorous challenges; and in this respect the FRG and Switzerland must, to a certain extent, be considered as models."[196] These arguments are mistaken in deriving policy prescriptions from a single model of economic structure and change. They neglect important political differences between the two countries. Austria, like Switzerland, is flexible in responding to change, but the way in which politics addresses economic change, and the consequences the form of response has for politics, differ. Strategies of adjustment respond to changes in economic conditions, but they are shaped politically. A simple economics requires a complex politics.

Like Switzerland and Austria, all of the small European states have adopted a flexible political strategy of industrial adjustment. They have found industrial policy a useful instrument for pacing the structural changes that international markets impose on the domestic economy. On questions of industrial policy they do not show the political indifference reinforced by protectionist policies that characterizes some of the large states, nor do they attempt to transform industrial sectors. Instead, the small European states combine international liberalization with domestic compensation. The liberalism of the small European states is, in John Ruggie's felicitous wording, "embedded" in a set of policies of domestic compensation.[197] Far-reaching policies of international liberalization can lead to severe social dislocations. Domestic compensation reduces these dislocations and both permits and requires the adoption of flexible policies of industrial adjustment. Industrial adjustment is thus embedded in a broad array of political responses that link liberalization with compensation. At the same time, there are important differences in how actively small European states pursue industrial adjustment.

One anomaly in the statistical work of economists supports the argument that the small European states have adopted a distinctive strategy of industrial adjustment. A large (and inconclusive) literature on the instability of export trade portrays the relatively open economies of the small European states as having a more stable export trade than the economies of the large industrial countries or of

Third World states.[198] Economists have tended either to neglect this counterintuitive result or to offer ad hoc explanations. Joseph Coppock, for example, says that "small open economies have to be more concerned about their export proceeds, so they may, through deliberate government policies or through built-in institutional arrangements, foster export stability."[199] This chapter has offered a different explanation for these economic data. The industrial adjustment strategy of the small European states stresses specialization in export markets. These states have generally succeeded in establishing comparative advantage in selected market niches where demand is relatively stable. The more price-elastic mass production for export markets of the large industrial states and the export of highly price-sensitive, unprocessed raw materials by Third World states leave the export proceeds of these two groups of states more vulnerable to fluctuations in the international business cycle.

Denmark provides an excellent illustration of this point. Confronted with the liberalization of the postwar international economy, writes Andrew Boyd,

> the Danes might have not merely missed their opportunities but been beaten to pulp if they had not recognized their limitations and used their imagination. . . . They developed the philosophy of the "niche." The Platonic ideal of this philosophy has much in common with that of the Danish open sandwich. You try to identify a gap which, although quite modest in size, evidently needs filling; and to fill it, neatly and quickly, with a product which requires only a small amount of material (local produce, as far as possible) but quite a lot of imagination. Freshness, high quality, portability, attractive design, and adaptability to customers' tastes are important. Mass production is inappropriate; a small team of craftsmen, working under personal supervision, usually gets the best results . . . but they cannot always hope to be left undisturbed in possession of their "niches." The trick then is to keep one jump ahead, by innovation or adaptability. The man who looks smugly settled into his niche is probably already trying to design an even better mouse trap, or planning for the time when he has to switch to something else, or both.[200]

The strategy of the small European states is flexible, reactive, and incremental. It does not counter adverse change by shifting its costs to others abroad; it does not attempt to preempt change by ambitiously reordering the economy at home. Instead, the small European states continually improvise in living with change.

CHAPTER THREE

Democratic Corporatism
and Its Variants

The Swiss joke that their air force is the world's champion in flying circles; the country is too small to learn how to fly straight. Size is, of course, one of the most obvious things to be noted about the small European states, but to be useful for analysis size should be considered a variable rather than a constant. Together with other factors it facilitates particular political outcomes.[1] Size affects, in particular, both economic openness and the characteristics of the political regime. Small countries are more open and vulnerable than large ones, economically, politically, and militarily. In small countries, moreover, political centralization tends to be greater and political arrangements tend to be more closely knit. These are powerful forces that buttress democratic corporatism. Yet the relationship between these variables is not inherent but historical: small size can, after all, be related to economic closure and authoritarian corporatism. But in the case at hand, Western Europe, small size has facilitated economic openness and democratic corporatism.

Economic openness reinforces the corporatist arrangements that distinguish the small European states from the large industrial countries. This corporatist difference is evident in the three defining characteristics of corporatism: an ideology of social partnership, a centralized and concentrated system of economic interest groups, and an uninterrupted process of bargaining among all of the major political actors across different sectors of policy. Corporatism also results from the distinctive party systems of the small European states. Political parties of the Right are divided, and proportional representation encourages a system of coalition or minority governments. As a result, political opponents tend to share power and jointly influence policy.

The argument requires that I establish systematic differences between small and large industrial countries in their economic openness, corporatist structures, and political party systems. The analysis
of the first three sections of this chapter is thus explicitly comparative.

But the small European states also differ one from another. The
fourth section distinguishes between the liberal corporatism of Switzerland, the Netherlands, and Belgium on the one hand and the social
corporatism of Austria, Norway, and Denmark on the other. Sweden
combines elements from both patterns. These two variants of corporatism differ in the strength and character of both business and
labor; that difference is illustrated in both where (globally or nationally) and how (privately or publicly) industrial adjustment occurs. The
fifth and final section compares Switzerland with Austria as the most
typical instances of, respectively, liberal and social corporatism. It also
shows how despite their differences, the two countries converge with
examples of both liberalism and statism among the large countries,
thus pointing to the emergence of a corporatist variant of capitalism
that combines both the market and state in distinctive ways.

ECONOMIC OPENNESS

In their openness to and dependence on the world economy the
seven small European states resemble one another. Small domestic
markets entail a degree of economic openness that is for two reasons
much greater in the small European states than in the five large
advanced industrial countries.[2] First, the small European states do not
offer the necessary economies of scale to a number of industries abso-
lutely critical to the functioning of a modern economy. They must
therefore import a wide range of goods that larger countries can
produce domestically. Secondly, small domestic markets lead the small
European states to seek their specialization and economies of scale in
export markets. Dependence on imports and the necessity to export
make the economies of the small European states both more open and
more specialized than those of larger countries.[3]

The import dependence of the small European states, as many
observers agree, reflects the absence of critically important industries
requiring large domestic markets. In the 1950s the relative output of
the small European states in industries with economies of scale (particularly basic metals, chemicals, metal products, and textiles) lagged
greatly behind that of the large states.[4] The same finding holds for the
late 1960s as well: the small European states lagged far behind the

large advanced industrial countries in the production of basic metals, chemicals, metal products, nonelectrical and electrical equipment, and transport equipment in 1965,[5] and of chemicals, petroleum products, rubber, iron and steel, metal manufactures, nonelectrical machinery, textiles, and transport equipment in 1970.[6] As these studies suggest, the industries of the small European states are less diversified than those of large industrial countries.[7]

This limitation in industrial structures leads to an import dependence that is much greater in investment than in consumer goods.[8] For example, the machine industry, with its large economies of scale, contributed between one-fifth and one-quarter of total production and less than one-fifth of exports of the small European states; corresponding figures for the five large industrial countries are almost twice as large.[9] In the late 1950s the import content of investment goods amounted to 52 percent for the small European states, only 10 percent for the large countries.[10] A more recent estimate of the average import content of gross domestic capital formation, though based on a different sample of countries and different methods of computation, arrives at substantially similar results: 49–52 percent for the small developed states, 17 percent for the large advanced industrial countries. The direct import content of consumption goods, by way of contrast, is less than 30 percent in both groups of states.[11] In the mid-1960s the small European states surpassed the large industrial countries in the total import content in fixed capital formation (transport equipment, machinery, and building and construction) by a factor of three.[12]

The import dependence of the small European states makes them far more open to influences from the international economy than the large countries. In the Netherlands more than half of total domestic demand for manufactures in the late 1970s was supplied by foreign producers.[13] The portion of the economy that must respond to international competition is eight times larger in Belgium and almost five times larger in Sweden than in the United States.[14] These examples illustrate the undisputed finding of virtually all studies on the subject.[15] As one statistical analysis concluded in 1970, small countries have high levels of imports *irrespective* of their level of income, while in the large countries the propensity to import tends to decline when income levels rise. Exposure to foreign competition in the small European states is, on average, more than three times as great as in the large countries.[16]

An openness to developments in international markets has strong effects on the movement of prices and wages. The small European economies import inflation from world markets—inflation that, in contrast to the large countries, not only has indirect effects through increasing demands for export or the balance of payments but also acts directly through price dissemination from imported goods and services.[17] In the 1970s, as the OECD's McCracken Report noted, external price influences were a major source of inflation for open economies. Even analysts who play down the consequences of an open economy nonetheless concede that the influence of the international economy on prices and wages is very strong.[18]

Swiss chemicals and Belgian steel illustrate the tendency of prominent industries in the small European states to seek economies of scale in international markets. The necessity of exporting has also brought corporations in the small European states, unlike in the large countries, to standardized and high-value-added products. They traditionally fill those market niches particularly well suited to their traditional economic strengths and resource endowments. During the last two decades, Switzerland and Austria have benefited greatly from the production of ski clothes and equipment. Sweden is exploiting its traditional strength in wood and furniture products in the computer market, through specializing in the exterior furnishings of minicomputers and in office design. Denmark has developed highly sophisticated marketing strategies in a wide range of consumer goods, best typified by the phenomenal success of Lego toys. Behind such illustrations lies a statistical truth: in the mid and late 1960s the economies of the small European states were much more specialized in their exports than were the larger European countries.[19]

Small European states have expanded their export markets in specific types of industry. While what constitutes a "modern" as compared to a "traditional" industry differs from one study to another, all studies suggest that the small European states have developed their comparative advantage in the latter. In the small states' "export basket" traditional industries such as food, beverages and tobacco, textiles, wood, paper, printing, and leather take a much larger relative share than do modern industries (rubber, chemicals and petroleum products, industrial raw materials, and metal products).[20] This imbalance is also reflected in the much greater import content of goods produced for export in modern industries.[21] Light industries are represented disproportionately in the industrial structure of the small European states.[22] In 1966 the share of exports in the industrial production of Sweden, Norway, Denmark, and Austria was twice as large as in the five large industrial countries. An analysis of the export orientation of several manufacturing industries in West Germany,

France, Britain, and six of the seven small European states arrives at the same figure for 1977.[23] In the postwar era the relative share of exports in GNP in the small European states has been more than twice as large as in the large countries.

This dependence, both on the import of modern investment goods and on the export of more traditional consumer goods, reinforces imbalances in the economic structures of the small European states. Economic specialization results in different sectors of the economy being less integrated than those in the large countries—an observation true throughout the postwar era.[24] Openness to international markets, specialization, and imbalance give the economic structures of the small European states a propensity, to borrow a phrase from David Riesman, for being "other-directed."[25] The small European states thus tend to develop two different economic sectors, one externally oriented and competitive, the other internally oriented and protected. The differences between these two sectors are usually greater in smaller than in larger societies.

Specialization for export is essential to cover the costs of necessary imports. Yet Hollis Chenery has concluded that diseconomies of scale in importing sectors are, statistically speaking, twice as important as economies of scale in production and (by inference) in exports.[26] Furthermore, specialization leads small European states to concentrate their export trade on particular countries and particular commodities—a concentration that during the last three decades has exceeded that of the large countries by a substantial margin.[27] This concentration can have important effects on politics: as Albert Hirschmann has shown for the interwar years, high degrees of trade concentration can become an enormous political liability.[28] For the small European states this has not been so since the war, a testimony to the more benign climate of the international economy since 1945.

That climate has favored not political liability but economic growth. Between 1938 and 1967 the value of the seven small states' export trade grew by a factor of eight as compared to a tenfold increase in imports.[29] Commodities that enjoyed a high growth rate in world trade between 1954 and 1969 increased by 14.2 percent in the five large industrial states but by only 9.1 percent in the small European states. Conversely, commodities with only an average growth rate declined by 0.8 percent in the five large countries while they increased by 7.4 percent in the small European states.[30] The import level of the small European states covered by gross international reserves is about one-third lower than in the large countries.[31] Furthermore, the small European states tend to run consistently sizable deficits in their balance of foreign trade: while the large countries found themselves in surplus two-thirds of the time between 1960 and 1977, the small European states ran a deficit in their trade balance two years out of three.[32] Overstating his case, one observer concluded that "small countries appeared to experience a comparative disadvantage in most manufacturing industries."[33]

Against these structural trade deficits we should set a substantial surplus that small European states generate in their invisible trade, the export of services.[34] Even though Swiss industry is in relative terms, larger than that of any other OECD member state, the export of services has remained essential to Switzerland's position in the world economy throughout the postwar era.[35] Norway's enduring trade deficit is partly offset by its sizable gross freight earnings. In 1960 Norwegian ships carried a larger share of American trade (15%) than did the American fleet; in the second half of the 1960s receipts from invisible trade were about one-third of Norway's total receipts from foreign trade.[36] And Denmark, hard hit by the economic recession of the mid-1970s, witnessed a very substantial growth in its invisible receipts even though it already had the highest proportion of invisible exports to total export earnings (29%) in Europe.[37] It is next to impossible to separate out the service component from merchandise trade, particularly in technologically advanced sectors where know-how, consulting, and service are integral parts of one product package; but it is striking that the small European states offer very different types of services, including finance and insurance (Switzerland), commerce (Netherlands), shipping (Norway), and tourism (Austria).[38] In 1976 receipts from invisible trade amounted to 12 percent of the GNP of the small European states as compared to 5 percent for the large countries; on a per capita basis the small states led by about three to one.[39] In short, the small European states exploit their comparative advantage in a sector that has kept pace with the worldwide growth of manufacturing trade throughout the postwar years.[40]

But the small European states also rely, and far more heavily than the large ones do, on the inflow of foreign capital. Direct foreign investment in these countries has increased very rapidly during the last two decades.[41] By the early 1970s the estimated share of manufacturing held by foreign enterprises was much larger in the small European states than in the large countries. On the average foreign firms controlled 26 percent of sales and 18 percent of employment in the small European states as compared to 15 and 11 percent respectively in the large industrial countries.[42] The inflow of long-term capital has

Table 1. Openness and dependence in small and large economies (percentages)

	Small states[a]	Large states[b]
Openness		
1. Exports of goods/GNP, 1955	24.4	11.3
Exports of goods/GNP, 1975	30.4	15.5
2. Exports of goods and services/GNP, 1955	31.0	13.8
Exports of goods and services/GNP, 1975	37.7	18.8
3. Foreign letters/total letters, 1955	13.6	6.0
Foreign letters/total letters, 1975	12.2	6.1
4. Foreign patents/total patents, 1965	82.5	39.8
Foreign patents/total patents, 1975	84.9	49.9
Dependence		
1. Balance of trade in goods/imports, 1955	− 16.6	0.3
Balance of trade in goods/imports, 1975	− 10.2	− 0.1
2. Balance of trade in goods and services/imports, 1960	− 0.7	8.7
Balance of trade in goods and services/imports, 1973	− 2.2	3.6
3. Direct foreign investment/GNP, 1967	4.4	3.1
Direct foreign investment/GNP, 1973	4.9	3.0
4. Energy imports/energy consumption, 1960	62.0	24.2
Energy imports/energy consumption, 1975	50.3	53.7

[a]Unweighted average for Austria, Switzerland, Sweden, Norway, Denmark, Netherlands, Belgium.

[b]Unweighted average for the United States, Britain, West Germany, France, Japan.

Source. Margret Sieber, *Dimensionen kleinstaatlicher Auslandsabhängigkeit*, Kleine Studien zur Politischen Wissenschaft nos. 206–207 (Zurich: University of Zurich, Forschungsstelle für Politische Wissenschaft, 1981), pp. 156–59.

accompanied the export of services in helping to balance the persistent trade deficit of small European states, thus bringing their basic balance of foreign transactions into equilibrium.[43]

If small European countries are unusually open to and dependent on a global economy that is beyond their control, however, they have also benefited from an increasing international division of labor (see Table 1). Between 1950 and 1981 the proportion of world exports to world GDP increased from 10 to 18 percent.[44] In the 1970s, in particular, an increasing dependence on imported energy put most of the large industrial states for the first time in a position comparable to that of the small European states. More generally, the growing liberalization of the international economy between 1955 and 1975 increased the dependence of large economies faster than that of the small economies.[45] This development accelerated in the course of the 1970s. Between 1970 and 1979, for example, the rate at which the economies of the five large industrial states opened to the international economy was about 50 percent greater than the rate for the small European states.[46]

Despite the growing openness of the large industrial states, however, the difference between the two groups of states is sufficiently large that for the foreseeable future the small European states will remain much more open to and dependent on the world economy. The reasons that support this prediction are plain. The economic structure of the small European states is less diversified than that of the large states. The small European states depend heavily on the import of investment goods and other products for which their small domestic markets do not offer sufficient economies of scale. Instead, they seek these economies of scales through a specialization in their exports, especially in relatively "traditional" industries. This pattern results in a structural trade deficit, which narrows temporarily only in times of recession. The small European states are thus forced to rely on their service sectors as well as the import of foreign capital to cover their perennial trade deficits. In sum, economic openness distinguishes the small European states from the large industrial states.

Democratic Corporatism

The inclusion of all of the major producer groups and political actors in corporatist arrangements creates a relatively dull and predictable kind of politics in the small European states. Predictability has its costs. Some political elites are excluded from basic policy arenas, for example, Swiss unions from questions involving foreign economic policy. Leaders impose strict controls on the spontaneous political participation of their followers, as is true, for instance, of the rank and file and middle-level cadres in Austria's unitary and highly centralized trade union movement. These concealed costs reinforce the political challenges to which the corporatist structures of the small European states have been subjected in recent years. Illustrations abound: the growing importance of rule by emergency decree in Swiss politics, the possible implantation of a Social Democratic regime in Austria, the trend toward class politics in the reordering of Dutch political life, the reappearance of militant ethnic politics in Belgium, and the instabilities in Scandinavian party systems. To date, however, these manifold political challenges have failed to change fundamentally any of the three defining characteristics of corporatism.[47]

The first characteristic of democratic corporatism is an ideology of social partnership, shared by both business and unions and expressed in national politics. The pervasiveness of that ideology since 1945 is mirrored in the infrequency of strikes. In his work on the political economy of strikes Douglas Hibbs concluded that the postwar era has seen a significant reduction of strike activity to negligible levels only in Denmark, the Netherlands, Norway, and Sweden. Had Austria and Switzerland been included in his study, they would have fallen in the same category. Only Belgium's decline in strike activity still allows for sizable industrial disputes. During the interwar years, by way of contrast, the small European states were much more prone to strikes than the large industrial countries. As Douglas Hibbs observes, "The withering away of the strike is a rather limited phenomenon confined largely to the smaller democracies of Northern Europe."[48] Even short strikes today have large repercussions, both real and psychological, in small open economies. In the open economies of the small European states a durable truce has since 1945 supplanted class warfare between business and labor.

Although it may appear paradoxical to outsiders, pragmatic cooperation and ideological conflict are not incompatible. Technical expertise plays an important role in the small European states. There is, however, no reason to believe that experts in the small European states are smarter than experts elsewhere, and so their prominent role evidently does not lie in the quality of the advice they give. Instead, experts matter because they provide a common framework and acceptable data, evidence of a pervasive ideology of social partnership. This ideology incorporates a continuous reaffirmation of political differences with political cooperation. In Harold Wilensky's words, "Such experts are preoccupied with rational argument and criteria; their technical competence compels opposing parties to be more careful and honest in the use of information and knowledge. It is still combat, but the spirit is, 'En Garde. We'll meet you with our statistics at dawn.' "[49]

This ideology of social partnership is a distinctive feature of all of the small European states. In Denmark, as Arend Lijphart has argued, ideological consensus is particularly evident in the search for compromise in Parliament. "The rule of the game prescribes that the top leaders of all four major parties do their utmost to reach a consensus. This is *glidningspolitik*. . . the politics of smoothness.' "[50] Austria's Socialist party, joined by the trade unions, continuously reaffirms in its political rhetoric and in its self-perception that it is building a better society in the name of democratic socialism. At the same time, though, the party pursues policies that focus on growth rather than redistribution and that are closely tied to West Germany's stability-conscious monetary policy. Conversely, together with the peak association of business and the most important newspaper in the country, Switzerland's liberal party (the Radicals) affirms the principles of a liberal capitalism with a great sense of urgency. Yet it accommodates itself easily to a coalition government with Switzerland's Social Democrats. Few Swiss and even fewer foreigners know that Switzerland's system of collegial leadership conferred the ceremonial office of prime minister upon the Social Democratic party three times in the 1970s. In the Low Countries a variety of political coalitions have been possible among the major political parties. Val Lorwin writes that "this general availability for cabinet coalitions we might, for the sake of a short and catchy name, call *Allgemeinkoalitionsfähigkeit.*[51]

The second characteristic of democratic corporatism is a system of centralized and concentrated interest groups. Philippe Schmitter has made this system the focus of his institutional characterization of corporatism. For Schmitter corporatism is a form of interest intermediation that is distinct from both pluralism and syndicalism.[52] It is theoretically possible for policy making to be corporatist without centralized institutions, but unprotected by firmly rooted institutions, corporatist bargaining is more susceptible to collapse under the stress of exogenous shocks. This at least is the lesson that one can draw from Britain's and, more recently, Italy's attempts to stabilize their economies through corporatist arrangements.

Both the centralization of society and the system of centralized producer groups are important. Normally, centralization and concentration are inversely related to the size of a country: "Other things being equal . . . the larger the country, the greater the number of organizations and sub-units it will contain."[53] Looking at the situation in which the small European states find themselves from the perspective of the management of the economy, Peter Wiles aptly notes that "it is never difficult to put through an agreed new policy. This is the phenomenon of 'willy-nilly Frenchy planning' in small countries: the *économie* is informally *concertée,* whatever may be the official arrangements or lack of them. This is as much as to say, there can be no laissez-faire in a rich small country with a market economy since the number of large enterprises is too small, and the intermarriage of elite families is inevitable, where the elite contains both enterprise directors and senior civil servants. Give a cocktail party, and you have to invite them all."[54] In larger states organizations are differentiated and functions are specialized; the functional substitute in small states is the "structural polyvalence" of organizations that play many different roles. As two Swiss analysts note, "Organizations in small societies find it especially profitable to keep themselves very open and available for possible alliances with many other organizations." Selectivity in problem definition, personalization of interorganizational relations, and versatility in response are some of the typical institutional reactions in the small European states.[55] But this fluidity of relationships within small states coincides with strong oligarchic tendencies. Political power is concentrated in the hands of a few decision makers and rests with strong interest groups and strong parties.[56]

Just as the main economic interest groups fully organize their respective social sectors, so political parties mobilize a very large proportion of the electorate. In the small European states between 20 and 25 percent of the registered or actual voters are typically party members, a proportion far greater than in the large industrial countries.[57]

Furthermore, strong and pervasive links exist between interest groups and political parties in the small European states. Small size and dependence on world markets thus has an effect not only on the centralization of domestic structures but also on the character of the policy process. "In a society as small and transparent as the Norwegian," writes Ulf Torgersen, "where the exercise of power is so much disliked, where equality is a dominant feature, and where evaluation on the basis of individual merit is avoided so consistently, the politics/ society configuration can present serious problems. This does not mean that power is not exercised, but characteristically the process is a difficult one."[58] Johan Olsen has similarly observed that anticipated reaction is a major form of policy coordination in small systems.[59]

The centralization of the major producer organizations in a system of "peak associations" is a corollary to democratic corporatism's characteristic centralization of domestic structures. Centralization is particularly striking in Switzerland's business community, as well as in Austria's trade union movement. Furthermore, the peak associations that characterize democratic corporatism are so broadly based as to approximate a representational monopoly of their constituencies, de facto if not de jure. The centralization and representational monopoly of these peak associations are important to the two ways in which the major producer groups coordinate their political objectives. Policy is primarily formulated between the leaders of producer groups, the state bureaucracy, and political parties at the summit. Policy is implemented within producer groups through middle-level functionaries as well as by the state bureaucracy. This combination of inter- and intraorganizational policy making is an elaborate effort to mobilize political consensus between and within organizations. It tends to blur the distinction between public and private.

Union membership levels illustrate the encompassing character of the main producer groups in the small European states. Among the large industrial states only Britain approaches the unionization rates common in the small European states.[60] No comparable and systematic statistical measures of the "organization of capitalists" are available. But what evidence we have suggests that conditions favor the institutional penetration of the business community in the small European states much more than in the large ones. The small size of domestic markets correlates highly with different measures of industrial concentration. Indeed, John Stephens classifies all seven small European states as having a high degree of economic monopolization and all of the large industrial states as having a low degree of monopolization.[61] It would, of course, be risky to infer a centralized institutional structure of the business community from a centralized economic structure. But a number of these countries lend some support to the notion that economic structure in this instance shapes institutional forms.[62] Finally, the entire literature on corporatist politics has assumed a symmetry in the degree of centralization of the unions on the one hand and of business on the other; in directly measuring the former, it is argued, we are indirectly measuring the latter. Summarizing his comparative analysis of industrial states, Stephens thus concludes that the countries "fall neatly into two categories, the small democracies and the larger democracies with a large gap between them."[63]

Perhaps the most frequently cited example of the centralization of democratic corporatism is the industrial relations system of the small European states. Incomes policy and collective bargaining were intimately linked both in Sweden's "private" central wage bargain and in the Netherlands' "public" official incomes policy in the 1950s and 1960s. In fact, all of the small European states, with the sole exception of Switzerland, have highly centralized collective bargaining systems. Even Belgium in the course of the 1970s moved to peak-level bargaining and conflict resolution, a movement clearly illustrated by the government's economic recovery plan of 1980–81. In the words of Anne Romanis, to summarize, "In five of the six smallest and most open small European states—and in only one large economy, West Germany—powerful coordinated employers' federations face coordinated labor unions. On the other hand, in six of the seven large industrial states uncoordinated labor unions face uncoordinated employers' organizations."[64]

The third characteristic of democratic corporatism is a voluntary and informal coordination of conflicting objectives. Coordination is achieved through political bargains struck between the major pro-

ducer groups, state bureaucracies, and political parties across different sectors of public policy, with trade-offs that are more or less
explicit.[65] Individual transactions in markets and hierarchical com-
mands by state bureaucracies do of course exist in democratic corporatism, but they are not of its essence. Instead, the important social
actors are systematically included in the policy network, thus acquiring a stake in the continued operation of that network even if they are
dissatisfied with particular policy outcomes. The "sectoral interpene-
tration" of state bureaucracies and interest groups gives way to a
process of "trans-sectoral co-ordination."[66] Interest groups participate
in the formulation and implementation of policies that go beyond
their specific sectoral interests to include such broad political objectives as full employment, economic stability and growth, or the modernization of industry. The consequence of this pattern of policy
making is clear: government bills account for a far higher share of
legislative proposals in the small European states than in the large
industrial countries (93% compared to 66%). The success rate of the
executive's legislative proposals is also greater (93% compared to
52%).[67] Among the large countries only Britain begins to approach
the figures of the small states.

The expectations that political actors bring to the process of coordination are shaped not only by the substance of the issue to be resolved
but also by acute awareness of how substantive differences between
groups affect corporatist arrangements. Disagreements on questions
of substance are mitigated by strong agreements on procedures because differences in power are carefully calibrated. In corporatist
policy making not only is the question that is on the table at stake—so
is the shape of the table. The very process of coordinating conflicting
objectives creates a climate of political predictability.

Political bargains over wages and prices are distinctive of the incomes policies of most of the small European states, and they provide
an excellent example of how a corporatist policy process works. In
Austria incomes policy is informal, protecting the leaders of the main
interest groups from being caught between bargains struck at the top
and demands made by the rank and file. It involves other policy
sectors—social welfare, taxes, and employment—and is significant
primarily for its political rather than its economic effects. Switzerland
does not have a formal incomes policy. There, a less explicit link exists
between a labor-market policy that leaves hiring and firing to the sole
discretion of businessmen and an understanding that foreign workers, of which Switzerland has a large number, will be laid off first. This
policy has virtually assured Swiss workers of full employment

throughout the last thirty years. What matters in these corporatist arrangements is the links between different political actors, which generate long-term expectations. In comparison to the large industrial states, political bargaining in the small European states resembles exchange rather than barter or control.

Is democratic corporatism distinctive of small rather than large industrial states? Several authors, using a definition of democratic corporatism partly at odds with mine, suggest that it is. For example, Philippe Schmitter ranks industrial states along the dimensions of fiscal effectiveness (a measure based on different indicators of the government's fiscal strength); societal corporatism (a measure of the organizational centralization and the associational monopoly of labor organizations); and citizen acquiescence (a measure of citizen-initiated protest or resistance as shown by collective protest, internal war, or strikes).[68] These three concepts bear some resemblance to the three defining characteristics of corporatism I discussed earlier. Fiscal effectiveness can be interpreted as an indirect, economic-outcome measure of the coordination of diverging political objectives across different policy sectors; societal corporatism is one way of measuring what I identified as centralized and concentrated economic interest groups; and citizen acquiescence is one indicator of the strength of an ideology of social partnership and a culture of compromise. On all three dimensions Schmitter's rank ordering consistently separates small European states from large industrial countries. West Germany and France, it is true, rank ahead of Belgium on the dimension of fiscal effectiveness (cross-sectoral coordination of policy). West Germany ranks ahead of Switzerland on the dimension of societal corporatism (centralization of domestic structure) and ahead of Belgium on the dimension of citizen acquiescence (social partnership). But only these 4 out of 84 possible pairwise comparisons (each of the seven small states compared to each of the four large states) fail to support the argument that corporatist arrangements are distinctive of the small European states.

Other comparative studies strengthen this conclusion, whether they rely on judgments about degree of corporatism or on more precise numerical indicators. After extensive comparative research on the political structures of advanced industrial states, Manfred Schmidt concluded that the degree of corporatism in the small European states is roughly twice that found in the large industrial states; J. E. Keman and O. Braun arrived at the same conclusion, and Gerhard Lehmbruch has also concurred.[69] Data in comparative studies of the welfare state lend further support to the view that, in contrast to the large industrial states, the small European states are distinguished by their corporatist arrangements.[70]

By contrast, the political arrangements in the large countries do not exhibit the characteristics of democratic corporatism. Paraphrasing Werner Sombart, students of American politics have repeatedly posed the question, "Why no corporatism in America?"[71] Their answer, like Sombart's, points to key features of American politics: decentralized political institutions, the strength of liberal ideology, and the prominence of political forces favoring market solutions rather than group concertation. Britain's class-based ideology and politics, as well as the decentralized structure of its trade union movement and producer groups, defeated repeated attempts in the 1960s and 1970s by both Labour and Conservative governments to construct corporatist arrangements. Japan's politics, it is true, features a close integration of business and government, close enough that the late Andrew Shonfield called it an example of corporatist politics.[72] In sharp contrast to the small European states, however, this Japanese variant exhibits "corporatism without labor" and bears little if any resemblance to the politics distinctive of the small European states.[73] French politics similarly lacks ideological consensus and a centralized system of interest groups. Among the large countries only West Germany's centrist politics and system of peak associations provides an approximation to the corporatist substance and style of politics that typifies the small European states.[74]

OPENNESS, CORPORATISM, AND PARTY SYSTEMS

In comparison to the large industrial countries, as the first two sections of this chapter have shown, the small European states are both more open to the international economy and more corporatist in their internal organization. Openness and corporatism are linked in distinctive ways to political parties. Here my argument converges with the conclusions of another analyst of European incomes policies in the 1940s and 1950s: "Students of neo-corporatism and incomes policy must pay more attention to the international dimension of national political economies."[75]

Analyses of how the small European states cope with economic openness and dependence typically emphasize that these countries are small and international markets are large. Because of their size, the small European countries are often viewed as harmonious manifestations of Bacon's New Atlantis—endowed with coherence, agility, and intelligence.[76] Simon Kuznets, for example, speculates that the social homogeneity and consensus on the one hand and the quickness and effectiveness of political adjustments on the other must be the main reasons allowing small states to overcome the disadvantages associated with their economic openness and dependence.[77] In a similar vein a Hungarian economist, Béla Kádár, points to characteristic features of the domestic policies of the small European states that encourage political interventions in the domestic economy and counterbalance a relative weakness in international markets.[78] Even David Vital's pessimistic appraisal of the viability of small states concludes that "the crucial factor in almost every case is the human one. . . . Where the society coheres and is strongly led very great obstacles can often be overcome."[79] In different ways these assessments concur that the small European states compensate for their economic openness and dependence on world markets through political efforts at home. But we need to replace mystical assumptions about social coherence and common purpose with an analysis of what shapes domestic structures and how domestic structures condition political choices.

As I shall argue in greater detail in chapter 4, past international crises and political vulnerabilities have repeatedly strengthened cooperative arrangements in the small European states. In the case of Belgium such arrangements already existed in the first hours of the new state: a coalition among Liberals and Catholics was established during that country's secession in 1830. In the Netherlands the "politics of accommodation"[80] over the hotly contested issue of religion and education was reinforced by the outbreak of World War I. The incorporation of the Swiss Socialist party in the federal cabinet in 1943 resulted from a convergence between Left and Right, a convergence forced during the 1930s and 1940s by fascism and war and strengthened by the long-standing Swiss tradition of proportional linguistic and geographic representation of different sectors of society. Austria, confronting occupation by the four Allies as well as overwhelming economic odds, established an all-party government in 1945.[81]

Since the middle of the 1950s the requirements of international competitiveness that stem from an increasingly liberal international economy have contributed to the maintenance of a democratic corporatism. Less dramatic and chaotic than events of the 1930s and 1940s, the structural trade deficits of the small European states have reinforced corporatist patterns throughout the postwar decades. Incomes policy, a frequently noted example of corporatist politics in the small European states, illustrates the point. Control over wages and prices is particularly urgent in the small European states, which import inflation from world markets. "Generally speaking," notes Lehmbruch, "corporatist incomes policies have mostly been a sort of crisis management where, under economic stress, organizations have been ready to cooperate."[82] A mixture of wage restraint and price control is often a requirement of international competitiveness, and the need for economic stability is pressing if an equilibrium in the balance of payments is to be achieved. In ten episodes of incomes policy in the 1940s and 1950s, Peter Lange has concluded, the logic of economic vulnerability prevailed over the logic of worker militancy in forcing political outcomes that stressed consensual wage bargaining.[83] Ulman and Flanagan reached a similar conclusion for the 1960s. At least in the short run, for the small European states "the currency crisis thus furnishes an example of the civilizing influence of common adversity on communal behavior. . . . Social problems that do not yield to competitive pressures arising from individual activity should be tackled, not by the state alone, but by 'interest group activities' which may have caused them in the first place."[84]

Confronted with the cleavage between externally oriented and domestically oriented economic sectors, the small European states have developed corporatist structures that enhance political predictability by facilitating cooperation and compromise. Even though he discusses only Norway, Robert Kvavik aptly characterizes the consequence of centralization for all of the small European states: "Decisions are made with reference to some acceptable national standard . . . in such a way that the goals of voluntary associations are realized by accommodating private interests to an accepted and visible national interest. . . . All participants (public and private) see themselves as responsible to both private and national constituencies. All participants in the system view themselves as sharers."[85] External pressures force domestic accommodation even in societies, for instance Switzerland, that feature less centralized political institutions and practices: "People forfeit opposition policies because they know, in the end, that their security and their wealth depend on the confidence they inspire elsewhere."[86] Gerhard Lehmbruch comes to a similar conclusion. "Even in countries where a class-conscious labor movement in this strict sense is absent (as in Japan), or where social class is less salient for the cleavage structure of society (as in Switzerland), perceptions of international dependency may push the elites to establish patterns of coordination of government and interest groups with functional affinity to the modal pattern of corporatism. This includes some form of integration of labor, but the mechanisms are different."[87] The small European states thus feature both widespread acceptance of the national interest and political accommodation among public and private actors.

How can we think systematically about these different mechanisms for integrating labor? Michael Shalev has usefully surveyed the most important studies done on this subject in the 1970s and 1980s.[88] A basic feature of what he calls the Social Democratic Model is the integration of the labor movement through strong socialist parties and strong labor movements into a national consensus. The modern welfare state is the result of class conflict; its major supporter has been the working class, and Social Democratic parties have been the main left-wing parties contesting public office with good chances of success. Thus the likelihood that Social Democratic parties will come to power and impose reform depends on the degree of working-class mobilization and its institutionalization in both unions and parties. The character of mobilization in turn depends both on the historically given features of society and on the political strategies of political elites. The Social Democratic Model remains fundamentally class-based even though it allows for the independent effect of state institutions and ideology in preventing the automatic translation of working-class power into policy outcomes. Corporatism has been no guarantor of the accommodation of diverging class interests. But in Scandinavia, for example, as Francis Castles notes, "the corporate pluralist system has been the instrument by which working-class organizations have been politically integrated into the fabric of capitalist society."[89]

Although numerous studies support Shalev's generalization, there exist significant exceptions. Strong corporatist arrangements, both Cameron and Wilensky conclude, can be found in the context of strong Socialist parties and of strong Catholic parties—or of the coincidence of both.[90] Corporatism, they conclude, is not strongly associated with the domination of a particular party and ideology. Data on working-class mobilization (as measured by the percentage of workers unionized and of the electoral strength of leftist parties) show that working-class mobilization is too high for Britain's weak corporatism, too low for the Netherlands' and Switzerland's strong corporatism.[91] Corporatism is thus not strongly associated with the mobilization of the working class. Cameron's conclusion fits with the argument I develop here: the openness of the economy has a stronger effect on the growth of the public economy than does socialist incumbency. For that growth, "leftist domination was not a necessary condition, since several nations experienced large increases in spite of the absence of a strong leftist representation in government. Included in this latter group are the Netherlands and Belgium . . . which share at least one common trait: their economies are relatively open."[92] Shalev concludes that "these various qualifications add up to an admission that the mechanisms by which the interests and collective leverage of the working class are conveyed to the state and influence policy are much more variable than one would expect by interpreting strength of the Left as simply the extent of democratic socialist tenure of government."[93]

The Low Countries illustrate a different mechanism for integrating labor into the corporatist arrangements of a capitalist society. In both countries, "working class interests are transmitted to the state and make themselves felt in policy in the absence of a governing working class party. In the Netherlands and to a lesser extent in Belgium, one observes a level of 'welfare effort' comparable to that in the Scandinavian nations and Austria, where for decades social democratic parties have enjoyed a dominant or very prominent position in government."[94] Lower levels of labor organization, shorter periods of socialist rule, and the breakdown of Dutch incomes policy since the late 1960s make the Netherlands an anomaly for those comparative studies of corporatist politics which focus on the strength of the Left as the prime determinant. Stephens, for example, is forced to call the Netherlands a "deviant case" of corporatist politics. "It may be that the Dutch system of bargaining centralization owes more to the combination of very heavy export dependency and the 'politics of accommodation' than to the political and economic strength of the labor movement."[95] The problem with dismissing the Dutch as deviant is obvious, for the effects of small size and economic openness on corporatism are no more exceptional in the Netherlands than in any of the other small European states. But the Dutch labor movement is nevertheless integrated into society on very different terms than in Scandinavia. In the 1970s, for example, Dutch employers' associations unified while the trade union federation became more decentralized, thus approximating the Swiss pattern.[96] In party political terms, moreover,

> in a re-organized and restructured party system, in which confessional strength is reduced to a third of the vote rather than a half, the Labour party, the only major party likely to mandate a greater voice for the trade unions, is still weak. Much to their frustration, Socialists, with a third of the popular vote, remain dependent on coalitions with the confessional bloc, regrouped in a single party, the Christian Democratic Appeal. Reflecting their centrist posture and desire to maintain a broad base of

support, the Christian Democrats are receptive to trade union concerns, but unwilling to accept or endorse fundamental reforms.[97]

Throughout the 1970s polarization and integration in the Netherlands were maintained in a delicate balance. The economic crisis of the 1970s kept Dutch industrial relations somewhere half-way between a decentralized system with conflictual and autonomous unions, toward which it moved in the late 1960s, and the restabilized corporative system of the 1950s. As in the 1950s the primary task since 1973 has been to restrain growth in wages, but the institutional and political forms for imposing restraint have changed. They no longer resemble explicit social contracts as much as a series of coordinated, specific measures designed to reach a compromise among diverging interests. Despite this difference in form, the Netherlands has responded to the economic crisis of the 1970s and 1980s, as was true in the 1950s, with wage restraints that are among the most effective in the industrial world.[98] It was symptomatic of this general pattern that in the midst of the first oil shock in 1973–74 Dutch citizens experienced a "crisis psychosis" that enhanced the willingness of political elites to cooperate.[99]

The Low Countries suggest that the integration of labor into corporatist arrangements is shaped by the need to construct governing coalitions in variegated party systems.[100] Francis Castles has paid attention to the importance of parties of the Right, and he concludes that no systematic relationship exists between economic openness and the frequency of Social Democratic incumbency.[101] His data show, however, that the influence of openness is mediated by political parties of the Right. Incumbency of the Right has a strong negative correlation both with economic openness and with the generous welfare spending in the 1960s and 1970s that signaled a close integration of labor into the political economies of advanced industrial states. "If a closed economy is propitious for the development of strong and united parties of the Right, once developed it will be those parties' ideological leanings which determine the content of public policy at least as much as any imperative structured by the nature of the economy."[102] Unified parties of the Right are to be found in all of the five large industrial states but only in Austria among the seven small European states.

"Parties of the Right," which in Western Europe means political Catholicism, is a label that means different things in different political settings. As Shalev argues,

> there is a distinction to be made between Catholic parties that stand to the left of a sizable conservative party and owe a special debt to working-

class interests, and those in which Catholicism enters the polity in the form of what is, in fact if not in name, a right-wing party. The first type of alignment is found in Belgium and the Netherlands, the second in Germany, Italy, and France. . . . The first type is ideologically egalitarian, frequently governs along with left-wing parties, and produces a large and fairly redistributive welfare state. The second type of party, when dominant, has been responsible for considerable expansion of welfare but as a concession to the Left during spurts of working-class mobilization and capitalist weakness. . . . The cost to rightist interests is minimized as far as possible in such cases by emphasizing nonredistributive programs and methods of finance.[103]

In the Low Countries the major labor parties are not as systematically excluded from state power as in some of the large countries, and they do not assume a confrontational stance toward employers and the state. Unsurprisingly, and in contrast to Italy and France, there exists in Belgium and the Netherlands a tradition of centralized, joint negotiations among representatives of labor, business, and government on questions of economic policy.

The electoral rules of the game heavily influence not only the dynamics of coalition formation among left-wing and right-wing parties but also how the working class is integrated into corporatist arrangements. Proportional representation, as Stein Rokkan has noted, is a characteristic feature of the small European states. Among the large industrial countries only West Germany's electoral system, often described as a mixture of plurality and proportional representation, comes close to the small states' electoral rules. The principle of proportionality, which political parties in the small European states embraced in the early twentieth century, encourages a sharing of power among different political actors. But "why should the smaller democracies on the whole tend to yield so much more readily, and with much less regret, to the pressures for PR than the larger ones? . . . To put it in abstract game-theoretic terms: is it theoretically plausible to assume that party leaders in smaller polities are more likely to depart from the zero-sum model of political competition than their opposite numbers in larger countries?"[104] My line of reasoning in this chapter and this book answers Rokkan's question in the affirmative. Furthermore, with the exception of West Germany the small European states have a much smaller number of national constituencies than do the large countries. Ronald Rogowski argues plausibly that "single-member districts, whether they elect by the Anglo-American method of plurality or by the French or Australian system of absolute majority

. . . generally subject representatives more to protectionist pressures from locally powerful interests . . . and they tend also to stimulate the inefficient public expenditures that Americans familiarly call 'pork barrel.' . . . Both tendencies—toward greater protectionism and bolder raids on the public fisc—must undermine the competitive effectiveness of an advanced trading state."[105]

A divided Right and proportional representation often lead to minority governments. The experience of the Weimar Republic as well as of postwar France and Italy, marked by radical opposition parties, has left the impression that minority governments form in deeply divided states and are unstable or conflict-ridden. But minority governments have also been of great importance in five of the seven small European states. Between 1945 and 1982 minority governments comprised more than one-half of all cabinets in Scandinavia and about 15 percent in the Low Countries.[106]

The effect of minority government on the policy process is very strong in all of the small European states. "The secret of governing in Denmark, one of Europe's most stable societies," the *New York Times* announces, "is not the creation of a working majority; it is making sure no majority is working in opposition."[107] Similarly, Hans Daalder writes, in the Netherlands, "the divisive effects of segmentation are softened by the circumstance that none of the subcultures has much chance of acquiring an independent majority, while there is at the same time little advantage to any two of them forming a lasting coalition against the third."[108] In Sweden, according to Nils Stjernquist, "the main aim of an opposition in a system of this kind would be to influence the policy-making process. The means available to the opposition would be compromises; its tactics, bargaining. . . . [After 1936] the opposition . . . adopted a new policy: in election campaigns the English approach; in Parliament and elsewhere, collaboration with the government in order to influence the political decision making as much as possible."[109] This quotation about Sweden also characterizes the role of the opposition in both Switzerland and Austria, governed for more than half the years since 1945 by all-party governments. There, as in the Low Countries and in Scandinavia, electoral victory is one of two important prizes; the other is the substantial influence over policy that the opposition exercises.[110]

Minority governments are, then, a rational response for parties that are oriented primarily toward influencing policy rather than accumulating patronage. They are the preferred choice of political parties especially in such states as Norway, Denmark, and the Netherlands, which witnessed sharp increases in electoral volatility in

Table 2. Differences in the party system of small and large states

(1) Electoral formula	(2) Number of constituencies, 1974		(3) Number of parliamentary parties, 1945–80		(4) Average vote for all parties excluding major party of the Right, 1960–77		(5) Average electoral turnout as % of eligible age groups, 1959–77		(6) Score of fragmentation of legislature by political parties, 1960–65		(7) Party-group linkage scores, 1964–75	
	Rank	Absolute	Rank	Absolute	Rank	%	Rank	%	Rank	Absolute	Rank	Absolute
Switzerland Proportional representation	6	25	1	5.0	6	78	12	53	1	82	6	45
Netherlands "	1	1	2	4.9	1	88	1	90	3	79	1	64
Belgium "	8	30	4	3.7	3	84	3	88	7	68	2	50
Sweden "	7	28	6.5	3.2	2	85	5	86	6	71	5	46
Denmark "	4	17	3	4.3	4.5	81	4	87	4	74	4	47
Norway "	5	19	6.5	3.2	4.5	81	7	82	5	72	7	40
Austria "	2	9	10	2.2	8.5	55	2	89	11	58	3	49
Small states' average	4.7	18	4.7	3.8	4.2	79	4.9	82	5.3	72	4	49
United States Plurality representation	10	435	12	1.9	11	52	11	59	12	49	12	20
Britain Plurality representation	12	635	11	2.1	8.5	55	8	74	10	59	8	38
West Germany Plurality-proportional representation	3	10	9	2.6	10	54	6	84	9	61	9	36
France Majority-plurality representation	11	489	5	3.3	7	65	10	70	2	80	10	34
Japan Single nontransferable vote	9	124	8	3.1	12	48	9	71	8	62	11	24
Large states' average	9	339	9	2.6	9.7	55	8.8	72	8.2	62	10	30

SOURCES. Cols. 1 and 3: Arend Lijphart, *Democracies: Patterns of Majoritarian and Consensus Government in Twenty-One Countries* (New Haven: Yale University Press, 1984), pp. 122, 152, 155.

Col. 2: Ronald Rogowski, "Research Note: Does Trade Determine Political Institutions?" (Stanford: Center for Advanced Study, 1984), p. 17.

Col. 4: Gary P. Freeman, "Social Security in One Country? Foreign Economic Policies and Domestic Social Programs," paper prepared for delivery at the 1983 Annual Meeting of the American Political Science Association, Palmer House, Chicago, 1–4 September 1983, p. 6.

Cols. 5–7: G. Bingham Powell, Jr., *Contemporary Democracies: Participation, Stability, and Violence* (Cambridge: Harvard University Press, 1982), pp. 14, 81, 90–91.

the 1960s and 1970s. In these three countries the incidence of minority governments increased almost threefold between the 1950s and the 1970s.[111] A system of minority governments is well suited to the party system of the small European states because, far from penalizing opposition parties, it offers these parties significant influence over policy.

The corporatism of the small European states is, in sum, linked to a distinctive party system that offers strong, though different, mechanisms for integrating the working class into a corporatist consensus. The party system of the small European states, compared to that of larger industrial states, is distinguished by a greater mobilization of the electorate, a greater degree of partisan fragmentation of the legislature, and stronger links between political parties and interest groups.[112] Table 2 presents comparative data on these three dimensions as well as on electoral rules, the number of constituencies, the average vote for nonrightist parties, and the number of parliamentary parties. On all dimensions the small European states rank substantially higher than the large industrial countries. Omitting one tied rank, 185 of the 210 pairwise comparisons (of each of seven small states with each of five large ones for six different columns), or 88 percent, support the expectation that the party systems of the small European states differ significantly from those in the large industrial countries.

Political partisanship on questions of economic policy is less important in the small European states than in the large industrial countries. "Reaganomics," "Thatcherism," and the new conservatism drastically changed the approach of the United States and Britain to questions of economic policy. The contrast with Sweden is striking on this score. A coalition led by the Conservatives wrested control from the hands of the Social Democrats in 1976, after forty years of SD government. In subsequent years, however, there has been no fundamental reorientation in policy—except for a large-scale nationalization of ailing private firms. Esping-Andersen concludes that "it is not entirely false to claim that the bourgeois governments were more social democratic than the SAP."[113] In the large industrial countries the effect of partisanship on the size of the public sector is pronounced. In sharp contrast, the great expansion in the public economy of both the Netherlands (governed through much of the postwar era by coalition governments led by Conservatives or Liberals) and of Sweden (ruled by Social Democrats) illustrates that in the small European states generally, "all governments—whether formed by leftist or non-leftist parties—have been impelled by the exigencies of the open economy to expand the role of the state. . . . The openness of the economy is the best single predictor of the growth of public revenues relative to the economic product of a nation."[114] Another observer concludes similarly that "the association between high spending and Social Democratic dominance in government—characteristic of the Scandinavian countries but not of the Netherlands—appears mainly to stem from the fact that both are the products of the same set of structural factors. . . ."[115]

Those structural factors include, as Cameron has argued persuasively, a high degree of economic openness that coincides with a concentration of industrial ownership, especially in the export sector, a small number of employers' associations, high degrees of unionization, few but effective national union federations, an extension of collective bargaining, and an increasing power of industrial labor unions—in short, with many of the structural conditions that facilitate democratic corporatism.[116] Government policy after the first oil shock confirms the importance of economic openness and partisan choice in corporatism.[117] Manfred Schmidt argues that while the expansion of the public sector was quite sensitive to whether power was wielded by leftist or rightist parties, some Social Democratic governments were fiscally conservative while some governments of the Right increased taxing and spending substantially. Of decisive importance in the 1970s, Schmidt argues, was the distribution of power *outside* Parliament.

Economic openness, corporatism, and a distinctive party system set the small European states apart from the large industrial countries. The correlation between these variables is so high that statistical analyses are unlikely to help us much further in disentangling relationships. A functional explanation of how corporatism maintains and recreates itself should instead be supplemented by a historical explanation of its origins, a task to which I shall turn in chapter 4.

LIBERAL AND SOCIAL CORPORATISM

The corporatist structures of the small European states are embedded in world markets. Reinforced by distinctive party systems, the pressures of the market have helped integrate labor, business, and government into firm, evolving, collaborative arrangements. Yet "corporatism," as Shalev correctly notes, "is after all only a description of certain institutional arrangements which can themselves hardly be understood without reference to class structure, power and conflict."[118] Systematic differences exist among the small European states in the relative centralization and orientation of business and in the power and centralization of labor (as measured by unionization rates, Left voting, and Social Democratic incumbency). Switzerland has a particular affinity with the Netherlands and Belgium. These three countries have politically strong, internationally oriented, centralized business communities and relatively decentralized and weak labor movements. They are liberal variants of democratic corporatism. Austria, Norway, and Denmark have strong, centralized labor unions and business communities that are politically weak, express a national orientation, and are relatively decentralized. They are social variants of democratic corporatism. Sweden mixes these two political patterns.

The relative strengths of business and labor are reflected in different political choices. Some favor programs that give maximum scope to private initiative and seek to modify market outcomes by providing supplementary income maintenance through means-tested welfare benefits; others, programs that encourage public intervention and attempt to structure or replace market processes, for example through the provision of public housing or public health and universal social insurance for which eligibility depends not on employment but on citizenship.[119] This difference is reflected in where and how the small European states adapt to economic change—broadly speaking, there are two clusters of responses. The global adaptation and private compensation of liberal corporatism contrasts with the national adaptation and public compensation of social corporatism. This distinction between the two responses shows that corporatism can appear in substantially different political contexts. Policy choices in a number of sectors illustrate the differences between countries from group I (Switzerland, the Netherlands, Belgium) and group II (Denmark, Norway, Austria). Sweden can exemplify the policy choices of either group.

Global vs. National Adaptation

Business in the small European states can vary strikingly in character. In Switzerland, the Netherlands, Belgium, and Sweden business has an international orientation and is more centralized; in the countries of group II it has a national orientation and is less centralized. The data in Table 3 illustrate the point. This difference among the small European states can be traced in the contrast between global

Table 3. The business communities of the small European states ranked by international orientation and centralization

	(1) International production in foreign subsidiaries as % of exports, 1971		(2) Direct foreign investment per employee in $, 1971		(3) Exports per employee in $, 1971		(4) Total balance sheet of the largest 3 banks/GNP, 1971		(5) Associational monopoly of business		(6) Sum of ranks of cols. (1)–(5)	
	Rank	%	Rank	Absol. no.	Rank	Absol. no.	Rank	Absol. no.	Rank	%	Rank	Sum
1. Switzerland	1.0	236	1.0	3,077	4.0	1,906	1.0	1.07	1.5	10.0	1.0	8.5
2. Netherlands	3.5	52	3.0	916	2.0	2,925	2.0	0.46	1.5	10.0	2.0	12.0
3. Belgium	3.5	52	4.0	822	1.0	3,122	3.0	0.41	3.0	7.0	3.0	14.5
4. Sweden	2.0	92	2.0	1,123	3.0	2,187	4.0	0.31	6.5	3.0	4.0	17.5
5. Denmark	5.0	16	5.0	128	6.0	1,527	5.0	0.29	6.5	3.0	5.0	27.5
6. Norway	6.0	8	6.0	58	5.0	1,646	7.0	0.17	5.0	4.0	6.0	29.0
7. Austria	7.0	3	7.0	13	7.0	1,046	6.0	0.22	4.0	5.0	7.0	31.0
Average (1–3)	2.7	113	2.7	1,605	2.3	2,651	2.0	0.64	2.0	9.0	2.0	11.7
Average (5–7)	6.0	9	6.0	66	6.0	1,406	6.0	0.23	5.2	4.0	6.0	29.2

SOURCES. Cols. 1–2: United Nations, *Multinational Corporations in World Development*, ST/ECA/190 (New York, 1973), p. 159.
Cols. 3–4: Herbert Ammann, Werner Fassbind, and Peter C. Meyer, "Multinationale Konzerne der Schweiz und Auswirkungen auf die Arbeiterklasse in der Schweiz," Institute of Sociology, University of Zurich, 1975, pp. 106–07.
Col. 5: This indicator varies from zero to 12 and measures the number of business organizations in different economic sectors which are included in the peak association of business. Vorort des schweizerischen Handels- und Industrievereins, "Der Aufbau der europäischen Industrie-Spitzenverbände: Ergebnisse einer Umfrage (Stand: Ende 1975)," unpublished ms. (Zurich, 1977), p. 16.
Col. 6: A combined ranking of cols. (1)–(5).

and national strategies of adaptation in the areas of foreign investment, research and development, foreign trade, and industrial concentration.

The variation in the experience of the small European states perhaps explains why analyses of all small advanced industrial states reach different conclusions about the relative importance of an internationally oriented business community in general and the role of multinational corporations in particular. Impressed by the prominence of firms such as Philips, Unilever, or Ciba-Geigy, some authors show that big business can exist without large domestic markets. Large firms in the small European states have succeeded in overcoming the restrictions a small domestic market imposes on their growth through early, rapid, and sustained moves toward exports first and the internationalization of production later. It thus comes as no surprise that the relative degree of internationalization of large multinationals in Switzerland, the Netherlands, and Sweden is greater than in the United States and that in Belgium it is only slightly less.[120] However, other analysts of international business in the small European states either do not discuss group I countries or stress the fact that the tendency to go multinational is much weaker in the small European states than in the large industrial states and that firms in the small European states typically tend to be much smaller.[121]

The two ways of adjusting to change are graphically illustrated by the extent to which business in the small European states locates production facilities abroad. In the late 1960s and early 1970s the average for Switzerland, the Netherlands, Belgium, and Sweden exceeded corresponding figures for group II countries by a factor of 30 in the total stock of direct foreign investment,[122] of 16 in the number of firms among the largest 650 multinational corporations,[123] of 15 in the annual flow of direct foreign investment,[124] and by a factor of 5 in the total number of multinational firms.[125] If measured in terms of the flow of direct foreign investment, the gap between these two groups of states widened substantially in the 1970s.[126] Among the states that invest abroad, a further distinction can be drawn: in Switzerland and in the Netherlands corporations are larger, have a greater preference for foreign production, and expand more rapidly abroad than those in Belgium or Sweden.[127]

The internationalization of production has had a central place in Switzerland's strategy in the international economy. The prosperity of Switzerland's chemical industry in the 1960s and 1970s contrasts with the great problems that have plagued the Swiss watch industry in recent years. Swiss watches were until the late 1970s produced only domestically, and so these different experiences are a poignant reminder of the benefits that can accompany internationalization.[128] Dutch multinational corporations play a central role in economic life in the Netherlands. Corporations with more than 500 employees account for most of the 190,000 jobs lost in Dutch industry between 1970 and 1976. In contrast to the autonomy-minded Swiss, however, Dutch foreign investment is often undertaken by very large international firms owned and managed, for example, jointly with Britain (Royal Dutch Shell and Unilever) and, for some years during the 1970s, West Germany (Hoesch-Hoogovens and VFW-Fokker).[129] Also in contrast to Switzerland, there are some signs that Dutch foreign investment was spurred in the 1970s in part by the growth of a welfare state at home.[130]

Frequent changes in government insurance of overseas production indicate that foreign investment comes less naturally to Belgium and Sweden than it does to Switzerland and the Netherlands.[131] But judging by the Swedish experience, at least, it is doubtful that changes in government policy on questions of direct foreign investment have had significant consequences in recent years. Neither government regulations offering risk insurance in 1968 nor legislation concerned with the structural and employment consequences of Sweden's direct foreign investment appear to have had much effect on corporate strategies.[132] One possible reason is the export-inducing character of Sweden's foreign investments, which has created a supportive attitude toward the international operations of firms shared widely across the political spectrum. At the beginning of the 1980s more than half of the employees of Sweden's ten largest firms worked abroad. These same ten companies sold between 60 and 90 percent of their products in foreign markets.[133]

The difference between the two groups of small European states shows up as well in the kind of services that they sell in international markets. Switzerland and the Netherlands depend heavily on receipts from international finance and insurance. In 1976 these were the only two small European states with banks (a total of five) among the largest fifty worldwide.[134] Switzerland joins the United States, Britain, and France as one of four countries controlling 70 percent of the international insurance business.[135] Switzerland and the Netherlands furthermore export twice as many services as they import.[136] Although Belgium and Sweden are also highly competitive in the export of services, their net receipts are much smaller.[137] In contrast to these four states none of the group II countries are important exporters of financial and insurance services.[138] Instead Austria earns its service income from mass tourism, Norway from shipping. These sources of receipts are more susceptible than finance and insurance to variations in the business cycle.

In research and development it is equally evident that the small European states differ in how they adapt to change. Studies of the first group of states and Sweden have been so impressed by the R and D policies of the small European states that they hold them up as models worthy of the attention of policy makers in the large advanced industrial countries.[139] On the other hand, studies of group II (as well as other small countries) typically point to weakness and dependence. Indeed, one of the key dangers that this second group of small European states confronts, it has been argued, is being squeezed out of international markets.[140] From the perspective of group II, the Netherlands and Sweden have "large-country characteristics" in their R and D performance.

"The essential element in national innovative performance," write two recent observers, "is less size and intensity of national demand for technological innovation than the entrepreneurial, organizational and technological resources within a country that are capable of identifying and responding to market demands for technological innovation anywhere in the world."[141] The resources and skills needed are not present to a sufficient degree in Austrian, Danish, and Norwegian business. Despite sharply growing expenditures on R and D in the 1960s and 1970s these countries, unlike group I, by and large did not succeed in transforming themselves into active innovators.[142] Indeed, a study of the first commercial exploitation of 110 significant technological innovations since 1945 found only one such instance in Austria, Norway, and Denmark, compared to nine in the other four states.[143] Another analysis discovered that between 1953 and 1971 group II countries found their comparative advantage in traditional, nondurable consumer goods and in standardized commodities that depend on the availability of domestic raw materials such as wood, iron ore, hides, and skins or fur.[144]

Switzerland and the Netherlands aggressively exploit the comparative advantage that the small European states tend to have in the early phases of the development of new products with a high engineering and scientific content.[145] They do so with the help of a small group of very large multinational corporations, which organize basic research, product development, and process innovations in their own research centers both at home and abroad.[146] On a per capita basis, for example, Switzerland ranks at the very top of all industrial countries, large and small, in the number of scientific authors and patents granted.[147]

Swiss policy has been consistent in trying to keep the government out of all aspects of R and D policy, with the sole exception of nuclear energy. In the Netherlands, because of the country's agricultural orientation prior to World War II, an R and D policy favoring industrial innovation has evolved under government auspices, but it does not displace, rather complements, the activities of Dutch multinationals. Two-thirds of all R and D are undertaken by five large firms (Philips, Shell, Unilever, Akzo, and DSM).[148] This strand of privatism explains why, in Anthony Scaperlanda's words, "the Netherlands does not have an aggressive R and D policy by any standard imaginable."[149]

Belgium and Sweden are also high spenders on R and D, but they have developed a somewhat more coordinated and planned approach to problems of research and development.[150] Belgium traditionally "depended less on innovation from its own research laboratories than upon successful enterprise, planning and management."[151] During the last two decades Belgium has placed great emphasis on attracting foreign firms in industrial branches with high research intensity, such as petrochemicals, and has attempted at the same time to fashion a national research strategy through a variety of programs that are sponsored by government.[152] Sweden, unlike all the other small European states, has remained committed to a technologically independent program of national defense. As a result, technological innovation has received a much larger amount of government support than in Switzerland, the Netherlands, or Belgium.[153] The Swedish government also has long-standing policies for the stimulation of innovation.[154] The success of its policy of borrowing foreign technological innovations has earned it, among some of its envious neighbors, the nickname of "the Japan of Europe."[155]

Group II countries have followed a markedly different R and D strategy. Austria has specialized in basic and semimanufacturing industries that are characterized by relatively slow growth rates and moderate changes in technology. Indeed, Austrian attempts to stimulate industrial innovation date back only to the late 1960s, when the Austrian government attempted for the first time to emulate the technological prowess of its Swiss neighbor.[156] In Denmark, oriented toward agriculture before World War II, policies favoring industrial innovation are also of comparatively recent origin.[157] Norway, on the other hand, began to develop an active innovation policy as early as the 1950s and established around 1960 its system of national research councils as part of a more encompassing strategy of economic development and industrialization.[158]

The contrasting strategies of adaptation of these two groups are reflected in a number of other indicators. Expenditure data on research and development provide some suggestive evidence.[159] In 1973 R and D expenditures in group II averaged only 0.9 percent of GNP, far below the 2.1 percent figure for Switzerland and the Netherlands and the 1.5 percent average for Belgium and Sweden.[160] These figures agree closely with other measures of national effort in R and D.[161] R and D expenditures, furthermore, tend to serve different purposes in the two groups. In the Netherlands their prime purpose is to increase competitiveness in high-technology and high-growth sectors. In Norway, by way of contrast, their purpose is to enhance economic and industrial development more broadly conceived.[162] Differences in the distribution of R and D expenditures also show up in a comparison between Sweden and Belgium, which lag a bit behind Switzerland and the Netherlands but lead group II. Belgium and Sweden invested 60 percent of their total industrial R and D in science-based industries, well above the 46 percent figure for Austria and Norway. In the mechanical industries, on the other hand, the 29 percent investment figure for Belgium and Sweden was well below the 40 percent figure for Austria and Norway.[163]

Data on scientific publications and patent statistics provide further evidence of significant differences between the two groups of small European states. In 1963 the average number of patents granted in foreign countries to Switzerland, the Netherlands, Sweden, and Belgium was 5,400 compared to fewer than one thousand for group II.[164] By way of contrast, the proportion of patents taken out by foreign applicants in the years 1957–61 and in 1974 was lower in group I and Sweden than in Austria, Denmark, and Norway.[165] With these figures to hand it is no surprise that the ratio of payments over receipts for foreign licenses for Austria and Norway is three times as great as for Belgium and Sweden.[166] While Switzerland, the Netherlands, and, to a lesser degree, Sweden deliberately try to attract foreign researchers, Austria and Norway lose a significant proportion of their native researchers, especially to neighboring countries. In the international exchange of scientists only Switzerland, the Netherlands, Belgium, and Sweden among the small European states can record net gains.[167]

The small European states have embraced liberalization in the international economy throughout the postwar years with varying enthusiasm. Group II countries have not opened their economies to foreign trade as much as the other four small European states. Norway, Austria, and Denmark had liberalized, respectively, only 65, 75, and 77 percent of their trade by 1958, by which year the other four countries had achieved full liberalization.[168] Compared to Switzerland, the Netherlands, Belgium, and Sweden, group II relied relatively heavily on the quota restriction of industrial imports.[169] In 1960–61 these three countries initially opposed the acceleration of trade liberalization measures with EFTA proposed by Britain, Sweden, and Switzerland, and they were granted temporary though largely symbolic exemptions.[170] In 1962 Austria and Norway were the last of the small European states to withdraw trade restrictions due to balance-of-payment considerations.[171] Between 1969 and 1977 only Denmark (twice) and Norway (four times) among the small European states brought antidumping cases to the GATT.[172] In the Tokyo Round of trade negotiations Austria and Norway showed relatively protectionist instincts: the depth of the linear cuts agreed to by all negotiating parties in principle and the actual offer they made for tariff reductions was greater than for any group I country.[173] In the 1960s only Austria and Denmark maintained quota restrictions on the import of manufactures or semimanufactures from less developed countries.[174] And in 1974 Austria and Norway had the lowest shares of all market economies of total imports from the less developed countries.[175]

Conversely, group II countries are conspicuous by their absence from the main OECD exporters in 25 industrial sectors. Denmark is listed twice (furniture and shipbuilding) and Norway once (shipbuilding); Austria does not appear a single time. The Netherlands, in sharp contrast, is listed eleven times, Belgium ten, and Sweden and Switzerland six times each.[176] Compared to the total value of their export trade, Austria's and Denmark's expenditures on export promotion in 1972 were three times as great as those of Switzerland, the Netherlands, Belgium, and Sweden.[177] Yet between 1960 and 1977 there was not a single year in which Austria, Norway, and Denmark had a positive trade balance; on average the other four small states broke even.[178]

The relatively protectionist orientation of group II is reflected in tariff rates that lie consistently above those of Switzerland and Sweden. (Because of their membership in the European Communities, the Netherlands and Belgium produce no national data.) In 1960, for example, tariffs on manufactured goods were about twice as high in Austria (20%) as in Switzerland (9%) and Sweden (11%).[179] The weighted average of the post–Kennedy Round tariffs was 7 percent for Switzerland and Sweden and almost 12 percent for group II.[180] Indeed, at the conclusion of the Kennedy Round, Austrian, Danish, and Norwegian tariffs on the fifteen major manufactured product groups were without exception higher than the tariffs of the other small European states. If we distinguish product groups by the stage of processing, we get similar results. While there is no discernible statistical difference in tariff levels for raw materials, systematic tariff disparities between the two groups become evident in semimanufactured and manufactured goods. In 14 of 22 categories of semimanufactured goods and in 16 of 17 categories of manufactured goods Austria, Denmark, and Norway have higher tariff levels than do Switzerland and Sweden.[181]

National adaptation in Austria, Norway, and Denmark and, at times, Sweden offers a way to counter some of the effects of economic liberalism in the international economy. Foreign ownership of capital, for example, can undermine national control over resources and limit political choices. Sometimes this loss of control is evident in government revenues foregone. The transfer pricing practices of U.S. oil companies were such that their Danish subsidiaries showed only deficits in the 1960s.[182] For the same reason, Sweden's first government report on industrial concentration focused exclusively on the petroleum industry.[183] At other times loss of control is due simply to the imperatives of market structures. In aluminum, an industry marked by vertical integration, the Norwegian government felt compelled in 1967 to achieve vertical integration in order to secure sources of raw materials and dependable outlets. It did not choose the risky course of developing a Norwegian firm, Ardal, into an independent, integrated aluminum producer, but played it safe by permitting Ardal to join Alcan, a large multinational corporation and its main supplier of alumina.[184] Similarly, if with different motives, the Austrian government decided in the late 1950s to privatize the electrical engineering industry (which it had nationalized in 1945). In the late 1960s it permitted the industry's takeover by Siemens, a German company that had dominated the sector during the interwar period.

The small European states that adhere to a strategy of national adaptation thus do not handle problems through restrictions imposed on the free flow of capital. Occasional exceptions do exist, such as the conflict between the Norwegian government and ITT in the 1960s and the Swedish government's defense of a minor electronics firm against an attempted Italian takeover bid in 1969.[185] But the typical response in group II states has been industrial concentration and the building of national champions. These policies are noteworthy not because they are unique to the small European states but because industrial concentration in these countries already tends to be substantially greater than in the large advanced industrial countries. In the late 1960s industrial concentration in Sweden and Austria was about 40 percent higher than the average concentration of industry in

Table 4. Strength and centralization of the labor movements of the small European states, 1965–80

	(1) Average % of total labor force unionized		(2) Organizational unity of labor movement		(3) Confederation power in collective bargaining		(4) Scope of collective bargaining		(5) Works council and codetermination		(6) Social Democratic vote, 1970s		(7) Social Democratic presence in government, 1965–81		(8) Sum of ranks of cols. (1)–(7)	
	Rank	%	Rank	Index	Rank	Index	Rank	Index	Rank	Index	Rank	Index	Rank	Index	Rank	Sum
1. Switzerland	7.0	24	5.5	0.7	7.0	0.4	7.0	0.8	7.0	0.3	7.0	26	6.0	29	7.0	46.5
2. Netherlands	6.0	28	5.5	0.7	4.5	0.6	5.0	0.9	3.0	1.0	5.0	34	7.0	22	5.0	36.0
3. Belgium	3.0	55	7.0	0.6	4.5	0.6	5.0	0.9	6.0	0.5	6.0	30	5.0	30	6.0	36.5
4. Sweden	1.0	70	3.0	0.8	2.5	0.7	2.0	1.0	3.0	1.0	2.0	49	2.5	69	2.0	16.0
5. Denmark	4.0	54	3.0	0.8	6.0	0.5	5.0	0.9	3.0	1.0	4.0	39	2.5	69	4.0	27.5
6. Norway	2.0	65	3.0	0.8	2.5	0.7	2.0	1.0	3.0	1.0	3.0	47	4.0	61	3.0	19.5
7. Austria	5.0	50	1.0	1.0	1.0	0.8	2.0	1.0	3.0	1.0	1.0	51	1.0	73	1.0	14.0
Average (1–3)	5.3	36	6.0	0.7	5.3	0.5	5.7	0.9	5.3	0.6	6.0	30	6.0	27	6.0	39.7
Average (5–7)	3.7	56	2.3	0.9	3.2	0.7	3.0	1.0	3.0	1.0	2.7	46	2.5	68	2.7	20.3

SOURCES. Cols. 1–5, 7: David R. Cameron, "Social Democracy, Corporatism, and Labor Quiescence: The Representation of Economic Interest in Advanced Capitalist Society," paper presented at the Conference on Representation and the State: Problems of Governability and Legitimacy in Western European Democracies, Stanford University, October 1982, Table 6. It should be noted that the unionization figure for Switzerland has increased sharply to about 38 percent since a large number of foreign workers departed in the mid-1970s.

Col. 6: Manfred G. Schmidt, "Die Regulierung des Kapitalismus unter bürgerlichen und sozialdemokratischen Regierungen," University of Constance, Fachbereich Politische Wissenschaft/Verwaltungswissenschaft, Diskussionsbeitrag 8/79, p. 58. The Danish data include votes for the Social People's party; Social Democratic vote averaged only 34 percent. This lower figure does not affect the rankings in col. 8.

the large industrial countries.[186] Because the concentration of business is viewed as a necessity to counter foreign competition, antitrust legislation tends to be fairly loose in these small European states.[187]

Norway has been in the forefront of developing national champions as a defense against foreign corporations. Large-scale nationalization in the late 1940s and 1950s was designed to further Norway's traditional exports in steel, aluminum, iron mining, and coal processing.[188] In the 1960s government policy underwent a subtle shift, however, and since 1968 the Norwegian government has explicitly chosen to develop national champions as a defense against Swedish- and U.S.-based multinationals and as a way of enhancing the international competitiveness of Norwegian industry.[189] The development of Norway's North Sea oil reserves in the 1970s further increased the government's influence in industry. Although Denmark's policy follows similar objectives, it has remained more cautious.

Informed by government-sponsored studies, the Swedish government also came to obey a concentration "ethic" in actively encouraging mergers since the mid and late 1960s, that is, during the period of greatest liberalization in the international economy.[190] In the postwar years four-fifths of Swedish mergers were "defensive" horizontal mergers within an industry while only one-fifth involved "offensive" vertical or conglomerate-type mergers.[191] Yet by the mid-1970s Sweden's largest companies were heavily concentrated in the growth sectors of the economy. This concentration policy coincided with an increasing Swedish debate on science policy and a trend toward a more "active" industrial policy. Modeled after Italy's largest state-owned corporation (IRI) and parelleling a similar development in Austria, a state holding company (Statsföretag) was founded in 1971 comprising 25 firms with about 34,000 employees and sales of about $800 million.[192] Even though Sweden's public-sector economy was relatively small through the late 1970s, the role of state enterprises in industrial and regional policy has increased.[193] Concentration policy became a weapon for warding off the undesirable influences of multinational corporations and, in the late 1970s and early 1980s, for rescuing firms hard hit by prolonged recession.[194]

Private vs. Public Compensation

Labor movements vary considerably in the small European states. In Austria, Norway, Denmark, and Sweden labor movements are stronger and more centralized than in group I (see Table 4). This difference can be traced in reliance on public or private strategies of compensation in the areas of economic planning, public expenditures, regional development, social welfare, and international economic diplomacy.

The economic planning policies of the small European states provide one instance of the characteristic difference between domestic compensation that relies primarily on market forces in group I or on state supervision in group II. Applied to the small European states "economic planning" thus describes widely dissimilar policies. It encompasses passive planning, such as Dutch contingency forecasts, as well as the active medium-term public-sector financial planning in Norway.

Even though the Dutch Central Planning Board has won international fame for its virtuosity, the trappings of technical skill and imagination should not be mistaken for the substance of political power. For five different reasons, Dutch planners are relatively impotent. First, Dutch economic planning is based on government policy rather than the other way around; budget decisions precede the publication of and debates on the economic plans.[195] Neither the long-term nor the short-term plans are in any way binding on any branch of government. Second, the board is separate from the state bureaucracy; its administrative integration into the executive branch of government is a mere formality.[196] At the same time, though, it has only tenuous links to the private sector; its tripartite planning committee is not a steering committee but merely a discussion forum. No government directives and no consultation with Dutch peak associations accompanies the work of the economic planners.[197] Third, while board publications must be cleared by the government before being released to the public, clearance tends to be apolitical. The semipublic character of projections and pronouncements stems from the coordinating role of the planning bureau rather than from political backing received from the government.[198] Fourth, while the close attention of Dutch planners to so-called instrument variables has been heralded as a major advance in the theory and practice of economic planning, the only variable over which, according to the work of the board itself, the government has had effective control in the past thirty years was emigration. Yet as early as the late 1950s, when the government was still encouraging emigration because of widespread fear of unemployment, the Netherlands, like most other European countries, began to recruit foreign workers.[199] Finally, in contrast to Japanese and French practices, Dutch economic planning has operated mostly at the macro rather than the sectoral level.[200]

The Norwegian approach to planning, illustrative of group II, provides a striking contrast to the Dutch experience. Norwegian economic planners have been less theoretically and technically ambitious than their Dutch counterparts. Norwegian planners have relied not on high-powered econometric analysis and a precise specification of instrument variables but on planning by trial and error in successive, iterative approximations during the budget cycle.[201] And the Norwegian government has relied on political clout rather than technical virtuosity to make its planning policies work. In contrast to the Dutch variety, Norwegian planning is incorporated into the government rather than being left to an independent agency or research institute. Furthermore, Norwegian plans are binding on public-sector spending.

As the government-supervised exploitation of North Sea oil began to generate significant revenues in the late 1970s, the political importance of the public sector increased further.[202] Despite a noticeable shift away from the direct economic controls of the 1950s, the programmatic (rather than prognostic) character of Norway's plans became stronger. Understandably, the five-year plan is less binding than the annual budget on either Parliament or government; yet its targets and guidelines are important determinants of policy.[203] Furthermore, the budgets of all levels of government are integrated into one national plan.[204] The prominence of the plan is greater because the Finance Ministry assures that plan directives are followed throughout the public sector. The permanent secretariat, which in 1966 replaced ad hoc groups, also increased continuity in Norway's efforts by making planning more flexible. Unforeseen exogenous changes, like the 1973 oil embargo, can now be incorporated in a revised plan. Finally, in contrast to the Netherlands, Norway's planning secretariat paid increasing attention in the 1970s to key sectors of the economy with heavy government involvement in aluminum, hydroelectric energy, mining, and most importantly, the development of North Sea oil.[205] Norwegian economic planning policies, in sum, differ from Dutch policies in the greater prominence they give to the exercise of state power.

The difference between private and public methods of compensating for change can also be seen in the way the Netherlands and Denmark have deployed their large public sectors. During the past two decades both countries have witnessed an astonishing growth in public expenditures. Measured as a proportion of GDP their public economies rank among the largest in the small European states. In Denmark public expenditures increased from 26 percent of GDP in 1955–57 to 46 percent in 1974–76. Corresponding figures for the

Netherlands were 31 and 54 percent.[206] But these aggregate figures conceal critically important differences affecting the Danish and Dutch positions in the international economy. In the mid-1970s Denmark spent 24 percent of its public expenditures on final consumption and only 17 percent on transfer payments. Despite larger public expenditures, the Netherlands, in sharp contrast, spent only 18 percent on consumption and 27 percent on transfer payments. If measured in constant (1970) prices, between 1962–64 and 1974–76 Denmark's share of public final consumption expenditure in GDP increased by 3.3 percent while it declined by more than 4 percent in the Netherlands.[207] These marked differences have by no means trivial implications for economic health. Sounding an increasingly familiar theme, one statistical study found the level of gross capital formation to be adversely affected by increased public consumption.[208] Among the small European states between 1961 and 1972, for example, Denmark's increases in public expenditure were among the highest while the annual average of gross domestic fixed capital formation was among the lowest. In Switzerland these relations were reversed. Among small European states with large public expenditures, the Netherlands approximates the Swiss case.[209] In contrast to Denmark, the Netherlands imposes virtually all of the cost of social security on workers' incomes. A large public sector in the Netherlands primarily reflects large transfer payments; it manages to support economic growth and private investment because it does not erode the productive base of the economy. Large public consumption in Denmark, on the other hand, signals a shift of productive resources into low-growth and relatively "unproductive" parts of the economy. As the Danish case shows, the shift eventually weakens both the government's ability to extract the necessary taxes and the economy's competitive posture in domestic and international markets. The relative size of public-sector employment also illustrates the difference graphically: in 1975 it was almost twice as large in Denmark as in the Netherlands.[210] The 1960s was the decade of most rapid expansion of the public economy in both countries; but among twelve OECD member states the Netherlands experienced the highest growth of market share in one sector crucial for economic health—engineering products—in that decade while Denmark experienced the greatest loss.[211]

Belgian and Swedish approaches to the problems of regional development and job creation also illustrate the difference between groups I and II. Belgium's concerted efforts to attract private foreign capital contrasts starkly with the Swedish emphasis on an active manpower policy funded from the public purse. The original impetus for

Belgium's regional policy was the recession of 1958, structural crisis in Belgium's coal mines, and decline in the Flemish textile industry.[212] Regional development laws passed in 1959 and 1966 created strong investment incentives for firms. In the 1960s direct foreign investment in Belgium grew faster than in any other Western European country, and about one-third of foreign investment benefited from the government's financial incentives. In 1965–66, for example, 20 percent of total gross industrial capital was by one estimate invested by foreigners. In 1967–68 two-thirds of new investments were located in regions defined as depressed in the 1966 legislation. By 1975, 90 percent of Belgium's pharmaceutical industry was under foreign control as compared to Sweden's 45 percent.[213] However, investment in relatively backward areas typically did not occur in new industries. As a result, the legislative intent—improving the economic structure of weak provinces and shifting factors of production out of declining industrial sectors—has had only mixed success.[214] The political distinctiveness of Belgium's regional policy, whatever its economic record of achievement, lies in the use of foreign capital as the major instrument by which the government has sought to achieve Belgium's regional employment objectives.

Sweden, by way of contrast, seeks to achieve the objectives of regional development and full employment through an active manpower policy. Swedish policy relies more than that of any other small European state on job creation through vocational training or retraining and public works[215]—in fact, one of the most important and original of Sweden's widely celebrated contributions to the theory and practice of modern economic policy. Drawing on a variety of public funds, the budget of Sweden's two manpower boards amounts to 2 or 3 percent of GNP and is spent largely with an eye to encouraging industrial adaptation and the development of impoverished or declining regions.[216] These regional and manpower policies are adjustment mechanisms designed to cope with technological and structural change in the interest of increasing productivity and prosperity.[217] Nine hundred thousand Swedish workers were retrained between 1960 and 1975, with the proportion of the total work force affected each year varying between 0.5 and 1.5 percent.[218] Because of these special employment programs, Sweden's official unemployment rate has amounted at no time since 1973 to more than one-third of the Belgian rate.[219] Even if the Belgian government had wished to lower unemployment drastically (which is by no means clear), the option was foreclosed in a regional policy that predominantly relied on foreign and private rather than domestic and public funds. Conversely, had the Swedish government wished to diversify through encouraging industrial redeployment and regional development with the aid of foreign capital, it would have proved impossible. The inflow of funds increased only gradually, from $86 million in 1970–72 to $145 million in 1978–80 as compared to a steep growth in corresponding Belgian figures, from $384 to $1,371 million.[220]

The social welfare systems of Sweden and Switzerland illustrate a further difference between groups I and II. Sweden more than any of its Scandinavian neighbors embodies for many observers a generous, publicly funded welfare state. Switzerland, by way of contrast, is often neglected in the political analysis of the welfare state because its public provision of social welfare has traditionally been paltry. Hence one index of social insurance coverage in the advanced industrial states shows Sweden near the very top while Switzerland comes in at the bottom.[221] Comparisons of expenditures confirm the impression of Sweden as a "leader" and Switzerland as a "laggard" in publicly funded social welfare programs. Sweden spends 23.8 percent of its GNP on social security while Switzerland spends only 11.8 percent.[222] Even the substantial changes introduced in Switzerland's publicly funded social security system in the early 1970s, which narrowed the gap between it and other small European states, did not affect Switzerland's relative position as a laggard.

The Swiss welfare reforms of 1972 provide an important contrast to Sweden's hotly contested pension reform of the late 1950s. More generous support levels figured in both episodes. But Sweden's General Supplementary Pension was designed as an instrument of capital formation in the public sector.[223] The Swiss reform, by way of contrast, presumed the continuation of a substantial though diminishing portion of welfare through compulsory private pension and insurance schemes.[224] This difference in the balance between public and private organization of social welfare is also reflected in the prominent role that private occupational pension plans play in Switzerland; according to one study, in the late 1960s such plans were six times as important in financial terms in Switzerland as in Sweden.[225] Sweden's emphasis on publicly funded welfare schemes has resulted in virtually universal coverage; in Switzerland only four out of five workers are covered by the obligatory public and private schemes.[226] Sweden's policy encourages rather than restricts labor mobility, and it has had much greater effects on capital formation.[227] In 1972–73 the Swedish pension fund accounted for 7 percent of GNP and 30 percent of total savings.[228]

While voluntary pension insurance is virtually unknown in Sweden, just under one-third of total insurance premia in Switzerland is generated by voluntary schemes.[229] Switzerland's traditionally high level of individual savings is deliberately fostered by a policy that keeps taxes lower than in any other small European state. While between 1972 and 1976 the average married male worker with two children paid only 7 percent of gross earnings in Swiss taxes, he had to pay 35 percent in Sweden, more than in any other small European state.[230] It is notoriously difficult to estimate the combined total of obligatory contributions paid into both public and private schemes.[231] In rough terms, however, Switzerland seems to lag somewhat, but not much, behind Sweden in total expenditure on obligatory public and private pension plans. What difference exists in the data would probably disappear if private savings were included in the comparison.[232] In short, Switzerland differs from Sweden not so much in the magnitude of total expenditure on social welfare as in its method of financing.

This difference between Switzerland and Sweden can also be found in the two countries' responses to the demands of the less developed countries. Prior to the first UNCTAD conference of 1964, both counries opposed the granting of trade preferences; all forms of discrimination would, they feared, threaten the liberal international economy from which they were prospering. If preferences were to be granted, then in Gardner Patterson's words they should be granted only "as sort of an advance installment on a general most-favored-nation reduction of duties."[233] Switzerland and Sweden were two of eight countries voting against the conference's final resolutions.

In more recent years two fundamentally different approaches to North-South relations have emerged among the small European states. These approaches express different attitudes toward private and public methods of adjustment. Switzerland's policy toward the less developed countries reflects a mixture of laissez-faire liberalism and export promotion grounded in a firm belief in the virtues of private initiative and market solutions. By way of contrast, Swedish policy has evolved since the late 1960s to a kind of Social Democratic welfare policy at the global level. The Swedes aim to counteract some of the harmful effects that market solutions entail for the less developed countries. Private investment in the less developed countries also provokes typically different reactions. Since 1970, inspired by the OECD's Draft Convention on the Protection of Foreign Property, Switzerland (together with the Netherlands, the United States, Britain, and West Germany) has been attempting to reduce uncertainty in international investment through a series of bilateral investment agreements.[234] Sweden, by way of contrast, will guarantee foreign investments only if Swedish firms conform to a code of good behavior with respect to workers in the developing countries. This code of conduct includes granting collective bargaining rights to unions; extending benefits for loss of wages during illness, injury, and layoffs; providing for pensions, health, and welfare; and assuring nondiscriminatory employment practices.[235] To give a further typical example, in commercial policy Switzerland is opposed to granting any preferential treatment to imports from less developed countries. Sweden, meanwhile, has opened a special import office to help overcome the marketing limitations of the LDCs.[236]

For ideological reasons Switzerland and Sweden differ greatly in how much publicly funded aid they program for less developed countries. Switzerland's uninspiring record in international aid expresses a distaste for government intervention in the economy. In 1977 public aid amounted to 0.19 percent of Swiss GNP, far below the OECD average of 0.31 percent and the OECD target of 0.7 percent.[237] The Swedish government, on the other hand, had committed itself in 1968 to sharp increases in public aid to LDCs and in 1974 was the first advanced industrial state to surpass the OECD target. In the following year Sweden was again the first country to pass the one percent target figure of the UN Development Decade. Furthermore, in the mid-1970s the Swedes tied a smaller proportion of aid to their own exports than the Swiss did.[238]

In the total net flow of resources from rich to poor countries, which includes private aid, loans, and investments, however, Switzerland ranks well ahead of Sweden.[239] The strategies that Switzerland and Sweden pursued in the Paris Round of talks between North and South were characteristic of the two countries. Prudence prevented any overt Swiss support of initially strong opposition led by the United States and West Germany to the demands of the less developed countries, but there can be little doubt that the Swiss agreed fully with a defense of market liberalism.[240] Sweden took the opposite position. On critical questions such as debt relief Sweden was alone among the developed countries, large or small, in backing the demand of nineteen less developed countries for a debt moratorium. Indeed, in October 1977 the Swedish government announced the unilateral cancellation of $200 million in debt. In the LDCs' final compromise with the developed countries in 1979, Switzerland agreed to cancel $69 million.[241]

The small European states respond differently to economic change. Switzerland shares with the Netherlands and Belgium an offensive strategy in world markets based on low tariffs, very high export intensities, and high R and D expenditures aiming at product innovations in modern industries. Austria, Denmark, and Norway, by way of contrast, rely on a defensive strategy based on somewhat higher tariff levels, a somewhat lower export intensity, and lower R and D expenditures aiming at process innovations in more traditional industries. Offensive adaptation is international in scope and is typically based on private-sector activity. Defensive adaptation is national in scope and relies heavily on the public sector. These two strategies of adaptation signal the existence of important differences in the strength and character of business and labor, differences that shape the two variants of corporatism that I call liberal and social. The one country that clearly deviates from this twofold pattern is Sweden. Because it has an internationally oriented, powerful business community and a strong, centralized labor movement, Sweden relies on a large and active public sector for its offensive adaptation.

It would be foolish to deny that the real world is more complex than this limited set of comparisons suggests. The Netherlands, for example, has large public-welfare spending and has been generous in assisting less developed countries; Switzerland has not. Austria has a large nationalized sector and an acquiescent tax-paying public; Denmark does not. And Belgium has both an internationally oriented business community and relatively militant unions. The point of this argument is not to force all of the political experiences of the small European states into one, and only one, of two descriptive categories. It is, rather, to suggest that, broadly speaking, the political responses of the small European states vary systematically rather than randomly.

COUNTRY VARIATIONS ON A CORPORATIST THEME

Liberal and social variants of corporatism result in substantial differences in where and how the small European states adjust to economic change. But it is easy to make too much of the similarities of countries grouped under these two labels. Their similarities in strategy and structure notwithstanding, the Low Countries differ from each other, as do the three Scandinavian countries. In the postwar period the Low Countries, for example, have been marked both by deep social divisions and by political stability.[242] But in the Netherlands one social division, religion, has waned while another, class, has waxed. In the 1970s Catholic and Socialist unions joined forces just as collective bargaining was becoming more decentralized. Union militance increased—and with it employer resistance to workers' demands. What is striking, concludes Wolinetz, is "the relative weakness of the trade union movement and the difficulties which the trade unions have in asserting their priorities."[243] As in the 1950s, the state has recently been drawn directly into the economic arena. Thus the Dutch have evolved a more overtly competitive politics within their corporatist structures. In Belgium social change has not replaced but reinforced the old linguistic division between Flemish and Walloons. Economic adversity has intensified the language conflict. Cutbacks in Wallonia's ailing steel industry are inevitable, and the divestment of foreign multinationals is creating new problems in Flanders. In 1978 even Belgium's Socialist party split along linguistic lines. But as Belgium readjusts to the economic realities of the 1980s and 1990s, it will do so with corporatist structures that have coexisted with the divisive issue of language throughout the postwar era.

Substantial differences similarly separate Denmark from its two Scandinavian neighbors.[244] Nineteenth-century history left Denmark with a system of horizontal crafts unions, a strong middle class, and a fragile alliance between the labor movement and the Social Democrats. Conversely, Sweden and Norway have vertically organized industrial unions, relatively weaker middle classes, and Social Democratic parties closely linked to the labor movement. Since Denmark's social welfare state was constructed before World War II with the active cooperation of all of the main segments of society, the Danish Social Democratic party has evolved its policies throughout the postwar years within a fundamentally liberal structure. In Sweden, and to a lesser extent in Norway, Social Democrats had a much greater role in constructing the welfare state, at times against the active opposition of the political parties of the Center and Right. After 1945 social policies thus evolved in structures that expressed social democratic rather than liberal principles. Furthermore, as Gösta Esping-Andersen shows, the Social Democratic parties in Sweden and Norway use social and economic policies to rebuild their social base. This is not so in Denmark. As a result, a coalition between blue- and white-collar workers is gradually replacing the green-red (farmer-worker) alliance of the 1930s in Sweden and Norway. In Denmark, however, Social Democracy is suffering from advanced decomposition of its political support.

These differences, between the Netherlands and Belgium and among the Scandinavian countries, are quite considerable. Twelve indicators of the character of business and labor in the small European states are summarized in Table 5. They suggest that there exist two distinct variants of corporatism. Liberal corporatism in Switzer-

Table 5. Business and labor in the small European states

	(1) Business community by international orientation and centralization, average rank of 5 measures	(2) Strength and centralization of labor movements 1965–80, average rank of 7 measures
1. Switzerland	1.0	7.0
2. Netherlands	2.0	5.0
3. Belgium	3.0	6.0
4. Sweden	4.0	2.0
5. Denmark	5.0	4.0
6. Norway	6.0	3.0
7. Austria	7.0	1.0
Average (1–3)	2.0	6.0
Average (5–7)	6.0	2.7

SOURCES: Col. 1: Table 3.
Col. 2: Table 4.

land, the Netherlands, and Belgium is distinguished by an internationally oriented business community; social corporatism in Austria, Norway, and Denmark by a strong and centralized labor movement. The distinctiveness of Sweden is that it combines an internationally oriented business community with a strong and centralized labor movement. This interpretation of Swedish politics matches that of Jonas Pontusson. He has argued that "conceived in organizational terms, 'strength of labour' is by no means coterminous with 'weakness of capital.' The Swedish case suggests that the organizational strength of one side in effect reinforces that of the other."[245] The internationalization of Swedish business is an often neglected aspect of this process. A more detailed pairwise comparison of Switzerland, the Netherlands, and Belgium with Austria, Norway, and Denmark yields a total of 108 comparisons (nine for each of the twelve indicators in Tables 3 and 4). Omitting five tied ranks, 99 of the 103 comparisons (or more than 96%) agree with the classification suggested here. Furthermore, the data in Table 5 suggest that Switzerland and Austria should be viewed as the most typical instances of respectively liberal and social corporatism.

Switzerland and Austria

Switzerland and Austria differ most markedly in the character of their social coalitions and the substance of the strategies they adopt in response to economic change. Switzerland's powerful, internationally oriented business community is opposed by a less powerful, relatively decentralized trade union movement. In its liberal foreign trade policy, heavy direct investment abroad, and importing of foreign labor on a large scale, Switzerland's strategy is one of global adaptation to economic change. In its limited public expenditures, privatized social welfare system, and R and D policies primarily pursued by large corporations, Switzerland's strategy is one of private compensation for economic change. Conversely, Austria's largely nationalized business community confronts a powerful, centralized trade union movement. Austria's pursuit of a cautiously liberal foreign-trade policy, its heavy subsidization of domestic investment, and its commitment to full employment and an active labor-market policy point to a strategy of national adaptation. In its large public expenditures, publicly funded social welfare system, and incomes policy on which both unions and business agree, Austria's strategy is one of public compensation for economic change.

Even though institutions in both Switzerland and Austria are centralized compared to those in the large industrial states, the two countries differ one from the other in degree of centralization. Swiss institutions tend toward decentralization; they evoke the image of a convoy of trucks steered by many drivers along the same highway. Austrian institutions are more centralized; they suggest a train operated by a single engineer. But in both countries political institutions are very stable and similarly effective in shielding the policy process from exogenous shocks.

An analysis of the policy networks linking interest groups with state bureaucracies in Switzerland and Austria suggests that the boundary demarcating state and society is virtually impossible to identify. Producer groups and state bureaucracies are inextricably linked through institutions. Both countries have well-organized, encompassing, and typically centralized peak associations. The fashioning of a durable consensus among often widely divergent views within these groups is a key to the stability of policy networks and the predictability of the policy process in both countries. At the same time the degree of centralization in both countries is somewhat greater in the dominant social bloc, Swiss business and Austrian labor, than in the subordinate bloc. The state bureaucracy is small and decentralized in Switzerland and large and centralized in Austria. But in both countries the state is relatively passive and lacks autonomy from the major producer groups. The political limitations under which both state bureaucracies operate are compensated for by the elaborate search for consensus both within and between peak associations.

The search for consensus is also reflected in party systems. In Switzerland the different political parties "fuse" in a system of all-party coalition. The federal executive seeks to fashion agreements acceptable to both Switzerland's powerful interest groups and a citizenry enjoying the rights of direct democracy. When Austria's "Grand Coalition" between the dominant political parties came to an end in 1966, the coalition reappeared almost instantaneously in a social and economic partnership that effectively grounds all ministries in a system of bipartisan checks and balances. This partnership requires the fashioning of a consensus among Austria's dominant political parties, the interest groups that travel in their orbits, and the rank and file that these groups represent. The fusion of power between state and society and between government and opposition thus occurs in both Switzerland and Austria. But the different constellations of social forces in the two countries lead to a depoliticized, private, and decentralized liberal corporatism in Switzerland and a politicized, public, and centralized social corporatism in Austria.

Finally, the policy process reflects the underlying social reality of liberal capitalism in Switzerland and democratic socialism in Austria. In Switzerland bargaining extends to noneconomic issues but excludes investment and employment; in Austria bargaining is largely restricted to economic issues but centers around investment and employment. Because the state is less involved in the economy in Switzerland than in Austria, the mode of political bargaining tends toward bilateralism in Switzerland and trilateralism in Austria. In Switzerland industry and finance deal with each other on questions of investment, business and labor on questions of wages and employment. The state steps in, if at all, only in situations of grave crisis. In Austria business, the state, and the labor unions address questions of investment, while business, unions, and indirectly the state deal with wages and employment. The state is thus deeply enmeshed in political bargaining between business and unions on a daily basis. The result is that the trade-offs across different sectors of policy tend to be more implicit in Switzerland than in Austria.

The significance of the policy process in both countries, although it takes a depoliticized form in Switzerland and a politicized one in Austria, lies in its recreation and reaffirmation of the consensus among major political actors on the legitimacy of political institutions and the choice of political strategies. Through their policy process Austria and Switzerland bridge the gaps that divide state from society and government from opposition. Interlocking corridors of power provide a substitute for the policy instruments that the state often lacks in Switzerland and rarely uses on its own in Austria. The result in both countries is a politically effective, though rarely efficient, way of choosing a stance in the world economy. Throughout the 1970s Switzerland's strategy of global adaptation and private compensation and Austria's strategy of national adaptation and public compensation did not encounter serious political challenges. The policy process in Switzerland and Austria succeeds in incorporating all important sources of potential opposition in an overarching consensus.

Despite the many differences between Switzerland and Austria, the policy process in the two countries differs more in political form (the scope and the mode of bargaining) than in political consequence. Conflicts over the questions raised by industrial change involve bargaining not only over a particular substantive issue but over the whole array of corporatist arrangements through which political elites in these two societies have adjusted to economic change for several decades. Analyzing the response of democratic corporatism to economic change thus entails analyzing the way different political actors relate to one another in a process that enhances the power of the weak in Switzerland and constrains the power of the strong in Austria. Politics organized along corporatist lines links long-term political thinking closely to short-term economic calculation. Because sharp distinctions are not drawn between perceived group interests and vague notions of the public good, the political process creates not "winners and losers" but "sharers." In short, in both states politics tends toward a narrowing of political inequalities among political actors—a narrowing that facilitates their corporatist arrangements. Table 6 summarizes the characteristic patterns of liberal and social corporatist arrangements.[246]

Corporatism and Large Countries

All advanced industrial states, be they large or small, must adjust to economic change abroad and at home. In countries such as Switzerland and the Netherlands, which accord pride of place to the working of markets, corporate adjustment policies assume a greater political significance than in countries such as Austria and Norway, which are more distrusting of market institutions. Furthermore, those countries which have located a large share of their productive capacity abroad (e.g., the United States, Britain, Switzerland, and the Netherlands) rely heavily on the global operations of large firms and have a distinct disadvantage in fashioning industrial policy at home. Corporations and governments have an incentive to adjust to change globally rather

Table 6. Two variants of democratic corporatism

	Liberal corporatism in Switzerland	Social corporatism in Austria
1. Social coalition		
a. Business	international; stronger	national; weaker
b. Unions	decentralized; weaker	centralized; stronger
c. Political strategy	global adaptation and private compensation	national adaptation and public compensation
2. Policy network		
a. Structure of institutions	less centralized; stable; effective	more centralized; stable; effective
b. Policy process		
Scope of corporatist bargaining	broader, but excluding questions of investment and employment	narrower, but including questions of investment and employment
Mode of bargaining	bilateral; trade-offs more implicit	trilateral; trade-offs more explicit
Consequence for politics	narrows political inequalities between actors	narrows political inequalities between actors

than within the context of the national economy. Policies that favor direct foreign investment leave all major decisions about industrial redeployment affecting employment, regional development, product mixes, and research and development to large private corporations. The hostility in Switzerland toward industrial policies and the strain they cause in Britain resonate with a growing American debate in the 1980s. But while large industrial countries like Britain flirt with exporting the costs of change through tariff protection, liberal corporatist states like Switzerland are willing to tolerate the costs of change that free trade imposes.

One political ingredient is essential for an active industrial policy intent on structural transformation: a Left that is weak and politically excluded from policy making at the national level. Since the late 1940s the two countries that have adopted a deliberate strategy of sectoral transformation, Japan and France, have met this condition. Theirs is not the kind of industrial adjustment policy favored by social corporatist states like Austria or Norway, where a reactive and flexible industrial policy aims at incremental adjustments in the structure, location, employment, research and development, and marketing of firms in domestic industries.

Although liberal and social corporatist states differ in where and how they adjust to change, both show a remarkable degree of flexibility in policy. A comparison with larger industrial states helps to reinforce the point. Among the large countries, at least on the surface, it is perhaps the United States that most closely converges, in both strategy and structure, with Switzerland, a country that most clearly typifies the traits characteristic of liberal corporatism. These are the two capitalist bastions of federalism, liberalism, and democracy. Both countries favor a global adaptation to change, which affords the federal government a comparatively weak role in policy making, and privately organized compensation policies at home, for example in the area of pensions. Furthermore, in both Switzerland and the United States an internationally oriented business community has great influence over foreign economic policy, while a decentralized labor movement suffers from political weakness. Such similarities are, however, balanced by two important differences. The hegemonic role that the United States has played in the international economy since World War II has at times elevated the pursuit of international liberalism from the realm of self-interest to the realm of ideology, thus giving the executive branch of government a greater role in the area of foreign economic policy than is true in Switzerland.[247] The coherence that hegemony imposes from time to time on American policy making is in Switzerland, at times, created by a spirit of collectivism. In Switzerland the tension between individual liberty and collective necessity is not resolved solely, as in America, through an accumulation of individual preferences into a *volonté des tous;* at times, that resolution also occurs through sublimation into a *volonté générale.* It is no accident that the Swiss constitution speaks of the "general well-being" while the U.S. Declaration of Independence celebrates an individualistic "pursuit of happiness."[248] Furthermore, Switzerland's policy network has traditionally been more integrated and more broadly based than America's, which has facilitated the development of the consistent policies with which the Swiss face the international economy.

Paradoxically, great similarities can also be found between this exemplar of liberal corporatism and the apparent opposite of the United States, Japan. Switzerland's and Japan's paternalistic systems converge at three points. First, both countries are single-minded in their pursuit of economic objectives: both occasionally play the role of a free rider in the international economy, shifting their costs abroad, either through the repatriation of foreign workers, as with Switzerland, or through informal restrictions on imports, as with Japan. Second, both Switzerland and Japan share the privatization of the welfare aspects of their compensation policies.[249] Finally, in both countries a politically united and strong business community enjoys a privileged position in policy making and faces a decentralized and politically weak Left. Yet a great difference separates the two countries: it lies in the prominent role that the Japanese state bureaucracy plays in the definition and implementation of policy. Japan hesitantly and belatedly adopted the liberal premises of the postwar international economy, and in its industrial policy it is the state bureaucracy that leads adjustment to change. Furthermore, unions and the political Left are politically included at the national level in Switzerland's corporatist arrangements; they are excluded in Japan.

At first glance the strategy and structure of Austria's social corporatism quite strikingly resemble those of France. Because they mistrust market institutions, both countries approached the increasing liberalization of the postwar international economy with hesitation and delay. In both countries the state, in terms of its political objectives and instruments, appears predestined to play an important role in the structuring of society. Furthermore, both countries have chosen to adapt to economic change primarily in domestic rather than in international markets. Indeed, in his successful electoral campaign for the French presidency François Mitterrand repeatedly pointed to Austria as a model for what a democratic Left might accomplish in France. However, these similarities are deceptive. The Austrian state is constrained in ways quite uncharacteristic of France. Students of the French bureaucracy have emphasized how its internal divisions and links to the business community shape its political choices; Austrian bureaucrats, however, experience a virtual absence of political choice. The fortunes of the Mitterrand government elected in 1981 depend, moreover, on how it balances its campaign promises to imitate the Austrian model against the temptations to build socialism without the workers. On this score the first three years of the Mitterrand presidency have had a sobering effect. There exists a world of difference between a deeply divided, radical French Left out of government throughout the 1970s, on the one hand, and a united, moderate Austrian Left in government, on the other. Austria's policy network has been more encompassing and integrated than that of France, fostering consistency in the policies with which the Austrians have met the international economy during the past two decades.

Interestingly, Austria's social corporatism also appears to resemble important features of British politics, even though Britain is often presumed to be the opposite of continental statism.[250] Politics in both Britain and Austria is largely coterminous with class politics. Both countries exemplify the power of organized labor to such an extent that they are often dubbed "trade union states." That power is reflected not only at the workplace but, to varying degrees, in the unions' relations to the working-class party as well. It is also mirrored in the growth of a public welfare state that has inspired emulation among such relative latecomers as the Scandinavian and the Low Countries. Here again, however, surface similarities prove deceptive. While Austria's powerful unions exercise a power firmly integrated with the country's durable and flexible policy network, British unions have been both contestants in and targets of unsuccessful attempts to bring such policy networks into being. Incomes policy and industrial policy, for example, provide opportunities time and again to legitimize existing institutions and political practices in Austria; in Britain they have provided arenas in which existing institutions and practices have been increasingly delegitimized by a perpetual tug-of-war, and new ones prevented from emerging. Finally, both countries have rapidly moved in opposite directions in the international divison of labor. While Britain is increasingly turning to protectionism and becoming accustomed to the living standards and production struc-tures of the European periphery, Austria's economic miracle is pro-pelling the country toward international liberalization and the standards and structures of the European center.

In its ideology, its interest groups, and its political bargaining, democratic corporatism in both variants compensates those who suf-fer from political weakness and economic dislocations. Social cor-poratism tends toward economy-wide bargaining and relies to only a limited extent on the social segmentation of its labor force. Liberal corporatism tends toward firm-level or industry-level bargaining and relies more heavily on economic and social segmentation, as illus-trated by the role of foreign and female workers. But because of their exposed postions in international markets, both variants share cor-poratist characteristics that are less typical of the large industrial states. Focusing on the role of the political Left and the trade unions, some analyses classify Austria, the Low Countries, Scandinavia, Brit-ain, and West Germany as "inclusionary," and Switzerland, the United States, Japan, Italy, and pre-1980 France as "exclusionary."[251] But an analysis that concentrates on domestic structures and neglects the different international contexts in which small and large industrial states operate creates anomalies. It groups together societies with cen-tralized and decentralized collective bargaining systems (West Ger-many and Britain), and with weak and strong states (United States and Japan). It distinguishes between societies that differ only in de-gree in their reliance on foreign workers, women, and the old (West Germany and France), and in their political incorporation of the Left and the trade union movement (Switzerland and the Netherlands). This book has advanced a different argument. The small European states distinguish themselves by their corporatist politics and industrial policy from industrial countries that are larger and hence less exposed to the international economy.

Switzerland's and Austria's paradoxical affinities to the political manifestations of both liberalism and statism among the large industrial states suggest that they have evolved a third variant of capitalism, one that combines elements of both market and state. What they have evolved is democratic corporatism.

Democratic corporatism has one central political consequence. By incorporating all major political actors and producer groups, it creates political coherence in the domestic structure and flexibility in political stategy. The small European states are liberal market economies; their antiliberalism consists in substituting, where needed, political mechanisms of compromise for the dictates of the market. Conversely, the small European states are statist in according their state bureauracies an important place in the making of policy; their antistatism is revealed by their neutralization of state institutions, which suffer from a relative lack of institutional autonomy and political interests of their own.

The argument of the last two chapters rests on a cumulative differentiation betweeen the political strategies and structures of small and large states as well as among the small European states. What unites the experience of the small European states, and what sets them apart from the large industrial states, is their flexibility when confronted with economic change. The main political actors view economic change as a way of life, an opportunity as much as an abnormality and a threat. Democratic corporatism is marked by particular political strategies. Because of the economic openness and vulnerability of the small European states, protectionist policies are not a viable political option. Instead these states can be counted among the stongest advocates of international liberalization. Although democratic corporatism did not emerge until the 1930s and 1940s, the small European states have favored international liberalization throughout the twentieth century. Economic openness rather than corporatism has been the decisive factor. But economic openness helps in maintaining corporatist arrangements. The political requirements of democratic corporatism account for the adoption of wide-ranging policies of domestic compensation by the small European states. Domestic compensation, I argue, responds primarily to the logic of domestic politics; it is not a deliberate response to the logic of the international economy.[252] Policies of domestic compensation, in turn, both reinforce and alter the politics of corporatism.

International liberalization and domestic compensation combine to produce the flexible policies of industrial adjustment with which the small European states respond to the constraints and opportunities of international and domestic structures. As protectionism is not an option, the strategy of the small corporatist states differs from the strategy of large liberal states, such as the United States or Britain, which typically seek to export the costs of change through selective protection. Conversely, policies that require a unity of purpose and an accretion of power contradict the political requirements of cross-sectoral political bargaining, distinguishing the small European states from the political strategy of Japan or France. A statist approach is built around preempting the costs of change through policies of selective intervention and protection undertaken in the name of structural transformation. As one comparative analysis of the political responses of four Social Democratic states (Britain, West Germany, Sweden, and Austria) to the economic crisis of the 1970s concludes, "Austria and Sweden seem to be institutionally rather better placed than either Britain or Germany to explore the full range of policy options potentially available to the government and the industrial relations system *acting jointly.* And they also seem to be fully capable of implementing jointly those policies on which they have agreed at the national level."[253] The small European states have learned how to live with the costs of change.

Flexible industrial adjustment is not a unidimensional response to changing market conditions or political pressures. Instead, as I have shown, democratic corporatism has two variants, one liberal and the other social. Both variants respond to the economic as well as the political requirements of adjustment. Liberal corporatism accepts market-driven change but makes the political gestures necessary to keep disadvantaged industry segments, firms, or regions integrated in an overarching consensus. Social corporatism seeks to cushion change within the limits that markets permit. The Swiss, Dutch, and Belgians put so much store in the institution of the market that they would find it reckless to disregard the political requirements of a flexible industrial policy. The Austrians, Norwegians, and Danes value highly the institution of the state, and they would find it equally foolish to disregard the economic requirements of a flexible adjustment.

Distinctive of both variants of corporatism is the calibration of the requirements of economic flexibility with those of political legitimacy.

Politics either does not impede a shift in the factors of production or does so in a manner that contributes politically to flexible adjustment over the longer term. Noteworthy in adverse economic circumstances is, therefore, what is least apparent: the political interventions of liberal corporatism in markets and the political toleration of market outcomes in social corporatism. Although liberal corporatism prizes efficiency more highly than equity, and social corporatism prefers equity to efficiency, both preferences are constrained by the shackles of democratic corporatism and the logic of markets.

CHAPTER FOUR

The Historical Origins of Democratic Corporatism

If we explain the industrial strategies of the small European states as results of the structure and functioning of democratic corporatism, we solve one puzzle while posing a new one. Why did democratic corporatism arise in its pure form only in the small European countries? The answer to this question lies in a historical excursion, but it first requires a simplification in our definition of corporatism. In this chapter I shall focus on the feature that played midwife at the cradle of democratic corporatism in the 1930s: cross-class collaboration. I shall neglect the two other defining characteristics of democratic corporatism. The centralization of politics, which stems from small size, existed before the 1930s as well as after and therefore appears to be of less decisive importance. The coordination of conflicting objectives across different issues, already evident in the 1930s, became a prominent trait only with the growth of the welfare state after World War II. There are also pragmatic reasons for simplification, which reinforce these intellectual ones. The historical answer that I shall offer is painted in very broad strokes; it will take us from the 1930s back to the twelfth century. This kind of macrohistory yields the best results when it addresses not definitionally complex issues but simple and big questions. Our question is this: why in the 1930s did cross-class collaboration arise in the small European states but not in the large industrial countries?

My intention is not to distinguish between necessary and sufficient conditions in a tight causal analysis. Instead, I hope to trace the historical antecedents that made possible the different outcomes of the 1930s. Small size is thus not treated as a master variable that somehow forces a particular political solution—the relationship between small size and democratic corporatism is historically contingent rather than logically necessary. What matters is a pattern of historical development that has resulted in different types of democratic politics in the twentieth century.

The corporatist compromise that distinguishes the small European states was struck, I argue, in the 1930s. This is a point of likely controversy. Students of European corporatism have mostly sought to explain or describe corporatism as part and parcel of a system of consensual wage bargaining in the 1960s and 1970s.[1] Although the evolution of democratic corporatism since 1945, as I have argued in chapter 3, is essential to any functional explanation of how this political regime recreates the conditions for its existence, it tells us nothing about the reasons that gave rise to corporatist structures in the first place. Alternatively, historical studies of the welfare state and of democratic party systems typically fasten on the intersection of the extension of suffrage with the introduction of the first social welfare measures around the turn of the century.[2] While my analysis acknowledges in the second section of this chapter the importance of the "electoral bargain" on proportional representation, the essence of democratic corporatism lies in its alignment of a territorially based parliamentary system of representation with a particular functional representation of interest groups. That system of representation emerged fully only in the 1930s and 1940s.

What historical antecedents made possible the corporatist compromise of the 1930s and the electoral bargain on proportional representation? The third section argues that the answer lies in the coincidence of two different conditions. First, the Right was weaker and more divided in the small European states than in the larger countries, thus creating political conditions favorable to compromise. Second, specialization for exports created links between different economic and social sectors in the small European states, links closer than those found in larger countries. The economic openness distinctive of the small European states thus plays an important dual role. Urban interests and international economic opportunities contributed to a relatively weak feudalism in the small European states; specialization for exports responded to the opportunities of growing international markets in the nineteenth century, thus creating close links across social and economic sectors.

These common experiences in historical evolution notwithstanding, political accommodation in the 1930s was achieved on different terms. The result was the differences between liberal and social corporatism so evident both in the adjustment strategy of the small European states and in the character of their corporatist arrangements. The fourth section focuses on how three variables—the timing of industrialization, international politics, and social structure—have shaped the character of business and labor. In the small European states these conditions are mutually reinforcing. Liberal corporatism is found in culturally heterogeneous countries that industrialized early and were favored by developments in international politics. Social corporatism emerges in culturally homogeneous countries that industrialized late and were less favored by international politics.

Finally, I relate this historical analysis to the book that inspired it, Barrington Moore's *Social Origins of Dictatorship and Democracy*.[3] The analysis establishes important commonalities in the historical origins of democratic corporatism in the small European states and of liberal democracy in some of the large countries. But it points to one fundamental difference. The small European states did not experience a revolutionary break with the past; the large countries that eventually turned toward democratic government did. The corporatist compromise of the 1930s and the democratic corporatism that has evolved from it thus fit a broader pattern of historical evolution—one that differentiates the small European countries from larger ones.

All analyses that deal with few cases and many variables face the acute problem of overdetermination. Although they are analytically distinct, a number of factors with presumed similar consequences occur together without us being able to disentangle them. Analyses like this one thus cannot meet the exacting standards of a social scientific test that asks for a distinction between necessary and sufficient conditions, a weighting of the relative importance of variables and, if possible, a proof of causality. In this chapter, as throughout this book, I am concerned less with proof than with increasing the plausibility of the argument by comparing, where relevant, the small European countries to the larger ones. In addition, however, the fifth section offers a stronger, indirect test.

Austria in the 1930s experienced civil war rather than a corporatist compromise. In the bulk of this chapter, therefore, I shall discuss only six of the seven small European states. Austria's historical evolution contrasts with that of the other six small European states, I shall argue, in that the Habsburg Empire favored economic closure, a strong landed aristocracy, weaker urban interests, and a united political Right. As a result, the Left found it difficult to strike political alliances with other classes and thus to moderate its militancy. With the collapse of the Habsburg Empire in 1919 Austria, alone among small European states, went through a revolutionary break with its past. It adopted proportional representation without debate, as a method of depersonalizing bitter political conflicts. Furthermore, in the nineteenth century Austria's industrial strategy of adjustment favored, with few exceptions, protectionism over free trade. Tempted by the fruits of empire, Austrian producers by and large eschewed the specialization for exports typical of the other small European states. Its industrial strategy thus did little to reinforce the links between different social sectors. Even if we were to exclude the adverse effects that the loss of World War I and the breakup of the empire had on the First Republic, the probability of striking a corporatist bargain in the 1930s was because of prior political developments significantly lower in Austria than elsewhere in Europe. In Austria all of the historical antecedents pointed away from rather than toward a corporatist compromise in the 1930s.

THE CORPORATIST COMPROMISE OF THE 1930S AND 1940S

The Depression of the 1930s triggered a profound crisis in all of the advanced industrial states. Liberal, democratic capitalism was confronted with the rapid growth of radical movements on both the Right and the Left. The small European states recorded unemployment rates that were staggering even by the standards of the interwar period. At the depth of the Depression in Scandinavia between one-third and one-half of the industrial work force was unemployed; one-third of the farmers were overindebted; and over a quarter of the population had to apply for poor relief at one time or another.[4] In the Netherlands and in Belgium unemployment among industrial workers varied between 15 and 35 percent.[5] Only Switzerland recorded lower, though still substantial, rates of unemployment.[6] The severe effect of the Depression on the small European states, with their open economies, is not surprising. As the larger countries rushed toward protection, the export-oriented small European states found themselves in a very difficult situation.

Against great odds the small European states succeeded in reconstructing the political bases of their regimes along corporatist lines. They did so through fits and starts rather than according to some conscious program. Experimentation prevailed over grandiose political plans or deliberate deficit spending. Indeed, what is striking about the political debates of the time is that, by and large, they did not force economic options into the opposed categories of market and plan. Commenting on Scandinavia in the 1930s, one reviewer concludes that

> policy (or at least those aspects which are of interest from the standpoint of the "new" economics) had no important effects. . . . It is extremely doubtful whether policy in any Scandinavian country played an important part in overcoming the crisis. . . . The Social Democratic governments of these three countries at the end of the 1930s neither did nor could pursue policies which were Socialist or Social Democratic in any special sense. They were rather some version of broadly based national policies which had to pay serious attention to the interests of other groups.[7]

Similarly substantial experimentation with policy occurred in Belgium, the Netherlands, and Switzerland. Even though the Left did not prevail politically as it did in Scandinavia, the management of the economy became a political issue to a degree unthinkable in the 1920s.

Policy, whatever its effect on the economy in the small states, had a profound effect on politics. Novel policies created new political possibilities for forging alliances across different sectors of society: between farmers and workers, between workers and Catholics, and between blue- and white-collar workers. In reacting to the Depression, political extremism, and the threat of war, political forces in the small European states accommodated themselves to the need to overhaul rather than to defend or overthrow capitalist society. That accommodation provided the political foundation for a democratic corporatism which emerged fully after 1945.

The political alliance between farmers and workers, typical of all three Scandinavian states, was formed in Sweden in 1932.[8] Only four years earlier Swedish Social Democracy had suffered a stinging electoral defeat. Defeat had prompted a fundamental reevaluation of the party's strategy, by Gunnar Myrdal and Richard Lindstrom. Both suggested broadening the party's base beyond the industrial work force, an idea first raised in the party's program of 1911.[9] Myrdal advocated a unionization drive among agricultural workers who had voted for the Conservatives and Liberals in 1928. Lindstrom favored a change in the party's ideological appeal to what Otto Kirchheimer in the 1950s was to call a "catch-all party." Elected in 1928, a Conservative-Liberal coalition government was progressively weakened by the onset of the Depression in 1929, by the Ådalen incident of 1931 (in which government troops were brought in to protect strike breakers and ended up killing four strikers and wounding scores of others), and by a corruption scandal in 1932 involving a prominent industrialist, Ivar Kreuger, and Prime Minister Ekman.

In 1932 the Social Democrats presented a program that stressed the need for both public works and agricultural supports, because workers and farmers depended on each other's buying power.[10] The year after their impressive electoral victory in 1932, Prime Minister Hansson negotiated an agreement with the Agrarian party. Quarrels over defense and pension issues in the spring of 1936 led to a brief falling out of Agrarians and Social Democrats, but the election of 1936 cemented the Red-Green (worker-farmer) alliance in a coalition government that would implant Social Democracy in power for the next forty years. This agreement, or "cow trade" as it was called by its opponents, was concluded in an atmosphere of crisis; many scholars have drawn the connection between Hitler's rising power and the crisis agreement.[11] Rustow's description of the situation in Sweden is apt for the small European states more generally: "The breakdown of the Weimar regime early in 1933 in the midst of an economic crisis further impressed on Swedish leaders the need for quick and decisive action."[12] The cementing of the Red-Green alliance of 1936 paved the way to industrial peace in the 1938 Saltsjøbaden agreement, concluded between the central organization of business and the labor movement. The Swedish business community acquiesced in a Social Democratic government, higher labor costs, a relatively expansive fiscal policy, and a growth of welfare services—in exchange for labor peace, the continuation of private control over property and capital markets, and openness to the world economy.[13] This was a "historical compromise," Swedish-style, between business and labor.

Although the Social Democrats came to power in Denmark earlier than in Sweden, Danish political developments were on the whole rather similar.[14] Danish Social Democracy's brief taste of power between 1924 and 1926 was followed in 1929 by a coalition with the Radicals; it kept Prime Minister Stauning in office for the next eleven years. The Depression brought Danish agriculture to the brink of collapse and increased unemployment among industrial workers to over 40 percent by 1933. The government responded with a devaluation in September 1931, foreign-exchange controls in January 1932, and public works as well as assistance for farmers. Government policy was evidently not successful, and business pressed for a 20 percent wage cut, adamantly opposed by both the unions and the Social

Democratic party. The government proposed legislation fixing wages for one year, but support for the proposed legislation required Prime Minister Stauning to make political concessions to some of his political opponents. Negotiations at the prime minister's house resulted in the "Kanslergade Treaty" of January 1933 between the Social Democrats, the Venstre, then the second-strongest party in Parliament, and the Radicals. The agreement included a further 10 percent devaluation, a variety of policies designed to help agriculture as demanded by the Venstre, and support of the Social Democratic wage legislation, as well as a variety of new social programs stressing relief and public works.[15]

This agreement between workers and farmers was directed against the Conservatives and their supporters in the business community. It secured the power of the Social Democrats, who won electoral victories in both houses in 1935 and 1936. As in Sweden, industrial militancy now gave way to industrial peace as the Social Democrats and the unions cooperated in developing methods of collective bargaining and arbitration that avoided strike action. New political alliances and the magnitude of the Social Democratic victory in 1935–36 were influenced not only by the Depression but also by the fear of fascism. Denmark had a small Nazi party. Spurred by the continuing crisis of Danish agriculture, rightist political agitation for union with Germany was increasing, especially in North Schleswig. The 1936 electoral victory of the Social Democratic party was won with the slogan "Stauning or chaos"; as Esping-Andersen concludes, "the Social Democratic realignment was very much a product of the looming specter of fascism on the right, and Communist mobilization on the left. In response to proto-fascist leanings among Conservative party youth, and a drift of young unemployed workers toward the Communists, the Social Democratic party placed special emphasis on strengthening its youth movement."[16]

Social Democracy in Norway was much more radical than in Denmark.[17] Its success, however, in forming a new political alliance with agriculture was remarkably similar. The victory of the reformers over the radicals occurred with the deepening of the Depression between 1930 and 1933. Following the Danish example, the Norwegian Social Democrats adopted a program stressing job creation, welfare reform, and agricultural subsides. The party campaigned in 1933 with the slogan "work for all."[18] Its program was rewarded by the party's best-ever showing at the polls. The unions responded; they decreased strikes to give the new policies a chance of success. The union movement recognized that its members depended in part on the taxes provided by the middle class from which the reform programs of the government were to be funded. In 1935 the Social Democrats made a formal agreement with the Agrarian party to support the reform program, and pragmatism became the order of the day.

This agreement gave Norway its first majority government since 1918 and secured the foundations of Social Democratic rule in the decades to come. In the same year unions and business signed a "Basic Agreement" that covered pay and labor agreements in three hundred trades through 1940 while leaving the details of precise wage determination to subsequent, routine rounds of collective bargaining.[19] The rapid transformation from labor radicalism to reformism and the urge to form a lasting alliance with agriculture received a powerful stimulus from the fascist tendencies of farmers supporting the Conservative party and from the support extreme right-wing movements, among them Quisling's Nazi party, appeared to be gaining in the early 1930s. In Norway, as in other small European states, the deterioration of international and domestic conditions strongly reinforced the pressure for cooperation.[20]

New political alliances also emerged in Belgium, the Netherlands, and Switzerland. In these three countries labor movements, though weaker than those in Scandinavia in the mid-1930s, also pushed hard for the adoption of concerted crisis plans. As Erik Harsen notes, "In a sense planisme . . . was taken more seriously and had a greater impact upon the social democratic left in Belgium and the Netherlands than it did elsewhere in Europe, with the possible exception of the Czech and Swiss experiences."[21] The debate over political options and the implementation of concrete crisis measures resulted in the same outcome as in Scandinavia: new political alliances between different social sectors—alliances, moreover, that provided the political foundation for the democratic corporatism of the postwar period.

Belgium's Social Democratic party (BWP) was, measured in terms of membership, about twice the size of the combined forces of the Dutch Social Democratic movement. Its share of the popular vote was also substantially larger (one-third as compared to one-fifth).[22] Belgian Social Democracy occupied an important position of ideological leadership for the democratic Left in both the Netherlands and Switzerland. The party had already participated in a government of national union during World War I and in five coalition cabinets in the 1920s before going into opposition in 1927.[23] With the deepening of the Depression, the party was eager to reenter a coalition government with Christian Democrats and socially progressive Roman Catholic forces. Dramatic increases in unemployment, from 28,000 in 1929 to

350,000 in 1932, and sharply declining wage levels (an estimated 30 percent drop for Walloonian coal miners between 1930 and 1934) favored the adoption of an economic crisis plan. In 1931 the party countered the government's fiscal conservatism by proposing measures to alleviate unemployment and to support farm prices. The proposals generated little enthusiasm; it took the intellectual force of Hendrik de Man, who returned from Germany to Belgium in 1933, to work out the *Plan van den Arbeid.* It emphasized deficit spending, public works, partial nationalization, new credit institutions, and greater government involvement in the economy.

In the year of the plan's appearance, 1935, the Social Democrats reentered a three-party cabinet headed by a progressive Catholic banker, Paul van Zeeland. This cabinet broke with the deflationary policies of the previous decade and set the stage for Belgium's economic recovery. De Meeüs concludes that "it was Paul van Zeeland's work of organization and reform that was largely responsible for bringing Belgium out of the old system of uncontrolled capitalism and into the new equilibrium that enabled her to come through the war and the postwar period unscathed."[24] The coalition of Catholics, Liberals, and Social Democrats successfully fought the fascist challenge of the Rexists headed by Leon Degrelle.[25] A by-election forced by Degrelle in 1937 pitted him against van Zeeland, whose candidacy was backed by all three parties and the Catholic church. In what amounted to a national plebiscite van Zeeland received 80 percent of the vote.

Social Democracy thus participated actively in reshaping Belgian politics after 1935, but de Man, minister of public works after 1935, did not succeed in implementing the core of the *Plan van den Arbeid.* The bourgeois majority in the coalition refused to go along. Even though the Social Democrats were represented in six consecutive cabinets between 1935 and 1940, they lacked the political leverage to get their program adopted as government legislation. That program aimed not at socialism but at a reformed capitalist society responsive to the need for economic recovery rather than deflation. In de Man's words, "we are no longer a revolutionary party, but a popular party, a democratic, government-majority party, a constitutional law-and-order party, a national party."[26] Economic improvements and political stabilization after 1935 reduced the importance of the plan for party members and officials. As in Scandinavia, it was policy experimentation that after 1935 created new political alliances.

In the Netherlands a coalition headed by the Catholic State party moved in July 1931 to support agricultural prices.[27] Import quotas were imposed in December 1931, and a policy of austerity was adopted. These measures constitute what the economic historian Brugmans has called "the great change" in Dutch economic policy.[28] The government opposed devaluation until 1936; it aimed to lower domestic prices and wages while at the same time offering support to sectors in distress.[29] Subsequent cabinets headed by Prime Minister Colijn adhered to the gold standard until 1936 and to fiscal austerity and deflationary monetary policy throughout the decade.

Unlike its Belgian counterpart, the Dutch Social Democratic party (SDAP) had not participated in government in two decades. But in the 1920s the party had been receptive to de Man's call for an ethical, humanistic, and democratic socialism and had assumed a parliamentary and democratic character. When the radical left wing of the party was expelled in 1932, the reformers gained further strength. Prompted by the party's shocking electoral defeat in 1933 and influenced by the political debate in Belgium, Dutch Social Democrats moved to formulate their own *Plan van de Arbeid,* which the party officially adopted in 1935. In the words of one of the principal authors, "the Plan was partly rooted in the view that the bad economic situation was a breeding ground for national socialism and fascism and that for this reason also it was desirable to bring about an improvement."[30] A massive propaganda drive, aimed at the 1937 parliamentary elections, was sustained over a two-year period. As in Belgium, the plan was presented as an anticommunist, antirevolutionary, and antifascist alternative to a liberal capitalism discredited by the events of the early 1930s. Also as in Belgium, the propaganda drive was "aimed at the new middle class of salaried employees, i.e., white-collar people, technical personnel, low and middle-level management, and professional people."[31]

The election of 1937 showed that the Social Democratic party's policy had failed, and as in Belgium the plan quickly faded in public and party life. Its message of class compromise and the rehabilitation of the existing economy did, however, survive. The Nazi threat eroded the pacifist leanings of the Social Democrats and made them accept the need for national defense and such national symbols as the monarchy. When the conservative coalition broke up in 1939, the Social Democrats were invited to join the cabinet (soon to be a government in exile). After agonizing debate the party had turned down a similar offer in 1913; this time it accepted with alacrity and in the hope of attracting votes away from the religious and secular parties to the Social Democratic cause.[32] As in Belgium, a new political alliance had emerged.

Developments in Switzerland paralleled the incorporation of Social Democratic parties into bourgeois majorities in Belgium and the Netherlands as well as the conclusion of industrial peace treaties in Norway and Sweden.[33] With the rapid deterioration of Switzerland's economic situation in 1930–31, the Federal Council adopted far-reaching emergency decrees in support of exports, particular sectors, and the unemployed. The government also restrained imports. Throughout the 1930s the government intervened directly in sectors as different as watches, shoes, retail trade, hotels, embroidery, agriculture, and finance. And where the government did not intervene directly, government-sanctioned crisis cartels were organized in growing numbers.[34] As in the Low Countries, the Social Democratic party in Switzerland participated in an alliance with progressive elements of the Conservative, Liberal, and Agrarian parties. It aimed to replace rule by emergency decree through a constitutional amendment by popular initiative. The amendment would have granted the federal government the legal competence to pursue an economic policy. Furthermore, as in the Low Countries and Scandinavia, the initiative proposed numerous measures that would have increased the purchasing power of workers, farmers, and salaried employees.

After intense debate this initiative was defeated at the polls in the spring of 1935, by a three-to-two margin. But, as in the Low Countries, defeat did not prevent Swiss Social Democracy's accommodation with an existing political order. The positive experience of cooperating with other political groups and the worsening of the economic and political crisis throughout Europe prompted the Social Democratic party in 1935 to eliminate from its statutes the programmatic demand for class struggle and to support increased spending for national defense. The experience of Swiss Social Democracy in 1934–35 thus resembled Denmark's, characterized by Esping-Andersen in the following terms: "The polarized ideological climate of the 1930s forced political moderation on the Social Democrats, ideologically substituting 'democracy' for 'socialism,' the 'people' for the 'working class.' "[35]

The integration of Swiss unions into the new national consensus occurred in 1937. The right wing of the labor movement had opposed viewing the crisis initiative of 1935 in a partisan context, and in 1937 it was thus ready to embrace the "Peace Agreement" concluded between the Swiss Metalworkers' and Watchmakers' Union and the employers' association.[36] The immediate cause for the agreement was a government-imposed price freeze and the possibility of mandatory wage arbitration sanctioned by a federal government that was intent on Switzerland's devaluation enhancing the competitiveness of exports. To forestall further government intrusion in the private sector, employers were now willing (as they had not been in 1929) to recognize the union as an essentially equal partner on questions of labor-market and social policy. In return the unions were willing to replace the unconditional right to strike with a system for mediating industrial grievances and taking them to arbitration.

New political alliances formed in the 1930s in all of the small European states. This reconstruction of political foundations was expressed in new relations among political parties and in transformed relations between business and unions. Sweden and Switzerland, for example, responded in identical ways to the economic and political pressures of the 1930s by concluding their industrial peace agreements in 1937–38. In all seven small states the sharp decline in the volume of industrial strikes between 1948 and 1967 from the high levels between 1927 and 1937 reflects these new alliances.[37]

By all historical accounts, World War II, German occupation, and the experience of government-in-exile consolidated the changes wrought by the Depression in the 1930s. Between 1940 and 1945 the Norwegian government-in-exile, for example, was an all-party government.[38] Even though Denmark, unlike Norway, did not resist German occupation, by 1944 Denmark's Freedom Council had succeeded in bringing a general strike against the German forces to a successful conclusion, against the wishes of more cautious political leaders.[39] The situation in Belgium was comparable. According to Val Lorwin, "under the Nazi occupation, clandestine personal contacts among leaders of industry and Catholic, Socialist, and Liberal trade unionists produced a 'pact of social solidarity' of symbolic and practical importance. The pact was implemented after the Liberation by wide advances in social legislation and collective bargaining."[40] In the Netherlands a similar rapprochement occurred. The Dutch analogue to Belgium's "pact of social solidarity" was a wartime agreement between unions and business that resulted in the establishment of the corporatist Foundation of Labor after 1945. The foundation expressed the rapprochement between Socialists and Catholics that provided the political basis for the "Red-Roman" coalitions between 1946 and 1958.[41] The situation was no different in neutral Switzerland and Sweden. The Swiss Social Democratic party supported military credits and offered no more than token opposition to the legislative ban on the Communist party. It saw its first member elected to the Federal Council in 1943. Similarly, after the outbreak of the Russian-Finnish War the Swedish Social Democratic government moved to form an all-party wartime government, which excluded only the Communists. The Conservative and Center parties wanted this coalition continued after the war, an idea to which Prime Minister Hansson is reported to have been open.[42]

Developments in the five large industrial countries differed greatly in the 1930s.[43] None of them experienced the formation of enduring bargains across different social sectors. Germany and Japan chose fascism, militarism, and the political repression of the Left. Political alliances in Britain remained basically unchanged, for the political strength of financial interests in the City favored fiscal orthodoxy rather than far-reaching political experiments. The small size of Britain's modernized agricultural sector eliminated a potential alliance partner either for the Left or for segments of business discontented with fiscal orthodoxy. It would have taken a shock from the international economy far more serious than Britain's merely disappointing economic performance to transform traditional "collectivist" sentiments into a corporatist bargain.[44] Britain's political leadership continued to favor group autonomy over the negotiation of encompassing political bargains.

Across the Channel French politics did witness the formation of new political alliances. These new alliances were, however, unstable, lacked institutional support (for example, in the area of collective bargaining), and were only temporary. German occupation, the policies of the Vichy government, and Liberation eliminated the very tenuous roots of democratic corporatism and left French political leaders free to construct the Fourth and Fifth Republics on different political premises. For a brief moment, though, power did shift from a conservative coalition supported by business, agriculture, and segments of the Catholic working class to the Popular Front, which combined unions with segments of agriculture and the liberal middle class. Léon Blum tried Keynesian-style economic policies—deficit spending, higher wages, social insurance. But Blum was defeated a year after his electoral victory of 1936, by the encroachment of other issues, by the heterogeneity of his political base, and by the absence of a sizable, politically liberal segment of business.

Among the large industrial countries only the United States saw the emergence of a new durable alliance in the 1930s that bears a superficial resemblance to the corporatist bargain struck in the small European states. The need for government help in times of economic crisis drove labor and agriculture away from the protectionist coalition that the Republican party had constructed in 1896. The first New

Deal sought to satisfy new demands with inward-looking policies that, in rough terms, combined corporatism and protectionism. The United States left the gold standard and broke up the London Conference. At the same time the Agricultural Adjustment Act and the National Recovery Act were passed to protect agriculture and industry from unrestricted market competition. Well before the Supreme Court had declared the NRA unconstitutional in 1935, the deep cleavages within this new alliance had become, as in France, very apparent. The cartelistic approach of the NRA created strong opposition even among the supporters of reform. After 1935 the second New Deal brought internationally oriented business into the new coalition. The Wagner Act of 1937 resurrected collective bargaining, as Charles Maier notes, "less as a corporatist enfolding of organized labor than as an effort to give unions the organizational power they would need to stand up against industrial employers."[45] The second New Deal was therefore consistent with the American tradition of pluralism rather than with consensual and centralized coordination of conflicting policy objectives across different issues.

In sum, in the 1930s the large industrial countries did not evolve new coalitions, as in Britain; or they created new coalitions favoring a nondemocratic politics, foreign expansion, and the repression of the Left, as in Germany and Japan; or they engaged in experiments with corporatism that can best be described as ad hocery, as in the United States and France. New political alliances in the large industrial countries did not last. Authoritarian Germany and Japan did not resist the temptation of foreign expansion, which brought down their regimes. New alliances in democratic France and America, as well as stable British politics, were less exposed to the pressures of the international economy and more responsive to internal sources of friction than were the small European states. No fundamental remolding of their democratic politics took place. After the crisis of the 1930s and 1940s had passed, ad hocery or conflictual, decentralized, and uncoordinated resolution of political conflicts were to prevail in the large countries (except West Germany). The contrast with the small European countries is very striking.

The Depression, fascism, and World War II moved the political regimes of the small European states down the corporatist path. In economic policy what is striking about the 1930s is a spirit of political experimentation rather than some fundamental innovation along the lines of Keynesianism. Norway, for example, exhibited no trace of Keynesian deficit spending, and between 1930 and 1939 the levels of national debt and debt service remained virtually unchanged.[46] Similarly, the crisis plan of the Dutch Social Democratic party provided for a balanced budget, through a reduction of government expenditures and increases in taxation. Here is one possible explanation for the Dutch public's lack of enthusiasm for the Social Democratic plan.

The small European states did not master the crisis of the 1930s and 1940s because they adopted a "correct" economic policy, however we might define correctness. Rather, all of these states were so open to international influences that they were compelled to experiment with economic and social policies. It was the discussion and implementation of these policy experiments that provided the opportunity for realigning political forces. Even in the Netherlands, the country sticking longest to received economic orthodoxy in the 1930s, "the economic and social policies and the legislation in which these were manifested were increasingly being fused into an indivisible entity. The cruel reality of crisis and depression was a spring, from which flowed a desire to bring about an improvement in the social and economic sectors in collaboration." Jan de Vries concludes that "there developed a form of order with permanent features." The same was true of Belgium and Switzerland. In the segmented small societies on the continent, "the mutual acceptance of the legitimacy of social, especially labor, organizations of opposing ideologies dates chiefly from World War II." Val Lorwin argues that "segmented labor organizations in the smaller European democracies have shown more sense of the public interest and more civic responsibility since World War II than the functional organizations of the United States and Britain."[47]

PROPORTIONAL REPRESENTATION

The corporatist compromise of the 1930s had historical antecedents that made its occurrence more probable in the small European states than in the large industrial countries. The corporatist compromise of the 1930s would have been difficult without an earlier electoral compromise. Around the turn of the century all of the small European states had moved to adopt proportional representation. The coalition agreements among political parties that result from this electoral formula require political opponents to share power—a practice that has become widespread in the small European states since the 1930s. The larger countries, by way of contrast, either did not adopt proportional representation, abandoned it quickly, or fared disastrously with it.

How did a parliamentary politics emerge in Europe? Stein Rokkan has investigated this subject and he describes the emergence thus:

> The smaller democracies have been much more prone to accept the principle of proportionality, the larger ones have either rejected it or been riven by controversies over its maintenance. . . . The ethnically and religiously most divided of the polities were the first to break with the old tradition of "winner-take-all" representation. . . . In the other smaller countries the rapid growth of the working-class parties immediately before or in the wake of the extension of the suffrage threatened the survival of at least one of the older parties and produced constellations where PR was the "saddle-point" solution in the game of opposition forces. This was true of Belgium in 1899, for Sweden in 1909, for the Danish Lower House in 1915, for the Netherlands, Luxembourg, Norway, Austria and the entire Swiss Confederation at the end of or just after World War I.[48]

Two phases can be distinguished in the adoption of systems of proportional representation. In the first phase, before World War I, proportional representation aimed at protecting minorities. In the second phase, during or immediately after World War I, proportional representation sought to contain the threat that socialist parties appeared to pose throughout Europe to the established order.[49] In such culturally divided societies as Switzerland and the Netherlands minority representation was essential to maintaining or consolidating the territorial unity of the state. In culturally homogeneous societies, such as Sweden, Conservatives made their acceptance of universal suffrage contingent on the adoption of proportional representation, as a guarantor of their continued existence as a substantial political force. Proportional representation was similarly adopted in Norway at the end of World War I because the radical-agrarian Left feared its elimination by the younger Labor party. In both Sweden and Norway the pluralism inherent in PR systems helped to preserve a nonsocialist diversity of political choice.[50] The two phases do not, however, distinguish between the small continental and the small Scandinavian states. Denmark, in an attempt to accommodate the large German-speaking minority in Schleswig-Holstein, was the first of the small European states to adopt proportional representation in 1855. The reasons for that choice fit with the logic of Swiss politics in the late nineteenth century. Belgium, on the other hand, adopted proportional representation at the turn of the century after the introduction of universal male suffrage, qualified by property restrictions, had threatened the political viability of the Liberals; the political logic was repeated by Swedish conservatives a few years later. Since some of these episodes illustrate how the party system of the small European states laid the basis for the corporatist compromise of the 1930s, they deserve to be told in somewhat greater detail.[51]

Denmark adopted proportional representation eight years before it lost one-third of its population and two-fifths of its territory to Prussia in the war of 1864. The adoption of PR set the stage for a prolonged battle over the principle of constitutional government.[52] After 1864 power shifted to the Conservatives, who drew their support primarily from large landowners and the upper and middle classes. By 1876 the line was clearly drawn between the reformers in control of the lower house (Folketing) and the conservatives who controlled the upper house (Landsting). The reformers interpreted the constitution of 1866 as granting the Folketing primacy over the Landsting. They thus held that the king was obliged to choose his cabinet ministers from among the majority party of the Folketing, which had less restrictive voter eligibility. The Conservatives and the king upheld the equality of the two legislative assemblies and the right of the king to appoint his cabinet without restrictions. The increasing power of the Social Democrats, which threatened the relative power of both camps, spurred them to compromise in the early 1890s, but only the erosion of conservative electoral strength in the Folketing would prompt the "Change of System" in 1901. When in that year only eight Conservatives were elected to the Folketing (compared to 76 reformers and 14 Social Democrats), the king picked a cabinet headed and controlled by reformers for the first time. Farmers, schoolteachers, and the lower middle class seized the levers of power. After decades of struggle 1901 brought Denmark a parliamentary form of government.

The Conservatives continued to lose electoral ground. The first Social Democrats had been elected to the Landsting in 1890, and in 1914, for the first time in Danish history, the Conservatives lost their majority in the Upper House. Facing the prospect of political marginality and eventual extinction, the Conservatives responded positively to demands for reforms in the election of the Landsting. In 1915 both houses passed an amendment that abolished all property qualifications for voting or serving in the Landsting. All citizens 35 years or older, as compared to 25 for the Folketing, including women and servants, acquired the right to vote for electors who in turn would choose the Landsting. The king ceded his power to appoint members to the Upper House, and the Landsting itself could choose one-quarter of its members.[53] Radicals and Social Democrats, it is noteworthy, agreed to electoral provisions that favored the Conservatives:

indirect election, longer term in office, and higher voting age. More importantly, they agreed to a system of proportional representation that they knew would favor the Conservatives, whose support was spread over a wide geographic area.[54] Continued adherence to single-member constituencies would have eliminated the Conservatives from Denmark's political life. The point was not lost on the Conservatives. They had shown political flexibility as early as 1906 when they cooperated in a reform of local electoral institutions. After 1914 the political leadership of the Conservatives recognized that the Landsting had ceased to be an effective check on the reformers. Conservatives thus began to look for an issue of reform that they could embrace in the hope of attracting new support from the middle classes and of shedding their image as the one force in Danish politics that always opposed change.[55]

Both Sweden and Norway, governed by the Swedish king in personal union between 1814 and 1905, also came to adopt proportional representation in the first two decades of the twentieth century. In both countries political sentiment among reformers as well as conservatives favored proportional representation because it protected political minorities. But the proximate cause differed. After Norway had adopted a parliamentary system in 1884, the extension of universal suffrage was accomplished between 1901 and 1913. As part of that extension the electoral system was revamped in 1906, with Norway adopting, for a few years, direct representation and single-member constituencies. In 1919, however, proportional representation, used in local government elections since 1896, was extended to national elections in order to protect minorities.[56] The fear of a thorough political radicalization of the Norwegian working class was very important in this change in electoral rules. Proportional representation was seen as a buffer against extreme political volatililty.

In Sweden proportional representation came first (in 1907–9), parliamentary government and universal suffrage later (in 1918–21). There was no disagreement between the coalition government of Conservatives and moderates and the Liberal opposition that PR would prevent the suppression of minorities. As Berndt Schiller argues, "Proportionalism guaranteed considerable conservative minority representation in the Second Chamber . . . and a conservative majority in the First Chamber."[57] In the election of 1910 the Social Democrats gained 29 seats, the Conservatives lost 29 seats, and the two parties each controlled 64 members of Parliament.[58] But the electoral gains of the Social Democrats between 1910 and 1921 were so large that the Conservatives and the Liberals, who had also fought for the principle of minority representation, never again raised the issue of returning to the old system of majority representation. The adoption of proportional representation in Sweden strengthened urban interests in right-wing parties and rural interests in left-wing parties, thus reinforcing a tendency to reach political compromises, as in the 1930s.[59] In sum, in Sweden as in Norway proportional representation "favored the multiparty system and laid the institutional basis for compromise politics."[60]

The system of proportional representation, adopted with universal suffrage in 1917, has also been an important influence on Dutch politics.[61] The Dutch constitution dates back to 1815; limited monarchy was introduced in 1848; and parliamentarism prevailed as early as 1868. Between 1878 and 1917 three different issues shaped the political relations between Protestants, Catholics, and the secular political bloc: church-state relations, suffrage, and the principle of collective bargaining. Once adopted, proportional representation was not modified or repealed to benefit larger parties, Lijphart argues, because of "the widespread conviction that proportionality is a basic 'rule of the game' in the politics of accommodation." Proportionality was accepted because it assured far-reaching guarantees to political minorities.[62] Indeed, the Dutch have adopted the purest form of proportional representation to be found in the small European states. The entire country is treated as a single constituency, and before 1956 a party needed only 1 percent of the popular vote to gain a seat in Parliament.[63] As a result, of course, the number of political parties is far greater in the Netherlands than in Scandinavia. Once adopted, proportional representation reinforced the tendency toward bloc formation, or "pillarization" as the Dutch call it.[64] Ideological polarization between different social sectors was strengthened in 1917, because proportional representation "fitted well with the isolationist tendencies of the various minority cultures."[65]

Switzerland adopted proportional representation in 1919. It was adopted at the federal level only after ten different cantons had successfully experimented with this electoral system. Ticino and Geneva were first in 1892; both cantons were looking for an institutional procedure for ending bitter conflicts between political parties that, in the case of Ticino, had prompted the intervention of federal troops.[66] At the federal level both the well-established Catholics and the young Social Democrats were increasingly discontented with the way that Switzerland's system of majority rule reinforced the political domination of the liberal Radicals. Proportional representation was expected to redress the imbalance in representation, defusing hostility among party leaders by replacing vituperative oratory with rational argumentation and effectively protecting minorities against majority rule.[67]

Between 1900 and 1919 three popular initiatives aimed at changing the electoral system. One year after the general strike of 1918 the third initiative succeeded. The strike had changed popular preferences. Fear of growing social conflict and political instability as well as a desire to coopt or accommodate opposition parties created a two-to-one majority in favor of proportional representation. The number of parliamentary seats won by the Radicals declined from more than one-half to one-third, with the Catholics and Social Democrats each gaining a roughly similar number of seats.[68] Yet the Radicals did not look back wistfully to the political domination they had lost. When the party leadership was asked in 1975 about alternative voting arrangements, it responded, in George Coddington's summary, that "the majority system remains an electoral system which could lead to injustices."[69] The respect for minority rights and the willingness to share power is as well established in Switzerland as in the other small European states.

The Belgian experience illustrates similar political tendencies. Suffrage extension was the main issue between 1880 and 1900, with the Socialists and the labor movement pressing it by developing the strategy and tactics of the political strike. Adopted in 1893, universal male suffrage with plural voting eliminated the once-dominant Liberals and entrenched the Catholics firmly in power. In 1894 the Catholics secured 104 seats, compared to 14 for the Liberals and 34 for the Socialists.[70] Subsequently the Catholics introduced PR, Lorwin argues, "to avoid a government-opposition duel with the Socialists alone."[71] The introduction of proportional representation in 1900 stabilized the position of the Liberals, and 31 Liberals, 33 Socialists, and 85 Catholics were returned to Parliament. With brief exceptions in the 1930s and 1940s, this three-party system has endured.

In the larger countries proportional representation fared less well. The United States and Britain have never tried it, though both have considered its merits. A committee of the U.S. Senate investigating the causes of the Civil War in the late 1860s concluded that the war might have been avoided had the United States had proportional representation, since the large unionist minority in the South would have been represented.[72] In the late 1970s and early 1980s Britain's longstanding debate about electoral rules heated up as a new Social Democratic party found widespread support among the voters but enjoyed only slender representation in Parliament.

Italy and France adopted proportional representation in the general wave of electoral reform that swept the industrialized countries in the wake of World War I. In both countries, however, proportional representation proved to have little staying power. Mussolini's fascism ended democracy in Italy, and the Italians chose not to return to PR after World War II. The French passed a constitutional amendment in 1928 abandoning their experimentation with proportional representation as evidently unsuited to the structure of French politics. During the first two decades of this century Japan attempted to contain mass political parties through large-scale electoral districts. In 1920, however, it adopted a single-member district system designed to curtail the growth of minor parties. Finally, a radical system of proportional representation grafted onto German politics at the end of World War I may have contributed to the downfall of the Weimar Republic.

The small European states, on the other hand, adjusted more easily than the large countries to the weakness of the executive and cabinet instability that proportional representation brought. Minority governments between 1920 and 1936 suggest the price that Sweden had to pay for the advantages of PR: a weak executive.[73] During the interwar period minority governments were also very common in Norway: eleven cabinets were formed in 22 years.[74] In the Netherlands political accommodation was forced as much by the arithmetic of coalition building as by the fear of social disintegration.[75] Between 1918 and 1940 there were only two years, 1922 and 1928, when the Belgian government did not offer its resignation. While changes in government may have been frequent, however, the continuity in personnel and policy was great.[76]

Proportional representation tends to insulate different parties from one another. As Stein Rokkan has noted, it fixes an existing balance of power among social forces.[77] While lessening incentives for full mergers among political parties, moreover, it encourages a sharing of power among political opponents. In the absence of a commanding electoral majority by any one social sector, this system of sharing power generated its own political predictability, enhanced the prospects for consensus, and thus facilitated the corporatist compromise of the 1930s. The electoral compromise was important for the corporatist one because, following Maier's insight, it led to an evolution of working-class representation "where unions and parties kept approximate pace with one another. But it was precisely the latter synchronization that most abetted long-term consensual or corporatist outcomes in the postwar generation."[78] In the large states, by contrast, the development of interest groups and parties was out of phase.

POLITICAL DEVELOPMENT IN THE SMALL EUROPEAN COUNTRIES

The electoral compromise on proportional representation was an important condition facilitating the corporatist compromise of the 1930s. PR, however, was less a cause of corporatism than an enabling condition, one that must itself be understood as the outcome of a historical evolution that distinguishes the small European states from the large industrial countries. Why was electoral compromise possible? Why did the Left in Scandinavia stop short of total victory? Why was the Right in other small European states so willing to seek accommodation? Why, in brief, did a winner-take-all mentality not take hold in the small European states? Answers to that question require us to look in somewhat greater detail at the character of both Right and Left. I shall argue that, in contrast to the large countries, the legacy of weak feudal structures (a weak landed aristocracy and strong urban interests) created a weaker Right and political divisions favorable to accommodation between Right and Left. In the nineteenth century the strong incentives that economic openness provided for export specialization reinforced economic and social links between sectors that in larger countries were more sharply opposed. It was the coincidence of these political opportunities and social convergences, reinforced constantly by economic openness and the perception of vulnerability, that inhibited the emergence of a winner-take-all mentality and thus made possible the corporatist bargain.

A Weak Right and Political Divisions Favoring Accommodation

Weak feudal structures distinguish the small European states from the large countries. Michael Hechter and William Brustein have suggested three major different regional modes of production in Europe around the twelfth century.[79] The sedentary pastoral mode stretched from Scandinavia through parts of the British Isles and what today we call the Netherlands to the Iberian Peninsula. It was marked by self-sufficient households linked only loosely by ties of kinship. Economic production was restricted to hunting, pastoralism, and intermittent agricultural cultivation. Labor was organized through the family, whether nuclear or extended, and class distinctions did not exist. The petty commodity mode of production, in Flanders, Switzerland, and south of the Alps, consisted of individual producers residing in communities. Oriented toward long-distance trade, these producers owned the means of production. Political authority was typically concentrated in the hands of producer-merchants. Finally, what we think of as classic feudalism was to be found in the cores of what were to become the most powerful European states: South England, the Paris basin, and parts of the Iberian Peninsula. Feudal arrangements pitted landlords against serf-tenants, and large landlords wielded political and economic power.

For a variety of reasons intensely debated by historians—technology, agricultural productivity, population, social and political organization—the feudal mode of production proved to be stronger to the other two. The reasons that the small European states survived in this competition are complex, but between the sixteenth and eighteenth centuries the small states variously combined strategic inaccessibility to available military technology, intense urban-commercial activity, and location at the intersection of two or more major centers of state making.[80] With these basic divergences in the historical development of feudal and state structures, the small European states subsequently differed from larger states. For one example, as Hans Daalder argues, traditions of representation were stronger in the small European states and more successfully resisted the force of bureaucratic penetration.[81]

The historiography of the small European states supports Hechter's and Brustein's taxonomy. In Stein Rokkan's words, in the small European states "there were, to be sure large estates . . . but such alliances as there were between urban and rural elites still left large groups of self-owning peasants free to join counter-alliances on their own."[82] Swiss peasants prevailed over the encroachment of feudal lords, both secular and religious. Their victory did not lead to the displacement but to the politicization of prefeudal corporatist institutions and attitudes.[83] In the Netherlands land holdings tended to be small and were closely linked to the urban economy. As a result, the burghers came to dominate the more important Dutch provinces. Jan de Vries has detailed the relative absence of a feudal tradition and the weakness of the landed aristocracy in the Low Countries. The shift in global trade from the Mediterranean to the Atlantic sea routes favored Dutch cities, increased the economic and political position of the trading bourgeoisie, provided the trade profits that could be invested in agriculture, and thus encouraged an early commercialization of the rural economy without the reintroduction of serfdom.[84] The switches were set for the Netherlands, in particular, to become a highly specialized agricultural economy. In Belgium, especially in Flanders, the pattern of modernization was conservative but without the antidemocratic elements that prevailed in the vast East Elbian estates of Prussia.[85] What emerged eventually was a preference for a consensual style of conservative politics (but to the exclusion of urban, socialist influence). Neither Switzerland nor the Netherlands saw the development of large land-ownership.[86] In both countries rural communities were closely linked to powerful, independent cities.

The absence of a strong feudal tradition is equally striking in Scandinavia. Until the Napoleonic wars Norway was ruled by Denmark. Norway's landed aristocracy was weak and consisted primarily of Danish civil servants, while indigenous Norwegian aristocracy often sought wealth in commerce.[87] Historians are in agreement that, among the Scandinavian countries, Norway was least affected by feudalism.[88] In Denmark the "Age of Nobles" ended in 1660, when a coup supported by burghers and clerics established an absolute monarchy that systematically eroded the position of the landed nobility. The "Danish Law" of 1685 standardized the payment of service dues, replacing a decentralized and personalistic system organized around the landed aristocracy with a centralized and bureaucratic one run by the state. The agricultural depression of the seventeenth century, as Øywin Østerud argues, "decisively enfeebled the old aristocracy."[89] The peasantry was liberated in the 1780s and progressive land reform passed in the early 1800s, after a century of political bargaining between crown and peasants. "The modernization of Danish society," Esping-Andersen concludes, "was helped by an early emasculation of the aristocracies."[90]

Sweden, by most accounts, is the country with the strongest feudal tradition among the small European states more generally. Yet Timothy Tilton, summarizing historical scholarship, argues that the starting point of Swedish political development differs from that of larger countries "in that Sweden never knew a fully fledged feudal society such as developed in Germany, France or Norman England."[91] Swedish nobles did secure privileges, which would later be recognized in their dominant social role. But whatever its social status, "the nobility owned only one tenth of the land. . . . The size and strength of the independent Swedish peasantry can hardly be overemphasized."[92] As in Denmark, the threat of aristocratic absolutism foundered in the late seventeenth century on the combined opposition of peasants and crown, and aristocrats lost control over huge amounts of land. Sweden may well have had status divisions deeper than in any other small European state, but compared to the larger countries even its feudal legacy appears to have been weak.

The weakness of the landed aristocracy was mirrored in the effect of economic openness on the strength of the urban sector.[93] Switzerland and the Low Countries straddle the most important trade routes in Europe, which encouraged the early development of mercantile cities. "Both in the Netherlands and in some of the more important Swiss cantons, cities thus gained a dominant position which they also extended over the surrounding countryside." In both countries there exist "long traditions of municipal and provincial or cantonal liberties and initiatives."[94] For reasons of geography, Denmark throughout its history has always retained close ties to the city belt that divides northern from southern Europe. Urban commerce was thus an extremely important factor in Danish development. Across the Baltic the situation was not very different. In Norway, one recent analysis argues, "the separation of wealth and land meant that, by the seventeenth century, a non-agricultural bourgeoisie had a strong foothold."[95] With some delay economic power also shifted in eighteenth-century Sweden, toward "the Skeppsbro-nobility of Stockholm and Göteborg, so named because these merchants strung their houses out along the waterfront, and the mill nobility of the iron-making districts."[96]

The small European states had a weaker landed nobility as the nucleus for the political Right in the nineteenth and twentieth centuries. Such an argument is supported by deductive analysis. David Friedman argues that states which derive their taxes from labor rather than trade or land will tend to be larger. "When several nations tax a mobile labor force, each is limited in its tax rates by the fear of losing population to others. One way to raise the costs of emigration is to make a nation larger. Another is to restrict mobility forcibly—to chain the serf to the land."[97] Friedman's analysis points to the same conclusion as mine: a weaker feudal legacy and in its wake a weaker Right is a distinctive feature of the small European states.

The weakness of the landed aristocracy combined with the strength of urban interests also helps to explain the emergence of a moderate Left in the small European states. The problem for any comparative analysis of working-class movements is too many variables and too few cases.[98] Martin Lipset focuses his attention on two variables: the nature of the class system prior to industrialization and the response of economic and political elites to the demands of the working class for the right to participation. First, Lipset argues that rigid status demarcations encourage radical working-class-based parties. A strong feudal past accentuates status demarcations in industrial capitalism; a weak feudal past erodes them. Second, domestic structures and elite strategies that tend toward political and economic exclusion encourage strong revolutionary movements. Conversely, the ready political incorporation of the working class tends to impede its subsequent radicalism. Both variables are helpful in characterizing the distinctiveness of states that would experience the corporatist compromise of the 1930s.

Working-class movements in the small European states evolved in domestic structures not divided by deep status divisions. This generalization fits the experience of moderate, multiclass, Social Democratic parties in Belgium, the Netherlands, Switzerland and Denmark.[99] Norway, on the other hand, seems to offer a clear exception, at least in the early 1920s. Norwegian society was less marked by aristocratic status norms than either Sweden's or Denmark's, yet between 1919 and 1923 Norway's main socialist party opted to join the Communist International. That decision, however, proves to have been a historical irrelevance. Before World War I Norwegian socialism was mildly reformist in character; at the height of the Depression the Norwegian Communist party polled less than 2 percent of the vote; and a comparative survey conducted in 1948 showed Norwegians to have less class feelings than citizens of the other eight countries examined. Norwegian working-class radicalism in the early 1920s is thus the proverbial exception that proves the rule.[100]

Domestic structures and elite strategies also help us to account for the moderation of the Left in the small European states. In some of the small European states universal male suffrage was extended early, thus moderating the claims of unions and socialist parties. Many Swiss cantons, for example, had adopted universal male suffrage by 1848. From the mid-1970s onward the system of popular referenda made it possible for Swiss workers to influence legislation; by 1877, for example, the Swiss electorate had approved a referendum regulating work conditions in factories. Institutions such as the militia army, which brought together all citizens irrespective of class and status, further integrated Swiss workers into the fabric of society. As in Switzerland, so in Denmark: the extension of Danish suffrage occurred as early as 1848–49, when the king granted the vote to three-quarters of men over 30 years of age. By the turn of the century 86 percent of male Danes had acquired the right to vote.[101] The reformism of Danish Social Democracy depended in part on the comparative ease with which a liberal franchise was accorded.

Norway, the Netherlands, and Belgium, however, saw a much later extension of suffrage. In Norway male suffrage was granted only in 1898, fifty years later than in Denmark. In the Netherlands and in Belgium suffrage was also extended late, and the number of eligible voters was considerably smaller than in Norway.[102] In the Netherlands the proportion of adult males eligible to vote was expanded from about one-quarter in 1887, to about one-half in 1896, to about two-thirds in 1914. In Belgium universal suffrage was extended in 1894, but the votes of those owning property were heavily weighted.

It is evident that neither the character of status demarcations nor the inclusionary or exclusionary tendency of domestic structures and elite strategies gives a satisfactory explanation of the moderation of the Left in the small European states. Norwegian radicalism after World War I occurred in a society marked by weak status distinctions between classes. A relatively late extension of the suffrage in Norway, the Netherlands, and Belgium, moreover, cuts against an analysis that explains leftist moderation by the inclusionary tendencies of domestic structures and elite strategies. Sweden confounds the analysis on both scores, but it also points to a third explanatory factor. Swedish society was more status-bound than the other small European states. Its nobles were numerous and enjoyed prestige and influence. In some parts of the country the nobility acted like a rural aristocracy, and it staffed the state bureaucracy as well as the army. As a result, as Lipset points out, "class position has correlated more strongly with party choice in Sweden than in any other European country."[103] Thus the character of status demarcations in Swedish society cannot account for the relative moderation of Sweden's working-class politics (relative, that is, to that of Norway). Furthermore, Sweden's privileged classes strenuously resisted the extension of suffrage. The reform of Sweden's electoral system in 1866 retained far-reaching qualifications attached to the ownership of property. At the turn of the century only one-quarter of adult males had the right to vote (compared to 91% in Norway).[104] The demand for universal suffrage was the core of political agitation by the Social Democrats and the unions. Important changes in Sweden's restrictive electoral laws were made in 1902 only after a general strike had been called.[105]

To account for the moderation of the Left in Sweden as well as the other small European states, we need to consider a factor not mentioned by Lipset: the effect that the structure of political opportunities had on the pattern of alliances that the Left could conceivably enter in the nineteenth century.[106] In none of the smaller European states, unlike the larger countries, did the Left deal with a united front of established political and economic elites. On the continent the division between city and countryside was not reflected in the development of party opposition. The conflict between church and state, landowners and tenant farmers, and workers and capitalists also shaped electoral alignments.[107] In the Scandinavian countries, by contrast, the democratic impulses of the peasantry in the nineteenth century were decisive for Social Democracy, which contributed so much to the power of the labor movement.[108]

Let us begin with Belgium where, Val Lorwin writes, "church-state issues had prevented a concentration of the possessing classes in the conservative party."[109] Belgian Socialists found themselves allies of the Liberals against the Catholics on questions of education and church-state relations. They were allies of the left wing of the Catholics on questions of suffrage and social policy. Finally, in subsequent decades Belgium's Socialists were also confronted by the divisiveness of the ethnic and linguistic conflict between Flanders and Wallonia. Militant Socialists thus had numerous opportunities to compromise with Belgium's conservatives, sparing Belgium the politics of aggressive class conflict at times so prominent across the French border.[110]

A similar structure of political opportunities was also conducive to the Left's moderation in the Netherlands. Between 1850 and the 1880s a coalition of Catholics and Liberals in opposition to the principle of absolute monarchy dominated Dutch politics and pressed for further extensions of the suffrage. In contrast to France, Germany, and Italy no fundamental split divided political parties of the Center and Left from Catholic and conservative parties.[111] From the late 1860s onward a new political coalition began to emerge. Uniting Catholics with Calvinists against the Liberals on the burning issue of state aid for education, it came to power between 1888 and 1913. The first working-class movements drew on the heterogeneous support of impoverished farmers and agricultural workers as well as of artisans and manual workers.[112] In pressing their fight for the extension of suffrage, the Socialists could simultaneously woo poor enfranchised farmers as well as a religiously divided working class. The reformism of the Socialists and their informal cooperation with the Liberals on suffrage had far-reaching effects.[113] In 1913 the Liberals offered the Socialists participation in a coalition government, an offer the party rejected. Switzerland's referendum democracy also created strong incentives for political collaboration between Social Democrats and other parties. Although Social Democracy was in opposition at the federal level until 1943, the complex structure of Switzerland's cantonal politics and the political opportunities in popular initiatives created numerous issue-specific and territorially delimited arenas for political collaboration.[114]

In the three Scandinavian countries the existence of distinct agrarian parties helped the Socialists in forming alliances with other parties. In Norway, working-class political mobilization could not overcome a deep territorial and cultural split between city and countryside. Between the old Left (rural populists and urban radicals) and the Right, Rokkan writes, "there was no basis for an understanding. . . . Even the threatening specter of a giant working-class party could not bring the two cultures into close communication with each other."[115] Founded in 1887 the Labor party could rely for support on a large, quasi-proletarian rural base; its very existence helped to overcome the deep division between city and countryside. But Norway's Labor party accepted democratic institutions because they provided an opportunity to collaborate with other parties. In its fight for the extension of suffrage it tended to support candidates for the bourgeois party in national elections rather than running its own candidates, and such cooperation survived the enactment of male suffrage in 1898.[116] Similarly, Swedish Socialists aligned themselves with the large bourgeois party, the Liberals, in a common fight for the extension of suffrage (which was won in 1909) and a parliamentary form of government. The latter was won in 1917, the same year in which Liberals and Socialists joined in a coalition government.[117]

In Denmark, finally, the working-class party also retained close links with other parties. The conflict between the United Left and the Conservatives increasingly polarized Danish politics in the 1870s and 1880s around the issue of parliamentary government. The Social Democratic party elected its first member of the Folketing in 1884 and joined the United Left in calling for parliamentary supremacy over the king. After the Venstre had succeeded in 1901 in bringing parliamentary government to Denmark, the party split in 1905 between Moderates (supported by farmers) and Radicals (smallholders and urban professionals). The Radicals soon moved close to the Social Democrats, with whom they ran a coalition government between 1913 and 1920.[118] Political opportunities for alliance formation were great throughout small European states and constrained left-wing militancy.

These examples support Rokkan's broad comparative analysis. During the Industrial Revolution the commitment of "nation-builders" to the interest of the urban and commercial as opposed to the agricultural sector was stronger in the small European states than in larger countries.[119] Where, as in Scandinavia, these nation-building elites aligned themselves with urban and commercial elites, "the 'Right' remained essentially urban and proved unable to establish any durable alliance with the Agrarians and the peripheral 'Left.' "[120] The clearest institutional manifestation of this divison of the Right is the emergence in Scandinavia and in the Protestant cantons of Switzerland of parties of agrarian defense to resist the alliance of nation-builders and urban interests. In the Scandinavian countries independent peasants were in a position to build their own political alliances in the party system: "In Denmark the urban Radicals left the agrarian Venstre; in Norway and Sweden the old 'Left' was split in several directions on moralist-religious as well as on economic lines."[121] Switzerland's system of direct democracy similarly gave maximum scope to the exercise of political choices by independent farmers before the formation of an independent agrarian party in the 1920s. Although Switzerland's Catholic cantons and the Low Countries lacked parties of agrarian defense, their complex histories of religious conflict, ethnic divisions, and territorial fragmentation resulted in a political Right split at least as much as in Scandinavia. In general terms, then, the political opportunities for alliances between Right and Left were very substantial.

Economic and Social Links between Sectors

Just as noteworthy as these patterns of political division are the close links between different social sectors, which are typically less sharply opposed than their counterparts in the large countries. These links were reinforced by the specialization for export markets imposed on the small European countries by their economic openness.[122] Nineteenth-century industrialization in the small European states differed significantly from the sheltered industrialization based on large home markets that characterized France, Germany, Austria-Hungary, and to some extent the United States. Export specialization in the small European states reinforced the preference for free trade. Comparative studies of nominal tariff rates show, for example, that the small European states had, almost without exception, lower levels of protection than the larger industrial countries. In 1902 the average rate of protection in the five large industrial countries was 2.5 times higher than in the small European states.[123] The average tariff level for Switzerland, Belgium, Denmark, and Sweden in 1913 was about 7 percent, compared to about 21 percent for Germany, France, and the United States.[124] During the interwar years tariff levels in the small European states were on average 30 to 40 percent below those of the larger countries.[125]

Ulrich Menzel has analyzed the industrialization strategies of Switzerland, Sweden, and Denmark.[126] His analysis suggests that a strategy of specialization for exports helped to create links between different social sectors in all three societies, characterized in the twentieth century, as I argued earlier, by the main variants of democratic corporatism. In the nineteenth century the leading economic sectors in Switzerland, Sweden, and Denmark experienced enormous economic pressures from foreign competitors. First confronted with the qualitatively more advanced and more efficient British spinning industry in the 1790s, what had been Switzerland's leading economic sector was virtually eliminated in less than two decades, and in the industrial cantons mass poverty resulted. The mechanization of the weaving industry forty years later led to mass emigration. For the Swedish iron industry the social consequences of international competition were less dramatic. The total number of workers in the industry was smaller, and many workers were also part-time farmers who in hard times could fall back on subsistence farming. In Sweden, as in Denmark, it was imports of overseas grain in the 1870s that led to serious social dislocations, sharply rising foreclosures on farms, and dramatic increases in emigration. In Sweden, moreover, the agricultural crisis was intensified by a crisis in the timber and iron industries. Generally speaking, it was the leading economic sectors in these three countries (measured in terms of contribution to GDP, employment, foreign-exchange earnings, and tax revenues) that experienced the most intense economic pressures from abroad.

All three societies met these pressures through export specialization. Specialization for world markets had an effect on economic and social structures at home, reinforcing the foundation on which the corporatist compromise of the 1930s was constructed. Export sectors were initially restricted to textiles and watches in Switzerland, grain in Denmark, and grain, iron, and timber in Sweden. Like the other small European states, however, Switzerland, Sweden, and Denmark succeeded in expanding the range and number of their export sectors. By building up the linkages between export sectors and the national economies, moreover, the share of local processing, originally high only in Switzerland, also increased sharply in both Denmark and Sweden. These linkages worked both "forward" (Swiss chocolates, Swedish matches, and Danish bacon) and "backward" (Swiss textile machinery and chemicals, Swedish machine tools and turbines, and Danish equipment for dairies, cold-storage depots, and slaughterhouses). The backward linkages, in particular, provided the basis for developing international competitiveness in selected export markets. Swiss machines, Danish cheesemaking equipment, and Swedish ball bearings, for example, encouraged further specialization and refinement in the search for sheltered market niches. The result was an industrial structure that through multiple economic linkages achieved a high degree of economic coherence despite its diversification and integration into world markets.

The coherence in the economic structure of the small European states is reflected in the unusually close links between industry and agriculture. A decentralized, rural pattern of industrialization is typical of Swiss, Swedish, and Danish modernization. Since Switzerland's textile industry required water power, a rural domestic industry developed in the eighteenth century. It permitted relatively large additions to agricultural incomes from part-time industrial employment.[127] Before about 1850 Swiss entrepreneurs, like their Belgian opposite numbers, could count on low industrial wages to be supplemented substantially by agricultural incomes. In the second half of the nineteenth century the factories followed Switzerland's one source of energy into the mountain valleys, thus preventing the emergence of a deep split between city and countryside. Switzerland's economic adaptability thus depended on the combination of factory worker and part-time farmer. To this day Switzerland lacks large urban conglomerates, and Swiss workers retain numerous close links with the countryside.[128]

In contrast to Switzerland, industrialization in Denmark occurred late rather than early. The settlement pattern of industry in the countryside is nonetheless remarkably similar to the Swiss model.[129] Even in the nineteenth century the links between agriculture and industry were very strong. Brewing, agricultural machinery, and food processing were all derived from agriculture. With only a few exceptions Danish firms, like those in the Netherlands, were small and tucked away in the green countryside. Swedish industrialization reveals a similar pattern. As Tilton argues, Sweden's industry was rural rather than urban. "Sweden had nothing to match Germany's *Ruhrgebiet* or the industrial districts of northern England. Instead . . . plants [were] dispersed in many small communities rather than concentrated in a few large industrial towns." As a result, Tilton writes, "the Swedish farmer could sympathize with urban workers' demands. He himself was often as much of a worker as a farmer, taking winter employment as a miner or lumberjack."[130]

This pattern of rural industrialization has been prominently discussed by economic historians. It has been rediscovered as a Europewide phenomenon under the heading of "protoindustrialization."[131] Throughout Europe between the seventeenth and nineteenth centuries entrepreneurs succeeded in manufacturing large volumes of inexpensive goods with traditional production techniques in extended, well-organized networks of households. Industrialization of the countryside before the Industrial Revolution occurred without the development of factories, without large accumulation of capital, and without a substantial working class concentrated in urban areas.[132]

Organized around a dense network of medium-sized commercial cities that were oriented to international markets, protoindustrialization acquired a distinctive importance in the small European economies because it lasted throughout the nineteenth century. Searching for market niches, their economies generated multiple backward and forward linkages. We have no way of knowing whether the links between agriculture and industry and between country and city were more important in small than in large economies, but it is plausible to assume that differences in scale made these links more visible to everyone in the smaller countries. Visibility must have had significant political consequences for efforts in the small European countries to construct political alliances between social sectors.[133]

The linkages between different social sectors that export specialization reinforced may well have had a strong effect on the structure of party systems.[134] In Europe's societies, both large and small, party systems were the residues of earlier conflicts between church and state as well as between rural and urban interests. The openness of small economies intensified the conflict between the old preindustrial elites and urban interests that increasingly depended on the export of specialized products. Large countries, less dependent on world markets, exploited their home markets more gradually and thus could effect a more gradual merger between the interests of city and countryside. The consequence, Francis Castles argues, may well have been that conditions in the larger countries "minimized the potential for lasting cleavages in the party system prior to the emergence of lower class opposition."[135] The terms of accommodation between urban and rural interests thus differed greatly in small and large countries; and this difference may have contributed to the difference in political regimes that would emerge in the twentieth century.

The discussion so far has been based on Menzel's analysis of Switzerland, Sweden, and Denmark. In some of the other small European states, it is worth noting, the connections between city and countryside are also very close. In Norway most city dwellers left the countryside no more than three generations ago and maintain close ties with relatives in rural areas. In fact, Norway's first Labor government in 1928 was headed by a farmer. Johan Nygaardsvold, who came to power at the head of the Red-Green coalition between workers and farmers, was a cottager's son with a strong sentimental attachment to rural Norway. In Norway, argues Eckstein, "the notion of interconnection [between industrial work and farming] . . . seems particularly suitable to explaining the curious coexistence of clear-cut division and great cohesion in society."[136] A similar situation prevailed in nineteenth-century Netherlands, where "there was less domestic industry than in Belgium, though there were numerous agriculture-based industries offering employment to part of the family."[137]

In Belgium industry was also linked intimately to agriculture. Farms in Flanders were so small that agriculture and industry often shared the same work force. Rural industry gained strength from the tendency of moving cotton works to small towns to avoid the rising power of trade unions.[138] In Wallonia, with its concentration of heavy industry, the continued link between agriculture and industry depended heavily on government policy. Government systematically sought to encourage internal migration by providing cheap season tickets. As a result, "the family remained in a rural area, usually with a small holding, and the father commuted, often considerable distances, to the factory."[139] John Stuart Mill, writing about the typical Swiss worker, identified the distinctive effect that industrial adjustment had on the social structure in all of the small European states: "The workman of Zürich is today a manufacturer, tomorrow again an agriculturalist, and changes his occupations with the seasons, in a continual round. Manufacturing industry and tillage advance hand in hand, in inseparable alliance."[140]

In the second half of the nineteenth century these links were reinforced by rural cooperatives, which, in the small European states, mobilized a traditionally independent peasantry. For the Swedish farmer, Tilton suggests, "participation in farm cooperatives accustomed him to the collective pursuit of social goals. Hence, he consented to his party's participation in the construction of the welfare state."[141] In the Netherlands cooperatives first formed for the purchase of feedstuff and fertilizer, but soon they became producers of butter, cheese, eggs, refined sugar, potatoes, flour, and even cardboard.[142] In the latter nineteenth century agricultural cooperatives also played a prominent role in Switzerland, and the best-known rural cooperatives in Europe could be found in Denmark. Relying from the very beginning on the expertise of agriculturalists hired by the state, democratically organized, egalitarian cooperatives capitalized quickly on new production techniques developed in the 1870s and 1880s.[143] As a result, "among the nations of the world Denmark is distinguished as the farmers' co-operative commonwealth." As Peter Manniche notes, "Co-operation was practically forced upon Danish farmers by an external factor: dependence on foreign markets."[144] In sum, economic openness and export specialization created strong and durable links between different social and economic sectors in the small European economies.

Conclusion

Historical analyses of small European societies as different as Norway and the Netherlands have emphasized the ideological preference of these countries for unity, despite their deep social divisions. In the twentieth century this preference sustained the willingness of Right and Left to bargain politically, avoiding the winner-take-all mentality characteristic of larger countries.

Norway is a highly stable democracy, yet it has political cleavages and divergences that are relatively conspicuous.[145] Peasants and subsistence agriculture aligned themselves against urban merchants and bureaucrats.[146] Clashing economic interests were reinforced by divergent cultural norms. In the nineteenth century a bitter controversy over Norway's national language divided the urban from the rural sector. Similarly great was the difference between religious fundamentalism in the countryside and secularism in the cities. The country was, moreover, split into five different regions, each with its own clear cultural identity. What holds Norway together? Harry Eckstein argues plausibly that the answer lies in the strong sense of community as reflected, for example, in the "ubiquitous corporatism" of life.[147]

Dutch society is divided into different confessional "pillars" rather than into territorially based cultural regions. Ever since the seventeenth century Dutch society has been deeply divided along religious lines. Students of Dutch politics have described how the mobilization of Catholic, Calvinist, and Socialist subcultures has, since the late nineteenth century, divided Dutch society by providing a cradle-to-grave system of voluntary associations and political parties guided by sharply diverging religious and ideological orientations. As a result there existed until the 1960s three different employers' associations and until the 1970s three different trade union federations. Dutch media and education have reinforced these divisions, both at the political and at the personal level. Yet some long-term historical legacies counteract these divisive influences.[148] The Netherlands, decentralized throughout its history, has encouraged political tolerance. The country has been hospitable to the formation from below, of many pyramids of sovereign political societies, described and analyzed by Althusius, the first theorist of a "consociational" politics. The far-flung trading interests of the Netherlands similarly constrained religious divisions: during the war with Spain the flood of refugees from the south prompted economic elites to play down ideological conflicts, which they regarded as inimical to trade.[149] In the Netherlands, Daalder writes, "even staunch isolationists have learned that a strong insistence on subcultural rights need not prevent day-to-day cooperation with representatives from rival groups."[150]

I have emphasized two aspects in the historical evolution of Right and Left that have favored political accommodation in the small European states during the twentieth century. First, one legacy of weak feudalism was a Right less powerful socially and less cohesive electorally than that in the larger countries. The result was the possibility for creating new alliances between Left and Right, enhancing the prospects for political accommodation. Second, rural industrialization reinforced by strong incentives imposed by economic openness favoring a strategy of export specialization, added a dimension of sociological reality to politically possible alliances. The two conditions did not converge in the larger countries.

The weakness of feudalism in those regions where the small European states were eventually to emerge contrasts strikingly with the strong feudalism elsewhere. Feudalism bestowed a comparative advantage in wealth and power on what would become Europe's large and powerful states. Similarly, Japanese feudalism lasted until late in the nineteenth century; large estates were not broken up until the 1880s and 1890s, and the strength of rural elites was embedded in Japan's structures of power until the land reform carried out under U.S. auspices at the end of World War II.

Britain's Right, though split in the early part of the nineteenth century, was relatively united as the century drew to a close. The nation's hegemonic position in the international system reinforced among the defenders of the status quo a sense of power rather than a willingness to compromise. In Germany and France the Right, though more powerful than in the small European states, was divided on questions of religion, education, regionalism, and foreign policy. It was united only intermittently by the charisma of a Napoleon III or the cleverness of a Bismarck. But unlike the situation in the small European states, political opportunities were not matched by a willingness on the part of the Right to form new alliances with segments of the Left. One important reason for this difference was the relative absence of economic linkages between different social sectors such as had emerged in the nineteenth century in the smaller European societies. A second reason was the difference in the character of the Left. The larger countries, with their stronger feudal past and greater status demarcations, generally featured a more radical Left with political demands that the Right found more difficult to accept. Finally, in countries less open and vulnerable to the influences of the international system, the pressures for compromising were also smaller.

The Japanese Right emerged united and strong from the Meiji Restoration. Urban money and rural votes made possible an accommodation that traded arms for pork-barrel legislation in the interwar period. (Important elements of this political accommodation also characterize the prolonged era of Liberal Democratic party rule after 1955.) Whatever political divisions existed within the Right—over Japan's objectives in Asia, its stance vis-à-vis the United States, and the needs of different branches of the armed services—were by 1936 fused as a group within the Japanese army seized control and ended civilian rule. There was never a need to compromise with a divided and weak Left. The Left, moreover, was tainted by its ideological affinities with the Soviet Union, one of the major adversaries Japan confronted in the early twentieth century from a position of international vulnerability.

The importance of international strength and its effect in lessening pressures for compromise is brought out very clearly in the case of the United States.[151] Lacking a feudal past but featuring a divided Right and a moderate Left, the American case points to the importance of a fragile international position and a sense of vulnerability. Because of the absence (rather than weakness) of a feudal past in American history, working-class politicians had overwhelming incentives to form alliances with the leaders of other social sectors. As a result they never successfully organized an independent Left in the United States. The social groups that in Europe constituted the Right were in the United States thereby freed to divide their allegiance between the Republican and Democratic parties. Weak feudal structures led to the absence of coercive violence in the conflicts between Right and Left in the small European countries. The United States, by contrast, experienced a civil war over the issue of slavery and for many decades exceptionally bloody and prolonged conflicts between management and workers. One major feature can account for these different outcomes: the restraints imposed by a vulnerable and exposed international position.

In short, some of the large industrial states, like the United States, had weak feudal structures and adopted universal suffrage and parliamentary government early. Others, such as Germany, had strong feudal structures and accepted universal suffrage and parliamentary government late. But in none of the large industrial countries did the coincidence of political opportunities and social convergences, reinforced by economic openness and the perception of vulnerability, weaken the winner-take-all mentality and enhance willingness to bargain with political opponents.

HISTORICAL ORIGIN OF LIBERAL AND SOCIAL CORPORATISM

Despite the historical similarities that led small European states to the corporatist compromise of the 1930s, there exist important differences in the historical evolution of the liberal and social variants of corporatism. It would be a serious oversimplification to argue that the interlocking crises of the 1930s and 1940s resulted in political accommodation because that accommodation was necessary for survival. The terms of political accommodation were shaped, rather, by the relative power position that different actors held in domestic politics.

In the social corporatism of the Scandinavian countries compromise resembled an act of political acquiescence by Center and Right in the presence of an increasingly strong labor movement. In the liberal corporatist regimes on the European continent compromise looked more like the imposition of political conditions by Center and Right on a labor movement too weak to dictate its own terms. This difference is mirrored in contrasting strategies for crisis management: early devaluation, deficit spending, and pragmatic experimentation with welfare policies in Scandinavia, late devaluation, an orthodox approach to fiscal policy, and the discussion rather than implementation of elaborate crisis plans in Switzerland, Belgium, and the Netherlands. In Scandinavia Social Democracy prevailed because it constructed successful alliances with farmers. On the continent Catholic and Liberal parties prevailed instead. But they moved, as the crisis endured, toward the sharing of executive power with the Social Democrats: in Belgium in 1935, in the Netherlands in 1939, and in Switzerland in 1943. Although new alliances between different social sectors emerged in all six countries, the terms of political accommodation differed substantially.

A closer examination of the electoral compromise points to the same conclusion. Two different political developments on the one hand prompted the Left in Scandinavia to stop short of total victory (which would have entailed choosing a majoritarian rather than a proportional system of representation) and on the other led the Center and Right on the continent to abdicate power voluntarily by agreeing to PR. In Scandinavia the electoral compromise and political accommodation reflected a truce in class conflict. On the continent the electoral compromise expressed a traditional consociational strategy for coping with conflicts between minorities, and political accommodation included the Left as one political party among several in deeply divided societies. These distinctions are, of course, not ironclad. Belgium adopted PR primarily for "defensive" reasons, Denmark for "consociational" ones; the two cases complicate the distinction without, however, invalidating it. The same is true for the Swiss experience with PR, which mixed "consociational" elements at the cantonal level before World War I with "defensive" ones at the federal level after the war.

The differences in the terms of the corporatist and electoral compromises were shaped by the historical evolution of business and labor in the societies concerned. The character of business was influenced by the timing of industrialization as well as the effects of international politics (the ability to avoid involvement in war and the possession of overseas colonies). Labor movements were shaped by the timing of industrialization and by the number and intensity of social divisions.

In his studies of comparative economic history Alexander Gerschenkron developed a hypothesis that linked the timing of industrialization to a variety of political and economic outcomes.[152] Gerschenkron argued, more specifically, that the degree of economic backwardness was decisive in shaping both the speed of industrialization and its organizational structure. He applied the proposition persuasively, if in general terms, to Britain, Germany, and Russia; more detailed tests gave at best ambiguous results.[153] For my broad purposes, however, Gerschenkron's insight remains very useful: the timing of industrialization in the nineteenth century shaped the type of business community to emerge in the twentieth.

The small European states have followed different paths to industrial modernity.[154] Switzerland in the late eighteenth century adopted a strategy of export-oriented growth and free trade. Like Belgium, Switzerland was one of Europe's early industrializers, suffering from a unique constellation of natural disadvantages: absence of essential raw materials, deficits in agricultural trade, lack of direct access to ocean transportation, until the late nineteenth century relative isolation from Europe's system of railways and canals, and political fragmentation. Despite this cumulation of natural disadvantages, Switzerland found success in a pattern of development that featured the importing of grain and raw materials and the export of high-quality manufactured goods (textiles and watches, among others). By 1913 exports accounted for 40 percent of GNP, and one-fifth of Switzerland's industrial production occurred abroad.[155] Swiss banks reinforced this international orientation. The inflow of Huguenot refugees in the seventeenth century and the financing of railways in the nineteenth century fashioned Switzerland's financial community, mixing the features of Britain's commercial banks and Germany's investment banks. Although London's bankers rightly called their colleagues in Zurich "gnomes" in the nineteenth century, when Zurich was dwarfed by London's financial market, Swiss banks enjoyed a strong position within Switzerland. Economic development and industrialization relied largely on private initiative and private demand, and began with light industry. The absence of raw materials inhibited the development of heavy industry.

Belgium also figures among the earliest industrializers on the continent. Unlike Switzerland, however, but like the larger continental states (France, Germany, Austria-Hungary), it sought economic growth through the development of its domestic markets—a development that included building the most extensive network of railway connections in Europe.[156] Furthermore, the availability of coal and iron in Belgium encouraged the early construction of heavy industry and the production of investment rather than consumer goods. Belgium was, however, an exception to the pattern of export-oriented growth for a relatively short time. By 1860 its strategy had come to resemble the Swiss pattern, and by 1890 Belgium ranked number one in Europe in per capita exports. The country's convergence with the small-state strategy of export-led growth was rapid and total.

There is less agreement among economic historians about the timing and character of Dutch industrialization. Industrially retarded, compared to Belgium and Switzerland in the first half of the nineteenth century, the Netherlands appears to have experienced a transitional period (1850–70) and full-fledged industrialization thereafter. Although industrialization occurred later than in Belgium and Switzerland, the strong legacy of Dutch merchant capitalism as well as a strategy of agricultural modernization reinforced the Dutch inclination for international adaptation and set its business community apart from those of Denmark and Norway.[157]

Norway and Denmark industrialized late and followed a very different path.[158] The early decades of the nineteenth century focused on the export of raw materials, agricultural products, timber, and iron ore. In subsequent decades both countries followed import substitution and relative protection, which accorded the government a greater role in the economy than was true of the continental countries. In Norway rapid industrial growth around the turn of the century was focused on the exploitation of natural resources, financed by foreign capital. Denmark's more gradual industrialization, by contrast, was oriented more toward its rapidly modernizing agricultural sector. Only since 1945 has this development path converged with export-led growth. The pattern is distinguished by a successful attempt to move gradually from the export of unfinished goods (Norwegian lumber or Danish grain) to high-quality manufactured products (paper and pulp or dairy products).

Although in many ways comparable to that of its Scandinavian neighbors, Sweden's industrial development has been early and uninterruptedly involved with world markets. Swedish industrialization after 1870 brought not only a broadening of industrial activities but a deepening of capital, a shift to higher-value-added products and, most importantly, the emergence of new and dynamic export sectors, especially in the engineering industries. Swedish industry took on an export orientation much earlier than its Danish and Norwegian counterparts. Sweden now has a much smaller service sector and experienced a relatively late development of domestic markets. Of critical importance to Sweden's development pattern was the early international competitiveness of its capital goods industries, which made notable technical advances in the late nineteenth century in such areas as turbines, electrical machinery, and ball bearings. As in Switzerland, Belgium, and the Netherlands, the business community in Sweden had an international orientation.

International politics has also affected the character of business in the small European countries. Protected by neutrality, Switzerland and Sweden managed to stay out of wars. They acquired foreign assets without suffering expropriation. Denmark was less fortunate and found itself entangled in numerous European wars. The Netherlands and, more briefly, Belgium controlled vast overseas colonies that encouraged foreign investment.[159] By contrast, the Scandinavian countries did not control significant overseas territories in the nineteenth century.[160] Norway had been ruled for centuries first by Denmark and in the nineteenth century by Sweden. Yet Swedish-Norwegian union was tenuous, and Sweden's phase of continental expansion had ended well before the Industrial Revolution. Throughout the nineteenth century Denmark controlled the Danish West Indies (which it sold to the United States in 1916) and Iceland (whose independence it recognized in 1918). But these overseas possessions left virtually no imprint on Denmark's business community, which was closely tied to agricultural modernization.

The timing and character of industrialization as well as the vagaries of international politics left liberal corporatist regimes in Switzerland, the Netherlands, and Belgium, as well as Sweden, with a business community with an international orientation. In 1913, for example, the relative importance of foreign investment was very much greater in these countries than in Denmark or Norway.[161] Large corporations developed and entered world markets with advanced industrial products substantially different from those of agricultural Denmark and resource-intensive Norway.

The terms of compromise in the 1930s were also shaped by the effect that the timing of industrialization as well as the number and intensity of social divisions have had on the militancy and centralization of the labor movement. In a classic sociological study Edward Bull sought to explain differences in the evolution of the Scandinavian labor movements by structural factors, foremost among them the suddenness of change brought about by industrialization. Walter Galenson subsequently developed this hypothesis in his comparative studies.[162] According to this view, Norway's rapid industrialization pitted a rootless working class against large, powerful foreign companies, thus helping to forge a militant working class in the early decades of this century. A more gradual industrialization in Denmark, organized around small-scale industry owned by the petite bourgeoisie and producing for domestic markets, caused little working-class militancy. Sweden with its greater dependence on world markets held an intermediate position.[163] (Its labor movement approximates the pattern of social corporatism, while its business community resembles the pattern of liberal corporatism.) Bull's and Galenson's appealing proposition has been found wanting; it cannot establish a neat rank-ordering of the Scandinavian countries.[164] But when recast to become compatible with the proposition that I derived from Gerschenkron's hypothesis about the timing rather than the pace of industrialization, Bull's original insight helps us explain the degree of militancy of labor movements in liberal and social corporatism and thus the different terms of political accommodation in the 1930s. Early industrializers, Switzerland, Belgium, and the Netherlands among them, have less radical labor movements than do the later industrializers in Scandinavia.

In Switzerland there was little room for labor radicalism. Surplus labor was gradually displaced from the countryside; it assimilated with a confident bourgeoisie that by the late nineteenth century had integrated traditional artisans with capitalist entrepreneurs. Alliances between labor and business in particular industrial sectors were expressed in the form of a growing corporatist strain in Swiss society rather than through any direct influence of the Left. Finally, open channels for political participation and vigorous democratic institutions led to an early political incorporation of workers. In the Netherlands the growth of the Dutch labor movement was preceded by the emancipation of both the Calvinist and the Catholic communities. The initially hostile reaction of the two communities to social problems gradually changed from within as both developed effective working-class organizations. At the same time, though, the active opposition of the Catholic church to workers joining socialist-led unions also helped contain the spread of worker militance.[165]

In the evolution of Belgium's labor movement Christian social organizations kept the demands of mobilizing groups at levels that, Lorwin argues, "often sacrificed social justice to social peace."[166] As in the Netherlands and in Switzerland some early and more militant labor groups that joined together Catholics and Protestants were dissolved by the opposition of the churches. Belgium's early industrialization and great dependence on world markets after 1860 also helped reconcile the working class to the existing social and political order.[167] Historical evolution thus helps explain why Belgium's labor movement, though heavily unionized, enjoys only a relatively narrow scope for collective bargaining, and why the provisions for work councils and codetermination are restrictive. But by the standards of the small European states Belgium's work force is particularly strike-prone. One plausible explanation for this exception lies in the "monocultural" character of Belgian industry, which is skewed heavily toward the production of iron and steel. The technology of production in that industry requires centralization, which facilitates the organizing of workers. Throughout the capitalist world, furthermore, steel workers have been among the most militant during the last hundred years. Industrial militancy, it could be argued, reflects the logic of Belgium's industrial structure.

Differences in the centralization of the labor movements in the small European countries stem from social structure. The small European states, in the words of one survey, "include not only some of the most homogeneous countries in the world, but also several countries with a very high degree of what Val Lorwin calls segmented pluralism."[168] In some countries the primary axis of conflict is cultural diversity (measured by variation in language or religion); they are divided vertically into different cultural pillars. In others the primary axis of conflict is socioeconomic diversity (measured by variation in occupation, education, wealth, and the like); they are divided horizontally into different classes. Three small European states are marked by a very strong cultural diversity: Switzerland (ethnically and religiously), Belgium (ethnically) and the Netherlands (religiously). The three Scandinavian countries, on the other hand, are in cultural terms relatively homogeneous. Their major conflicts derive from socioeconomic diversity.[169] These fundamental differences in social structure offer a crude explanation of the degree of centralization of the Left in the small European states. The fissures that cultural heterogeneity opens in the organizational strength of the working class lead to a notable weakening of the position of organized labor in Switzerland, the Netherlands, and Belgium. Conversely, the relative unity of the working class in culturally homogeneous states has favored more centralized labor movements in the three Scandinavian countries.[170]

The Industrial Revolution reinforced the differences between liberal and social corporatism that already existed. As mentioned before, Hechter and Brustein distinguish between two nonfeudal modes of production: petty commodity production in that part of Europe which later became Switzerland and parts of the Low Countries, sedentary pastoral production in Scandinavia. Stein Rokkan's typological map of Europe similarly locates Switzerland and the Low Countries as transition areas in Europe's city-belt, run by oligarchies or provincial estates; Denmark and Norway were parts of a periphery that later experienced absolutist rule; and Sweden had a landward empire with a continuous operation of organs of representation.[171] In *The Modern World System* Immanuel Wallerstein has focused primarily on the commercially active, internationally oriented regions in the European city-belt. By contrast Perry Anderson in his *Lineages of the Absolutist State* pays much of his attention to the growth of the Habsburg Empire and to the aborted empires in Scandinavia.[172] The differences in focus point to important structural differences in the historical legacy of liberal and social corporatism. Hans Daadler has summarized these differences well:

In some countries responsible parliamentary government came early, at a time when politics was still dominated by pluralist elites in the absence of strong political parties. In Switzerland and the Netherlands (and to a lesser extent in the other two Benelux countries), an autochthonous tradition of the 'politics of accommodation' provided the framework in

Table 7. Historical determinants of the character of business and labor in the small European states

	(1) Industrial work force, late 19th century		(2) Industrial production per capita, 1898–1902		(3) War avoidance since 1815		(4) Possession of an overseas colonial empire		(5) Ethnic and linguistic division, as a measure of cultural heterogeneity, 1960–65		(6) Religious division, as a measure of cultural heterogeneity, 1960–65		(7) Sum of ranks of cols. (1)–(6)	
	Rank	%	Rank	Index	Rank	Index	Rank	Index	Rank	Index	Rank	Index	Rank	Sum
1. Switzerland	1.0	48	2.0	150	1.0	–7	5.0	0.0	2.0	.50	1.0	0.01	2.0	12.0
2. Netherlands	3.0	36	4.0	97	5.0	5	2.0	0.3	6.0	.07	2.0	0.03	3.0	22.0
3. Belgium	2.0	39	1.0	230	3.0	0	1.0	1.0	1.0	.53	3.5	0.98	1.0	11.5
4. Sweden	5.5	28	3.0	104	2.0	–3	5.0	0.0	4.0	.10	5.5	1.00	4.0	25.0
5. Denmark	5.5	28	6.0	85	6.0	9	3.0	0.1	5.0	.09	3.5	0'.98	6.0	29.0
6. Norway	4.0	33	5.0	93	4.0	4	5.0	0.0	3.0	.19	5.5	1.00	5.0	26.5
Average (1)–(3)	2.0	41	2.3	159	3.0	–0.7	2.7	0.4	3.0	.37	2.2	0.34	2.0	15.2
Average (5)–(6)	4.8	31	5.5	89	5.0	6.5	4.0	0.0	4.0	.14	4.5	0.99	5.5	27.8

SOURCES. Col. 1: Simon Kuznets, *Modern Economic Growth: Rate, Structure, and Spread* (New Haven: Yale University Press, 1966), p. 106. For Sweden the data are reported in G. A. Montgomery, *The Rise of Modern Industry in Sweden* (London: King, 1939), p. 141. For Austria the data refer to the western half of the Dual Monarchy in 1890 as reported in Karl Heinz Werner, "Österreichs Industrie- und Aussenhandelspolitik 1848," in Hans Mayer, ed., *Hundert Jahre österreichische Wirtschafsentwicklung 1848–1948* (Vienna: Springer, 1949), p. 369.

Col. 2: Paul Bairoch, *Commerce extérieur et développement économique de l'Europe au XIXe siècle* (Paris: Mouton, 1976), p. 137.

Cols. 3–4: Herbert Ammann, Werner Fassbind, and Peter C. Mayer, "Multinationale Konzerne der Schweiz und Auswirkungen auf die Arbeiterklasse in der Schweiz," Institute of Sociology, University of Zurich, 1975, pp. 106–7.

Cols. 5–6: Charles L. Taylor and Michael C. Hudson, *World Handbook of Political and Social Indicators* (New Haven: Yale University Press, 1972), pp. 271–74.

NOTES. Col. 1: measured by the percentage of the total labor force employed in industry, late 19th century.

Col. 2: volume of industrial production divided by total population.

Col. 3: measured in number of years; for every 25 years of declared neutrality and peace, one negative unit was scored.

Col. 4: colonies weighted according to market size, abundance of raw materials and foodstuffs, and political links to the imperial power.

Col. 5: the data are the mean values of the two indicators of ethnic and linguistic homogeneity presented and explained in the *World Handbook*.

Col. 6: measured as the absolute difference between the proportion of Catholics and Protestants divided by the sum of the proportion of Catholics and Protestants.

Parallel figures for Austria are given in chapter 4, footnote 203.

which later mass movements developed. . . . In a second group of countries (Sweden, Denmark, Norway) a much stronger centralized establishment which centered on King and bureaucracy co-existed with representative organs which did not succeed in obtaining responsible government early or easily. In Norway, Denmark, and Sweden, responsible government came about through a process of mass-mobilization of counter-establishment forces.[173]

The historical reasons that account for the terms of accommodation in the 1930s lie in the effects that industrialization, international politics, and social structure had on business and labor, reinforcing prior differences in evolution. Liberal and social corporatism have roots that go far back in history.

This brief discussion of the historical determinants of different kinds of democratic corporatism is summarized schematically in Table 7, which presents statistical data on the three variables that have shaped business and labor: industrialization (cols. 1–2), international politics (cols. 3–4), and social structure (cols. 5–6). A ranking of the six small European countries yields differences between Switzerland, the Netherlands, and Belgium on the one hand and Denmark and Norway on the other—differences that are consistent with my analysis (see col. 7).[174] A more detailed pairwise comparison of each state in the first group with each state in the second generates a total of 36 comparisons for the six data columns in Table 7. Omitting two tied ranks from the calculation, 30 of 34 comparisons (or 88%) follow the expected ranking with Sweden holding an intermediary position. Liberal and social corporatism, we can conclude, have discernibly different historical foundations.

No Revolutionary Break with the Past—and the Austrian Exception

Arguments that, like mine, derive important consequences for the structure of contemporary politics from the characteristics of preindustrial society build on Barrington Moore's path-breaking work on the emergence of democracy, fascism, and communism in large countries.[175] Yet Moore dismissed the experience of the small European states because, he argued, external influences on that experience decisively outweighed or somehow overcame internal ones. This view is mistaken, I shall argue, because it is based on an excessively narrow definition of the term "external influence."

At first glance, the evolution of democratic practices in the small European states seems to illustrate Moore's claim, for it was intimately linked to the revolutionary transformation of larger societies. The American Revolution, the French Revolution, the July Revolution of 1830, and the Revolution of 1848 all posed external pressures. To these pressures Switzerland, Denmark, and, to a lesser degree, Sweden had to respond, and the July Revolution led to the very creation of Belgium. A brief revolutionary war in Switzerland in 1847, a bloodless revolution in Denmark in 1848–49, and Sweden's reform of 1867 all resulted in constitutions that reduced the power of the established elite sufficiently to make it only one of several important political actors. In all three societies an agreement on the democratic rules of the game was increasingly accepted in the second half of the nineteenth century, but it was only when confronted with severe external pressures that these societies "made room" for new political actors and fashioned new political rules.

But other examples drawn from nineteenth-century history illustrate how external influence acted as an opportunity as much as a constraint. The Austrian Netherlands, to emerge after 1830 as the Kingdom of Belgium, was incorporated into the Napoleonic Empire and thus given access to a very large market free of tariffs. Switzerland benefited from the protection that the continental blockade provided for a brief period. Excluded from the French market soon after 1815 and confronted with formidable British competition, Belgium and Switzerland discovered that without substantial domestic markets, and heavily reliant on transit trade, they should seize the opportunity to export to European, and later overseas, markets. Exports became of decisive importance for their further industrialization. For later industrializers in Scandinavia, the situation was very similar. "British politics determined to a large extent what happened in the Norwegian economy during the 19th century," according to Sima Lieberman, and indeed the foundation of Norwegian shipping was the British Navigation Act of 1849. Similarly, Danish agriculture benefited enormously from the abolition of the Corn Laws in 1846.[176]

External influences operate as both constraints and opportunities.[177] Such influence can take the threat of revolutionary violence or of the prospects of variable degrees of dependence on others for markets, goods, capital, and labor. Typically international opportunities and constraints are intertwined. For example, in the late nineteenth century massive emigration provided an important safety valve as Norway and Sweden experienced rapid industrialization and massive social dislocations. Between 1881 and 1910 emigration accounted for 20 percent in Norway and 16 percent in Sweden of their total populations in 1910.[178] A change in American immigration policy converted this torrent to a trickle after 1919; partly as a result, domestic unemployment rates in both countries soared. The small European states have adjusted to international constraints throughout their history; but they also have exploited the opportunities that derive from economic openness. If we avoid a narrow conception of external influence we may understand better the political innovation that the small European states have made in the last half century.

In his historical analyses Moore was interested in isolating the conditions that favored the emergence of democracy, fascism, and communism in the twentieth century. What interests me are the conditions that differentiate democratic corporatism from other forms of democracy. One of the crucial steps in Moore's analysis is the identification of the way in which social relations in the preindustrial era affect the strength and the cohesion of the middle classes. Thus he writes, "no bourgeois, no democracy."[179] Yet even his sympathetic critics have pointed out that the strength of the bourgeois impulse is a key variable that Moore does not measure.[180] I have followed Rokkan and Castles in this chapter, arguing that because of the economic openness of the small European states, the political position of the urban sector was stronger than in larger countries with more closed economies. Lacking strong feudal structures, the small European states closely approximate the conditions that Moore identified as marking a democratic road to modernity: early commercialization of land, a commercially oriented upper class, independent peasants, weakened landed elites, and growing cities. More precisely, Moore identified five conditions necessary for the emergence of democratic regimes in the large states. Four of these conditions deal with the strength and autonomy of a free peasantry and urban elites. These social sectors were also strong in the small European states, and the coalitions among them and other political actors also inhibited the emergence of fascism and communism. Yet "a revolutionary break with the past," essential in Moore's explanation, does not appear to have been essential in the political development of the small European states. Jonathan Tumin's study of the Netherlands and work on Sweden by Timothy Tilton and Frances Castles converge in the conclusion that these democracies followed a peaceful road to democracy not charted by Moore.[181]

Tumin analyzes three phases in Dutch history that might be viewed as revolutionary breaks with the past: the revolt against Spain, the French Revolution, and the prolonged conflict over suffrage and education throughout the nineteenth and into the early twentieth centuries. The revolt against Spain froze Protestant supremacy as well as urban autonomy and created what G. J. Renier calls a "dictatorship of the upper middle class."[182] The revolt was not, however, a political revolution by the middle class—though prolonged, there was little bloodshed and violence. On balance, Tumin concludes, in Dutch politics "there was far more continuity than discontinuity." The American and French revolutions and the French occupation had a profound influence on Dutch society and politics, yet the "Dutch Revolution" differed fundamentally from the French Revolution. The democratic movement, expressing the preferences of the middle class over lower-class support for the House of Orange, affected a change in the structure of political institutions and rules. Yet the relations among different social classes remained relatively unchanged and the position of the Dutch elite, the upper middle class, was not threatened. In the 1820s Catholics joined forces with Liberals against the king, and this coalition dominated Dutch politics between 1850 and 1880. The year 1848 created neither a revolutionary movement nor serious disturbances in the Netherlands, yet the king granted a new constitution that opened the door to a subsequent, peaceful democratization. The balance of political power shifted gradually without a social revolution or a radical break with the past.[183]

Analyses of the origins of Swedish democracy reach the same conclusion. Before the nineteenth century the shifting balance of power among different social sectors did not lead to anything resembling a revolutionary break with the past.[184] In fact, institutional struggles between the sixteenth and eighteenth centuries gave freeholding peasants the power to tip the balance between nobility and monarchy. Aristocratic, constitutional, and hereditary obstacles checked claims to absolute rule.[185] In the eighteenth century a bureaucratic nobility came to rule uneasily together with powerful landowners. Only toward the end of the century did Gustav III's monarchical coup, based on popular support, drastically curtail the power of the nobility. In the nineteenth century, Tilton argues, "Swedish democracy does not owe its origins to a revolution but to a series of reform acts in 1866, 1909 and 1918 extending the franchise in a way reminiscent of the English Reform Acts." Popular pressure was very strong in 1866 and 1909. In 1917–18 social revolutions in Russia, Germany, and Austria-Hungary gave the threat of revolution in Sweden sufficient credibility for the Conservatives to permit a nonviolent transition to full democracy. As in the Netherlands, political developments in Sweden point to a "radical liberal model of democratic development . . . between timid liberalism and revolutionary violence."[186] Castles reaches the same conclusion: "Sweden has never experienced a revolutionary break with the past, and in this respect, at least, Moore's thesis seems simply inapplicable to Sweden's political development."[187]

Revolutionary moments may have existed briefly in the other small European states at particular junctures—for example, in Denmark in the 1880s, in Norway in the 1890s, in the Low Countries in the first decade of the twentieth century, and in all of the small European states, including Switzerland, in 1917–18. But these moments were remarkably brief, both in the small culturally heterogeneous states on the continent and the homogeneous ones in Scandinavia. This absence of a revolutionary break with the past is suggested by the titles Arend Lijphart and Dankwart Rustow chose for the two books on the small European states best known in America—*The Politics of Accommodation* and *The Politics of Compromise*. Rustow's *Politics of Compromise* is named after the 1907 Swedish legislation that specified the details of the "great compromise," a formula that combined the Liberal demand for a more democratic suffrage with Tory guarantees of proportional representation and bicameralism."[188] Lijphart's *Politics of Accommodation* centers on the great compromise of 1917 that resolved the three major issues debated in Dutch politics between 1878 and 1917. State aid to parochial schools, the extension of the suffrage, and labor's right to organize all came to a head in 1910–13, leading to a peace agreement, the *Pacificatie* of 1917.[189] These two books point, then, to the fact that the small European states have managed to arrive at twentieth-century democracy without the revolutionary break essential to the political development of larger countries.

For Arend Lijphart a moderate politics results from deep social conflicts. The consociational theory that he helped to develop stresses the intense polarization among different social sectors in the continental small European states. Instead, I have focused on a pattern of social divisions that has made possible a nonrevolutionary passage to the present. For me a moderate politics results from social conflicts that are less deep and that have afforded elites the political opportunity for striking new alliances. To sort out these different interpretations will take more detailed historical research than I have been able to undertake. Ilja Scholten has made a beginning, however, and argues in an article based on Lijphart's and Rustow's work, that in the early decades of the twentieth century the rules for achieving political compromise were remarkably similar in the Netherlands and in Sweden.[190]

I have stressed the global context of the small European states, their historical experience, and the specificity of their domestic structure when viewed in comparative perspective. Weak feudalism and relatively little domestic coercion favored peaceful transformations. These states evolved domestic structures conducive to the establishment of political alliances across different social sectors and hence to the moderation of the political Left. Proportional representation both reflected and reinforced the tendency toward compromise. In short, the political settlements of the 1930s and 1940s that provided the foundations for the democratic corporatism of the small European states since World War II are part of a long-term historical evolution that has distinguished the small European states from larger countries.

The small European countries, I have argued, have brought economic openness and domestic structures into a viable balance. I thus disagree with Barrington Moore's emphasis on the simplicity of the political circumstances of the small European states as well as the uniqueness of their political experience. Moore writes that "the fact that the smaller Western countries depend economically and politically on big and powerful ones means that the decisive causes of their politics lie outside their own boundaries. It also means that their political problems are not really comparable to those of large countries."[191] I hold, on the contrary, that the historical experience of the small European states has been more than mere passive reception of great-power influences. Indirectly, their experience illuminates those of the larger democratic states. The fortunes of the small European states are not simply determined by the great powers. Like the large advanced industrial states, "the weak in the world of the strong" must somehow succeed in making the requirements of international politics conform to the requirements of their domestic politics.[192] This is a predicament shared by all modern states. Under conditions in many ways less favorable than those in the large advanced industrial countries, the small European states have worked out a political solution that is neither simple nor unique.

This argument can be supported indirectly. The historical path that I have identified as leading to the corporatist compromise of the 1930s and 1940s was not preordained. Things could have turned out differently for any of the small European states, and in the case of Austria they did. Austrian history is, for the argument I have sketched, the exception that proves the rule. The Habsburg Empire was large, not small. Its economic openness was a matter of choice, not a necessity of life. Its domestic structure differed substantially from those of the other small European states: the landed aristocracy was relatively strong, urban interests were relatively weak, and the political Right was relatively united.[193] In the First Republic, Rokkan writes, "the Christian Social Party recruited the bulk of its support among the Catholic peasantry but was able to keep the rural-urban tensions within bounds through elaborate organizational differentiations within the party."[194] Between 1960 and 1977 the vote for the major party of the Right averaged 45 percent in Austria, the same as in the five large industrial countries, compared to 17 percent in the six other small European states.[195] Only Austria's two westernmost provinces, Tyrol and Vorarlberg, with their long traditions of independent peasantry, approximate the political pattern of the small European states. In fact in 1919 these two provinces expressed in a plebiscite their desire to join with Switzerland rather than the new Austrian republic. Austro-Marxism was a radical political and ideological force in European politics, which reacted to a strong feudal past, a relatively late extension of suffrage forced through general strikes in 1896 and 1905, and a structure of opportunities for political alliances and an attitude among its opponents that did not enhance the appeals of political moderation.[196]

Nor did Austria's industrialization strategy help in building bridges between different social sectors.[197] Because of Austria-Hungary's size, the Habsburg Monarchy eschewed export specialization. The industrialization of the German and Czech provinces—Lower and Upper Austria, Bohemia, and Moravia—accelerated greatly in the 1850s and 1860s, but even in these decades of lower tariffs the empire never embraced a free-trade policy that looked to exports as the stimulant for growth. Instead, Austria's industry developed its Eastern European markets behind high tariff walls. Until 1918 Austrians preferred to reap the benefits of empire behind tariff walls rather than prepare themselves for free trade and export specialization. Austrian tariffs were high in the middle of the nineteenth century when the Habsburg Empire proved to be too weak to counter Prussia's economic strategy of free trade in preparation for German unification. By European standards Austrian tariffs were very high in 1913.[198] Austria's industrial strategy thus never became, as it did in the other small European states, a reinforcement of tighter economic and social structures. Like the other small European states, Austria did adopt a system of proportional representation after the Habsburg Empire had collapsed.[199] But in sharp contrast, the adoption of PR elicited virtually no political debate. Instead, Christian Socials on the Right and Socialists on the Left hoped that in a deeply divided society proportional representation would make their debates less vituperative, electoral campaigns less personalistic, and politics more pragmatic. With a number of conflicts close to the boiling point in the early years of the First Republic, this was a prospect all political leaders welcomed. For when the empire crumbled at the end of World War I, Austria had the revolutionary break with the past that did not occur in the other small European states. In the words of Hans Daalder, "responsible government arrived in the wake of a revolution which left a heritage of dissensus about the very existence of the state."[200]

Historians of the First Republic typically explain the civil war of 1934 as a conjoining of forces: the loss of World War I, the crumbling of the empire, hyperinflation, unemployment, and the rise of fascism. These factors clearly had a major impact on Austrian politics in the 1930s, but my analysis places them in a broader historical perspective. If we picture Austria and the other small European states as trains and history as a set of switches, the Austrian train was at every branch switched in a direction opposite from the other small European states. The result in the 1930s was not class collaboration and the sharing of power in times of crisis, but civil war, repression, defeat in war, and foreign occupation. Austria's corporatism after 1945 emerged from these experiences rather than from long-term historical developments.

This interpretation of the Austrian case dissents from established interpretations in some ways and reinforces them in others. Austria has often been viewed as perhaps the most typically "consociational" regime in Europe. Since 1945 it has exhibited with particular clarity the coincidence of deep social cleavages and intense elite collaboration.[201] Yet I have argued that in its historical evolution Austria, far from being typical, is atypical. At the same time, though, there are parts of Austria's historical profile that fit extremely well with those of other social corporatist regimes. Austria's delayed industrialization was a "spurt that failed."[202] Its empire was continental rather than maritime, which reinforced, especially after its breakup, a national rather than an international orientation of business. Further reinforcing this national orientation, Austria has participated more than any other small European country in Europe's wars since 1815. Late industrialization encouraged worker militancy, and the absence of serious religious or ethnic cleavages after 1919 has favored the centralization of the labor movement. Had we included Austria in Table 7, it would have ranked last in five of the seven statistical indicators.[203] From this perspective, the comparison of Austria with the Scandinavian countries that feature social corporatism is entirely appropriate. Viewed in historical perspective, Austria's convergence with democratic corporatism after 1945 has been both instantaneous and total. In Austria, democratic corporatism is built on both a community of fate *(Astgemeinschaft)* and a community of fear *(Angstgemeinschaft)*.

The historical argument that I have outlined in this chapter seems to me to be both persuasive and plausible. Yet I recognize that historical analysis always has to entertain the possibility of alternative explanations. The difference between liberal and social corporatism in particular suggests an argument that deserves serious consideration. Social corporatism in Scandinavia emerged primarily because of the effects of worldwide Depression. The rise of the Left had been in the making for decades in Denmark, Norway, and Sweden; it was not helped by Nazi occupation or war. By contrast, liberal corporatism emerged primarily as a *result* of the threat of war, war itself, or Nazi occupation. Without these powerful international pressures, the Left in Switzerland, the Netherlands, and Belgium might have been incorporated into national political life on less favorable terms or not at all. In Austria it was the coinciding of both Depression and war that (against the background of the collapse of the empire, hyperinflation, and civil war) forced a belated convergence with the structure and strategy of democratic corporatism. This argument would explain why after 1945 democratic corporatism has been interpreted as both a consequence of the rise of the Left, which needed to be harnessed firmly to the enterprise of democratic capitalism, and as a morsel that remained for the Left after it suffered a fundamental defeat in its attempt to bring about democratic socialism. What first looks merely like a contradiction reflects a deeper historical truth. Different aspects of the crisis of the 1930s had different impacts on the small states. Unsurprisingly, the lessons people learn from history also differ.

The lesson I draw from this historical excursion is, however, quite clear. The corporatist compromise of the 1930s and 1940s was part of the broader historical evolution of the small European states. The domestic structures of the small European states were prepared for the possibility of compromise by distinctive characteristics: a weak landed nobility, relatively strong urban interests, and a divided Right; a moderate Left; no revolutionary break with the past; and a willingness to share power among political parties as illustrated by the adoption of proportional representation. In their industrial strategies of adjustment the small European states typically opted for export specialization. Structure and strategy interacted to make possible the compromise of the 1930s; thus they provided the political foundations for the democratic corporatism of the postwar period.

Viewed from this historical perspective, the 1930s and 1940s have multiple meanings for political life in the small European states. Depression and World War II forced the historical trajectories of the small European states into a common corporatist mold. These decades helped reveal important commonalities among different political actors and across diverse social sectors. Taking stock in 1939, Sir Ernest Simon concluded that the small European states afforded "definite proof that when the existing tide of barbarism has subsided, men will succeed in building a new and nobler civilization."[204]

CHAPTER FIVE

Conclusion

In the 1970s and 1980s, it is often said, the rate of economic change is accelerating while the capacity for political adjustment is shrinking. Throughout the advanced industrial world this divergence has become both a rallying cry for conservatives demanding fewer state intrusions in the market and a challenge to liberals seeking more effective state intervention. In the case of the small European states, this book has argued, economic flexibility and political stability are mutually contingent. The corporatist strain in the evolution of modern capitalism no longer yields readily to interpretations based on such established dichotomies as market and plan, private and public, efficiency and equity, Right and Left.

Under conditions of increasing vulnerability and openness, the large industrial states are groping toward workable solutions for the economic predicaments of the 1980s. The incremental, reactive policy of the small European states and a stable politics that can adjust to economic change provide a point of orientation that is both helpful and hopeful. Students of the international political economy are undecided whether the most important development of the 1970s lay in the predictable growth or the astonishing containment of protectionism. Similarly, students of domestic politics focus their attention both on the cartelization of politics in the hands of party, group, and bureaucratic elites and on the challenge that new social movements pose to established institutions. In analyzing the democratic corporatism of the small European states this book dissents from the view that capitalism is being driven by structural crisis toward collapse, nor does it support the view that capitalism is being resurrected by the vigors of market competition. Contradictions are inherent in all forms of political and economic domination. But democratic corporatism has been able to tolerate contradictions because of its accommodation rather than resistance to market competition and because of its inclusion of all significant actors in the decision-making process.

PROSPECTS

In the democratic corporatism of the small European states is a response to international pressures. Its proximate historical origin lies in the economic and political crisis of the 1930s and 1940s, its enduring strength in the postwar era in the liberal international economy of the 1960s and 1970s. the fear of authoritarianism, depression, and war contributed to its emergence in the 1930s. The enjoyment of democracy, prosperity, and peace contributed to its maintenance after 1945. The factors that create political regimes are not identical with those that maintain them.

At the beginning of the 1980s, however, it was no longer far-fetched to inquire whether the small European states were, for the first time since the 1930s, confronting external pressures so serious as eventually to effect a fundamental reorganization in their corporatist arrangements. How will the small European states fare in the emerging international economy?

Béla Kádár has listed some adverse developments that are putting the small European states under increasing strain.[1] A 50 percent decline in the growth rate of world trade (from 8.6% in 1960–73 to 4.2% in 1974–80) has created a decidedly less hospitable economic setting for small countries dependent on trade with others. Nonetheless, in all of the small European states except Denmark, foreign trade in goods and services continued to increase slightly between 1973 and 1979. Furthermore, sharp increases in the price of oil and unfavorable conditions in markets in which the small European states specialize (light industrial goods, semifinished products, and consumer durables) have caused adverse changes in relative prices. Between 1973 and 1980 the terms of trade declined by about 15 percent for Denmark, 11 percent for Belgium, and 7 percent for the Netherlands, Austria, Sweden, and Switzerland. By contrast, average terms of trade in Western Europe declined by less than 6 percent, and in West Germany they remained unchanged. Unsurprisingly, compared to 1973–78 the increase in total foreign indebtedness in 1979–82 was greater in the small European states than in the large industrial countries.[2]

The small European states are also facing entirely new problems, which stem from a doubling of the relative market share of the developing countries in less sophisticated industrial products. More poorly endowed with raw materials than large countries, the small European states have typically relied heavily on the processing and reexporting of imported primary products, areas into which newly industrializing countries are moving very rapidly. Changes now under way in the international economy thus point to the likelihood of an increasing "small-country squeeze."[3] During the last decade large advanced industrial states have shifted their R and D emphasis away from basic research in high-technology sectors toward applied research in more traditional industrial sectors. At the same time, a small group of rapidly developing countries has begun to wage a determined and effective export offensive with competitive products in some traditional industrial sectors.[4] Both developments will make it more difficult for the small European states to maintain their long-standing comparative advantage in these sectors. Thus the five small European states (Switzerland, the Netherlands, Belgium, Sweden, and Denmark) that account for the lion's share of engineering exports from small countries have been losing market share since 1973 in computers, office machinery, electrical-power-generating equipment, telecommunications, and scientific instruments.

The general economic climate facing the small European states has become harsher. From the vantage point of the mid-1980s this turn of events looks to be structural rather than cyclical. In the long term these adverse international pressures may affect the corporatist structures of the small European states in ways that are largely unpredictable today. Should the competitive pressures of the international economy create not sectorally specific crises but one crisis engulfing all of society, it is conceivable that democratic corporatism will be replaced by other political structures. The traditional advantage that corporatism enjoyed in the race for international competitiveness might turn into a severe handicap as liberal, statist, or authoritarian regimes find ways of reducing labor costs to a degree politically not feasible in corporatist systems. The pressures on business to move toward neoliberal arrangements and on the unions to favor state intervention may then become overwhelming. Once a solution to the problems of structural adjustment in a rapidly changing global economy, corporatism may then be viewed by business and labor as part of the problem. But these are speculations. Only fortune tellers claim to know when another major crisis will reshape the domestic structures of the small European states as fundamentally as did the events of half a century ago.

It is, however, important to keep in proper perspective the impact

Table 8. Economic performance of advanced industrial states, 1960–80

	(1) Annual unemployment as a percentage of total labor force				(2) Annual increase in real gross domestic product				(3) Annual changes in the consumer price index				(4) Balance of payments on current account as percentage of GNP			
	1960–80		1974–80		1960–80		1974–80		1960–80		1973–80		1960–80		1974–80	
	Rank	%	Rank	%	Rank	%	Rank	%	Rank	%	Rank	%	Rank	%	Rank	%
Switzerland	1	0.1	1	0.4	11	3.0	12	0.3	2	4.2	1	4.0	1	1.2	1	3.5
Netherlands	7	2.1	7	4.1	6	4.0	8	2.2	6	5.6	4	7.1	2.5	0.7	2	0.8
Belgium	11	3.3	10	5.7	5	4.1	5	2.4	4	5.2	5	8.1	6	0.1	9	−1.7
Sweden	6	1.9	4.5	1.9	10	3.3	9	1.8	8	6.6	9	10.3	10	−0.5	10	−1.8
Denmark	9	2.8	12	7.1	9	3.4	10	1.6	11	7.9	10	11.0	11	−2.5	11	−3.5
Norway	5	1.8	3	1.8	3	4.4	1	4.7	7	6.4	6	9.0	12	−3.4	12	−6.4
Austria	3.5	1.7	2	1.6	4	4.2	3	3.0	3	4.9	3	6.3	9	−0.4	8	−1.6
Small states' average	6.1	2.0	5.6	3.2	6.9	3.8	6.9	2.3	5.9	5.8	5.4	8.0	7.4	−0.7	7.6	−1.5
United States	12	5.5	11	6.8	8	3.5	6.5	2.3	5	5.3	7	9.2	5	0.3	4.5	0.1
United Kingdom	9	2.8	8	4.7	12	2.3	11	0.9	12	8.8	12	16.0	8	−0.3	6.5	−0.8
West Germany	3.5	1.7	6	3.5	7	3.7	6.5	2.3	1	3.9	2	4.8	2.5	0.7	3	0.6
France	9	2.8	9	4.8	2	4.6	4	2.8	9	6.8	11	11.1	7	−0.1	6.5	−0.8
Japan	2	1.5	4.5	1.9	1	7.7	2	3.7	10	7.4	8	9.7	4	0.4	4.5	0.1
Large states' average	7.1	2.9	7.7	4.3	6	4.4	6	2.4	7.4	6.4	8	10.2	5.3	0.2	5.0	−0.2

SOURCE. OECD, *Historical Statistics, 1960–1980* (Paris, 1982), pp. 37, 40, 77; David R. Cameron, "On the Limits of the Public Economy" (paper prepared for delivery at the Annual Meeting of the American Political Science Association, New York, September 1981), Table 11. W. D. McClam and P. S. Andersen, *Adjustment Performance of Open Economies: Some International Comparisons* (Basel: Bank for International Settlements, Monetary and Economic Department, December 1983), p. 10.

of these adverse economic changes on the small European states. Since the mid-1970s journalistic accounts of the declining fortunes of the small European states have often failed to take account of the economic and political success, measured in terms of both prosperity and legitimacy, that derive from a flexible strategy of adjustment. Eye-catching headlines portrayed, for example, Denmark as "heading for hell" and suggested that its "labor strife could bring national chaos."[5] Yet, as Andrew Boyd argued in 1978, "there is no reason that the Danes cannot look facts in the face. . . . Even in their fragmented political pattern there is a broader unity of purpose than before."[6]

In an article entitled "How Sweden's Middle Road Became a Dead End," *Forbes* magazine incredulously reported that under a conservative government Sweden's national budget deficit had increased from less than $1 billion in 1976 to $12 billion in 1981. To impress on its readers the disastrous consequences of a social welfare state run rampant, the article pointed out that "in the United States a comparable budget deficit would run $200 billion."[7] A ludicrous example in 1981 had, under a conservative Republican administration, become a political reality two years later. The borrowing record of the seven small European states in international capital markets has, moreover, been more favorable than that of the large industrial countries. Measured against the total value of international bonds issued to the five large industrial countries in 1978 and 1983, the share of the small European states declined from one-half to one-quarter.[8] The search for last month's or last year's "sick man of Europe," a favorite journalistic pastime, in the late 1970s mistook recalibration of political strategies of adjustment in a rapidly changing economic context for a crisis in the very structure of democratic corporatism.

Economic statistics measuring unemployment, growth, inflation, and the balance of payments are summarized in Table 8. They do not support the argument that the economic position of the small European states deteriorated in the 1970s relative to that of the large industrial countries. A rank-ordering by economic performance shows that, on average, the small European states performed better than the large industrial countries in containing inflation and unemployment, that they are holding their own in economic growth, and that they are lagging in their balance of payments. As the small European states experienced more adverse changes in the international economy in the 1970s than did the large states, the relative superiority of their economic performance is all the more noteworthy. It supports the view expressed in chapter 1, that a flexible strategy of adjustment is linked to economic and political success.[9]

Yet the new era of high interest rates, forced on the small European states by economic policy decisions in larger countries, has led to even greater difficulties than the two oil shocks of 1973 and 1979. The economic clouds over Europe have visibly darkened in recent years. Large budget deficits and high interest rates reinforced the fear that inflation is a long-term problem, and unemployment has risen to heights not seen since the 1930s. Belgium suffers from a structural crisis of industry. Denmark, like many other industrial states, is struggling to realign its generous welfare policies with projections of lower economic growth. The Netherlands and Norway—blessed by access to North Sea gas and oil—are temporarily cushioned from some of their neighbors' economic hardships, but at the risk of lagging behind their competitors in rationalizing production and consumption. Even Austria, which came through the 1970s strongly, is now being forced to put Keynesianism on ice.

Since the early 1980s all of the small European states have been tightening their belts and contemplating uneasily the prospect of stable or declining living standards in the 1980s. High levels of public consumption need to be readjusted to the requirements of smaller budget deficits and a reduced reliance on international capital markets. None of the small European states is contemplating a large-scale change in policy. Instead, these countries prefer to cut and trim as they consciously seek to improve their international competitiveness. Although social and political conflicts have increased, the inclination to seek piecemeal solutions persists. Political consensus is being strained and modified, but the small European states have resisted the temptation to discard the corporatist compromise.

One Danish banker, reflecting in the early 1980s on the economic crisis of his country in the global economy, remarked that "we have been living too well on borrowed money. We were on the way to hell, but we were doing it first class."[10] Since the mid-1970s the conservative Peoples party has become Denmark's second-largest. For the first time since 1901 a conservative, Poul Schlüter, became prime minister in 1982. Schlüter curtailed spending programs no longer compatible with Denmark's declining international competitiveness, and within a year the country's economic performance improved. In 1983 the inflation rate was halved to 5.5 percent, and interest rates dropped from 22 to 12.5 percent. For the first time in many years the country did not run a deficit in its balance of trade, and the unemployment rate appeared to have peaked at 11 percent. In 1984 the Danish electorate honored the conservative argument that change was in order to save the welfare state. It elected a four-party minority coalition government, still fourteen votes short of controlling Parliament. A modification of welfare policies is thus possible under conservative leadership; a dismantling of the welfare state is not.[11]

Similar political developments are also occurring in the Low Countries.[12] In both countries relatively unknown prime ministers, Ruud Lubbers in the Netherlands and Wilfried Martens in Belgium, both Christian Democrats, are fashioning economic policies designed to bring established welfare policies into line with new economic realities. In the Netherlands in 1983 Prime Minister Lubbers put into effect spending cuts, a work-sharing scheme, and a 3.5 percent reduction in public-service wages. As in Denmark, the majority of the electorate accepts the need for scaling down, but as one recent summary avers, "all large parties and leading politicians advocate the continuance of the Welfare State."[13] In Belgium the government prevailed in its confrontation with public-sector unions. There, as in the Netherlands, the growth of social security spending has been stopped. Even Austria's Socialists, in coalition with a small liberal party since 1983, are pruning welfare expenditures to contain a further growth in public deficits. Sweden's Social Democrats, returned to office in 1982, have emphasized the need for profitability in the public sector. In the words of a spokesman of the Department of Industry, "the state-owned companies had been saying for years that either we wanted them to operate politically or profitably, but that they could not do both. They have all been told explicitly that profitability is now the overriding aim."[14]

The calibration of welfare policies with international competitiveness has intensified political conflicts in the small European states. Prime Minister Olof Palme has called Sweden's businessmen "baboons and elephants." Nevertheless, while in Sweden "it seems clear that the old magic of the thirties won't work again," Arne Ruth writes, "there is no sign that any sizable portion of the Swedish population is seriously disaffected with the basic virtues of the welfare state, even if an increasing number complain about its cost."[15] In the autumn of 1983 Prime Minister Lubbers was jostled in public by angry protesters, an act of enormous social defiance in a country as orderly as the Netherlands. But considering the intensity and magnitude of conflict that the small European states experienced before World War II, these episodes should be viewed not as a prelude to class warfare but as part of a political struggle redefining the boundaries of legitimate expectations and demands in corporatist bargaining.

In the Netherlands, as in other small European states, "people dependent on state spending have been sheltered from changes in the world economy," the *New York Times* argued at the end of 1983, " and over the past few months what we have witnessed is social shock therapy."[16] The announcement of the death of Dutch corporatism in the early 1980s may be as premature as was a similar announcement in the early 1970s. Recent interpretations of Dutch politics, for example, emphasize that in the late 1970s extensive cooperation persisted, together with intense conflict, encouraged by the vulnerability of the Dutch economy and concealed by a rhetorical conflict at the national level.[17] "The rise and fall of the postwar social contract in the Netherlands," writes Steven Wolinetz, "suggests that such corporatist arrangements can be durable but not immutable."[18] But such a focus on the instabilities and temporary breakdowns of corporatist arrangements misses an essential point. Democratic corporatism is not an institutional solution to the problems of economic change but a political mechanism for coping with change.

The political staying power of corporatist structures is reflected in the way that these structures constrain the building of political coalitions that might fundamentally challenge existing institutions and policies. Such coalitions are made possible by recurrent cycles of industrial innovation, maturation, and imitation that redefine the economic and political interests which different actors have in the international economy.[19] Major firms and industry associations react to new circumstances by fashioning new coalitions to press for political changes that may be as specific as particular industrial adjustment policies or as general as broad regime characteristics. Because corporatist structures encourage flexibility, collaboration, and the absorption of the political consequences of economic dislocations, alternative political coalitions are not easily formed. The political logic inherent in the corporatist structures of the small European states instead enhances political predictability and incremental adjustment.[20] These structures narrow power differences and link state and society intimately. They thus succeed in capturing potential coalitions among changing political forces and in channeling political energies into the relegitimizing of corporatist arrangements.

More severe international constraints will make the domestic politics of the small European states more cohesive, at least in the medium term. The formal, "consociational" arrangements made between political parties in the 1960s in several of the small continental European states have rapidly eroded, and Social Democratic hegemony in Scandinavia partially decomposed in the 1970s. Both developments, however, have so far left the democratic corporatism of these seven states remarkably unchanged. Should economic crisis intensify, inter-locking interests, political practices, and institutions in the small European states may well yield, as Charles Sabel argues, "to the idea of a community of the vulnerable [in] a general commitment to share equitably the burdens of adapting social institutions to a continuously changing world."[21] In the years ahead a growing sense of vulnerability should, on questions of strategy in the international economy, unite political opponents in the small states who disagree on many other substantive issues. At the same time the policy networks of the small European states show few signs of change that would deprive policy makers of the sizable number of policy instruments that they now control. The emergence of alternative political structures of participation and representation in the 1970s, for example citizen initiatives or single-issue movements, may well complement rather than replace the corporatist arrangements that have developed since the 1930s.

Changes in the form of corporatist collaboration thus do not necessarily signify its disappearance. After 45 years Sweden decided to move to a more decentralized and possibly conflictual form of labor negotiations in 1984.[22] But this decision does not necessarily ring the death bell for democratic corporatism. In the Netherland the move toward decentralized labor negotiations has been under way for two decades without creating noticeably higher numbers of strikes or impairing, in the 1970s and early 1980s, a voluntary incomes policy that has been remarkably successful. The Swedish decision signals instead that both unions and business are looking for new institutional ways for coping with Sweden's economic difficulties. In the optimistically sentimental words of Flora Lewis, "The vision of progress is no longer blinding, but neither is it dead . . . once again, Sweden's example can inspire confidence. It is certainly not a model. It has taken some wrong turns and it is unique in ways that others cannot and would not wish to copy. But it is a reminder that rational argument and warm-hearted resolve found ways to leave the bad old days behind, and doubtless can again."[23]

COMPARISONS

Small states with open and vulnerable economies can respond effectively to changes in the global economy. A fairly wide range of responses is possible, as illustrated by liberal and social variants of democratic corporatism.

As the outbreak of a bitter strike in Sweden illustrated in 1980, democratic corporatism does not magically transform social and political hostility into harmony. Instead, it offers an institutional mechanism for mobilizing the consensus necessary to live with the costs of rapid economic change. For the small European states a reactive, flexible, and incremental policy of industrial adjustment occurs together with an astonishing capacity to adjust politically to the consequences of economic change. The small European states adapt domestically to economic change imposed by an international economy that they cannot hope to control. The structure of the small European states is not well suited to a political strategy based on liberal or statist premises. The relations between business, the unions, and the state are organized in a manner that compromises the logic both of unmitigated market competition and of decisive state intervention. Elaborate institutional networks and a complex policy process yield easily to marginal compensations for affected interests but strongly resist a single-minded devotion to entrepreneurial initiative or bureaucratic leadership. In sum, the small European states embody the politics of neither liberalism nor statism, but of corporatism.

The economic openness and corporatist structures of the small European states have had a strong effect on their political strategies. Open economies inspire a fear of retaliation, foreclosing protection as a political option for coping with adverse economic change. But in facilitating the emergence of corporatist domestic structures, economic openness encourages political compensations for change, foreclosing, if indirectly, strategies of structural transformation. Thus the two strategic responses with which liberal and statist industrial countries deal with change are not open to the small European states. Instead of seeking to export or preempt the costs of change, the small European states have chosen to live with the costs of change by compensating for them, politically and economically. An open economy and a position of international marginality generate a common outlook shared across the main political divisions in domestic politics. In 1937–38 both capitalist Switzerland and socialist Sweden witnessed the signing of peace agreements between business and unions. These agreements prepared the ground for a pattern of political accommodation in the postwar period that has been responsive to the requirements of international competitiveness.

As the large, advanced industrial states grope toward more adequate ways of responding to the risks and opportunities of the international economy, the example of the small European states will vary in relevance for them. Germany provides perhaps the closest approximation to the political practices characteristic of the small states. West

Germany's corporatism derives as much from openness, dependence, and a sense of vulnerability brought about by the diminished size of the Bonn Republic after 1945 as from the implantation of its political parties in fresh democratic soil.[24] Throughout the 1970s German politics fostered a consensual style of policy making among political actors who conceived of one another as social partners and controlled relatively centralized institutions, especially on questions of economic and social policy.

West Germany looms very large in the economic fortunes of its smaller neighbors. For example, political choices in Bonn and Frankfurt on questions of inflation, unemployment, and the value of the deutsche mark are of enormous consequence for Switzerland and Austria. More generally, Germany has a profound effect on the other small European states. During the interwar years and in the early 1950s Germany's most prestigious economics research institute issued a series of monographs dealing with the economic development of the small European states. These studies provide a rich source of data for tracing the economic dependence of the small European states on the German economy since the middle of the nineteenth century.[25] Marcello de Cecco has recently extended this interpretation to the 1970s. He argues that "one cannot fail to be struck by the central role these countries have played in recent years in stabilizing the international trade balance of Germany. . . . These countries play a vital role in generating demand for the German investment goods industry."[26] In 1980, for example, West Germany registered massive trade deficits with both the United States and Japan. But the small European states absorbed two-fifths of total German exports and their total trade deficit with Germany was more than $11 billion, more than twice as large as the overall trade surplus of Germany in the same year.

On the surface, the close relation between economic openness and dependence, on the one hand, and the corporatist structures of the small European states, on the other, suggests an analogy to the "dependent capitalism" in Third World countries on which much theoretical and empirical work was focused in the 1970s. Latin American authoritarianism, for example, is viewed as a concomitant or consequence of the penetration of relatively weak domestic structures by the forces of global capitalism, the multinational corporation its most dynamic agent. Overlooking some important qualitative differences, scholars in the small European states have pointed to similarities between the position of their states and that of many Third World countries.[27] But the small European states are not in the periphery of the world capitalist system. Their insertion into the international economy occurred at an earlier date, when political and economic conditions favored national autonomy. This early development is reflected in the structural characteristics of their foreign trade. The geographic and commodity concentration of foreign trade and the imbalance between the import of raw materials and the export of manufactured goods, as well as between the export of "traditional" as compared to "modern" manufactured products, are greater in the small European states than in the large ones; but they are smaller than in the developing countries.

Developing countries depend on the import of goods, capital, and technology. The small European states depend on exports. Their economic openness and dependence on global markets shape free-trade policies that are conducive to the international competitiveness of their export industries and a politics that is geared to contain uncompetitive wage settlements and price increases. Stephen Krasner has shown that in the small European states and in the developing countries there exists a strong statistical relationship between changes in trade and changes in government revenue. However, in 1974–75 five of the six small European states included in his analysis increased government revenues in real terms, compared to only 19 of 38 developing countries. Krasner concludes that "the revenues of small industrialized countries are susceptible to changes in their trade, but these countries appear able to at least resist an absolute decline . . . while almost half of the developing countries that experienced a decline in trade also suffered a decline in government revenues."[28] It is thus not surprising that in the 1970s the small European states (with the exception of Austria) relied less on established ways of raising tax revenues than did the large industrial countries.[29]

Furthermore, and in contrast to the developing countries, the small European states have in their service sectors a valuable set of economic activities that significantly narrow the perpetual trade deficit imposed by the structure of their economies. Although the small European states depend heavily on foreign investments both for a continuous modernization of their economies and for further reductions in the deficit of their trade balance, the constraints that derive from this dependence remain latent. Austria is one small state that relies on foreign corporations to modernize and diversify its industry, but it has succeeded in making these corporations adhere to a code of conduct, for example in the area of employment, that apparently agrees with the political objectives of the government rather than the narrower economic objectives of management. Finally, the small European states, unlike many of the developing countries, have been able, through their domestic structures, to maintain a great degree of autonomy from foreign influence. This autonomy accounts for the great differences in strategy with which Switzerland, the Netherlands, and Belgium confront the world economy, compared to Austria, Denmark, and Norway.

The pressures of world markets on the domestic structures of the small European states are less intense and less direct than on the developing countries. In the latter countries there frequently emerges an alliance between the state bureaucracy, the military, and segments of the business community. Authoritarian structures that exclude labor in time of crisis may adopt repressive strategies. None of this has occurred in the small European states since 1945. But external pressures have been greater in the small European states than in large industrial countries. The openness and dependence of their economies explains the prevalence of strong corporatist structures rather than liberal or statist forms of capitalism.

Daniel Chirot has suggested that dependence and economic backwardness have created true examples of social corporatism in small socialist countries undergoing rapid development, countries such as Romania. Chirot's argument is provocative because in the 1930s Romania produced perhaps the most important theorist of corporatism, Mihaïl Manoïlescu. His theories, Chirot argues, can be found in the development strategies of both Left and Right throughout the advanced peripheral and semiperipheral parts of the world. In contrast to the authoritarian Romanian regime of the interwar period, this socialist variant of corporatism is freed from the shackles of traditional class structures and thus can move decisively rather than halfheartedly to new political arrangements. "Manoïlescu was correct. The twentieth century is the century of corporatism. But he was wrong to think that the weak and fraudulent steps taken by fascism in the 1920s and 1930s were significant. It is only now, outside the old capitalist centers, that societies which proudly proclaim themselves marxist are building genuine corporatism."[30] Although Chirot is wrong to dismiss the relevance of corporatist arrangements to the political practices of capitalist states, his argument dovetails with mine. Authoritarian corporatism, he argues, can be viewed as a political formula for mobilizing resources in the name of either fascism or socialism. Social or liberal variants of corporatism, I have argued, are political formulae with which to mobilize political consensus in the name of either democratic socialism or liberal capitalism.

However, dependence on the international economy limits how far the two variants of democratic corporatism can differ. The convergence in Switzerland's and Austria's exchange-rate policies serves as a good illustration. Although the two countries differed in the methods by which they permitted a sharp appreciation of their currencies in the 1970s, the methods with which they pursued a "hard-currency option" began to converge in the late 1970s.[31] Throughout most of the 1970s Switzerland specified strict targets for monetary growth and let the franc float autonomously upward in foreign-exchange markets. Only when in 1978–79 the rate of appreciation reached levels that threatened to price Swiss exporters out of world markets did the Swiss National Bank step in and tie the franc informally to the deutsche mark, the currency of Switzerland's most important trading partner. The director of the powerful and market-oriented Crédit Suisse concluded in his reflections on the 1970s that "the value of money, unlike almost everything else under the sun, cannot be left to the free play of market forces but needs to be regulated by the State."[32]

Austria, by way of contrast, never attempted to maintain monetary sovereignty in the 1970s. The governor of Austria's Central Bank acknowledges that "Austrian monetary policy is made in Frankfurt."[33] Market forces were never permitted to determine the value of the schilling; instead, the Central Bank intervened in foreign-exchange markets to maintain a stable exchange rate with the deutsche mark. The Austrians refer to this as a hard-currency option, misleadingly in years such as 1978–80 when the deutsche mark, and with it the schilling, depreciated against the dollar and other major currencies. When either the steadiness or the strength of the deutsche mark is in question, as respectively in early and late 1980, the debates over Austria's policy reveal the same sorts of confusions that existed in Switzerland in the late 1970s and early 1980s. Although Austria and Switzerland differed in how they pursued their foreign-exchange policies throughout most of the 1970s, in the end market pressures forced the Swiss to abandon their autonomous policy and led to a convergence in the policy of the two countries.

This book reflects on a basic theme of contemporary political analysis, the interaction of historically shaped domestic structures with the world economy. That interaction has political consequences which are far from trivial. The political tensions and changes that the small European states experience in their relations with the world economy have led to the convergence of different forms of corporatism. Corporatism emanates both from the internal logic of the domestic structures and from the external requirements of the international economy.

LESSONS

What, if any, are the lessons America can learn? The increasing openness of the economy has made American industry ever more aware of the problems of international competitiveness—problems that have long been familiar to business in the small European states. Between 1970 and 1980 the ratio of U.S. exports to final sale of goods in U.S. markets more than doubled, from 9 to 19 percent; the increase in imports was sharper still, from 9 to 22 percent. Even in product categories or industry segments covered by America's restrictive trade policies, import penetration increased sharply between 1960 and 1979: from 4 to 14 percent in steel, from 6 to 51 percent in consumer electronics, and from 2 to 10 percent in apparel.[34] These figures understate the extent to which America has become an integral part of world markets. By 1980 more than two-thirds of the industrial goods produced in America were actively competing with foreign products.[35] The growing dependence of the American economy on global markets reinforces a sense of vulnerability. Since the mid-1970s the success of Japan's export offensive on the American market has convinced a growing number of Americans that national competitiveness is determined by more than endowment with natural resources and the workings of the market. The strong position that Japanese steel, automobile, and computer industries achieved within two decades suggests that the economic security of American workers and American firms is threatened by Japan's superior ways of organizing for international competition.

Growing economic openness also marks large advanced industrial states in Europe. According to World Bank data, between 1970 and 1980 the share of manufacturing imports grew from 16 to 23 percent in France, from 19 to 31 percent in West Germany, from 16 to 28 percent in Britain, and from 9 to 15 percent in the external trade of the EEC.[36] Geoffrey Shepherd and François Duchêne show similar increases in Europe's major industrial sectors. Glenn Fong has calculated that in the 1970s the rate of change at which the economies of the five large industrial states opened to the international economy was about 50 percent faster than for the small industrial states. America is thus not alone in experiencing sharp increases in economic openness and vulnerability.[37] Under these novel conditions the notion of steering the economy (with all relevant variables under direct control) may, according to Fritz Scharpf, be less useful than the notion of small-boat sailing (in which the captain keeps the boat afloat through skillful adaptation to and exploitation of circumstances beyond control).[38] We could do worse than look to the example of the small European states for lessons in how to react politically to conditions that are new to us and old for them.

Beset by mounting economic troubles during the last decade, the United States has found foreign success stories increasingly attractive. It is evident in America's recent infatuation with and resentment of Japan. Like small boys at a local fair pressing hard against the back of the tent, curious American intellectuals and politicians are often reduced to primitive forms of political voyeurism. Confronted with the astonishing success of the small European states in the 1950s, one economist observed ruefully (and unconvincingly) that "policy has been somewhat more sensible in the relatively open economies."[39]

Switzerland and Austria stand out as the two clearest examples of the liberal and social variants of democratic corporatism to which the other small European states approximate in different degrees. In order to account for the exemplary success of these countries in the 1970s some propose explanations that reflect what a friend of mine calls the Seven Dwarf Theory of Central Europe: the Austrians and the Swiss are both so successful because they depart for work each morning with a happy yodel. In one newspaper column George Will subscribed to the audaciously commonsensical notion that Austrians like to work and are, therefore, economically successful.[40] The explanation will no doubt please Catholics in Austria, dismay Calvinists in Switzerland, confound faithful readers of Weber's *Protestant Ethic* everywhere, and leave unconvinced those who value evidence; in the mid-1970s the Austrians worked shorter hours than the Swiss. Representative Henry Reuss, chairman of the Joint Economic Committee, expressed this bafflement: "When you put America's economic performance up against this country's, one is certainly compelled to seek what there is about the Austrian structure which enables your much better performance to occur."[41]

In an article entitled "Are There Any Swiss Lessons for the U.S.?" one of Switzerland's most powerful bankers offered scant hope. He concluded, "My country's institutions are tailor-made for a small nation with the historical peculiarities of Switzerland."[42] Another analysis links Austria's success to political commitments not easily transferred to other societies: "The lesson which can be learned is that tripartite bargaining offers prospects for the attainment of some of the objectives of the working people. The particular forms, machinery, and administrative arrangements are of less importance than the desire to achieve certain broad policy goals in an unstable world."[43] Without linking his prescription for America to the political experience of the small European states, Robert Reich summarizes aptly the secret to their success in arguing that "we need political institutions that are as versatile as flexible-system enterprises—less concerned with making 'correct' decisions than with making correctable ones; less obsessed with avoiding error than with detecting and correcting for error; more devoted to responding to changing conditions and encouraging new enterprises than to stabilizing the environment for old enterprises."[44] In the political parlance of one conservative economist Reich's prescription is nothing more than "fashionable fascism," an unfortunate oversimplification.[45]

This book offers no easy solutions to America's problems. Economic performance measures have influenced the argument at several points, but they are not the book's primary concern. I have argued, rather, that the small European states frame political choices in a distinctive way. Their choices are conditioned by two sets of forces: historically shaped domestic structures and the pressures of the world economy. These two sets of forces interact. And it is in the process of interaction—the unending and limited conflicts over economic and social issues—that the requirements of domestic and international politics converge in a flexible strategy of adjustment.

We cannot apply the "lessons" of the small European states for the simple reason that we cannot remake our history. The very attempt of a Republican president drastically to recast the shape of America in the 1980s illustrates the narrow political limits in this country of "unlimited opportunities." Yet even while writing this book, I could observe history changing America. The declining fortunes of America's steel and automobile industries, as well as the wood stoves reappearing in New England, illustrate our increasing economic openness and vulnerability. Suzanne Berger and Michael Piore have rightly pointed to the disadvantages of a narrow conception of political possibilities. This book was motivated by an idea that they have put well: the largest problem we face, they write, is "our beliefs about the limits of the possible. In order to release both imagination and will from the constraints of false necessity, we need a vision of the diverse possibilities that can be realized within industrial societies."[46]

Looking at the politics of unfamiliar countries may be confusing, but it can also be illuminating, even liberating. The small European states offer us an intriguing perspective because in an era of shrinking economic resources their political conflicts do not resemble the image, so familiar in Washington, of wrestlers in a china shop. "Bigness in a nation has certain advantages," writes Andrew Shonfield, "but it does sometimes succeed in swamping the national perception of what is obvious to smaller people."[47] That national perception is a distinctive trademark. The small European states acknowledge that policy is an essential ingredient in reaffirming and modifying an always evolving consensus, that victory in any battle must be balanced against the need to assure the loser of another round in a protracted, limited war. It is of course a sobering thought that other countries, especially small, powerless, and vulnerable ones, are better equipped than the large, powerful, and less vulnerable United States to deal politically with the economic dislocations and uncertainties of the 1980s. The record of the 1970s, however, and the argument of this book suggest that such a thought cannot be dismissed easily. But in this case the bad news brings good in its train. Our difficulty in grasping the political and economic achievements of the small European states reflects a lack of political imagination—a lack more easily remedied than many another.

This book has focused on the political consequences of economic openness and international vulnerability. "Adversarial politics" typical of the United States is constrained in the small European states by awareness of common interest and the "unitary politics" it creates.[48] Typical of small European states is decision making by consensus, which supplements majority rule. A "unitary politics" can of course emerge, at least for a time, in large industrial states: with technocrats through a logic of things that reduces politics to administration; with Weberians through the institutionalization of charisma; with Marxists through the struggle for socialism; and with conservatives through wise statesmen determining the collective good in the realm of moral philosophy rather than individual preference. Typically, though, all such appearances are temporary; as Jane Mansbridge argues, "Like war itself, efforts to create a unitary 'moral equivalent of war' lose their glamor."[49] America provides ample illustrations. On economic questions policy initiatives are often couched in the language of national security. The National Defense Highway Act, the National Education Act, and a variety of energy programs are all described aptly by what Theodore Lowi has claimed of American foreign policy more generally: in overselling the threat it also oversells the remedy.[50]

Since the 1930s the small European states have experienced in economic openness and international vulnerability at least a partial substitute for the "moral equivalent of war" (when not experiencing war itself). A flexible economy and cooperative politics has been one consequence. A second consequence, not stressed here, is the danger inherent in corporatist arrangements. The widespread notion of a common good, suggested by international economic pressures, makes political conflicts over basic political choices illegitimate for longer periods of time than in large industrial states. It is no accident that Parliament, as the institutional arena where such choices are typically fought out in liberal democracies, has less importance in Switzerland and Austria than in any other advanced industrial state.[51] As large industrial states increasingly experience those consequences of economic openness and vulnerability to which the small European states have had decades to adapt, the trend toward democratic corporatism will undoubtedly alter the style and substance of democratic politics.

In some sectors of American society formal or informal corporatist arrangements have appeared as a natural response to the economic crisis of the late 1970s and early 1980s. Chrysler's Loan Guarantee Board was staffed by members of the federal government, management, and the unions. New York City's fiscal crisis was managed by informal cooperation between bankers like Felix Rohatyn, trade union officials like Victor Gotbaum, and state officials. Less spectacular attempts have occurred in other situations with mixed success. Industry advisory committees, set up during the Tokyo Round of trade negotiations, collaborated successfully because of the threat posed by foreign competition. By contrast, the Steel Tripartite Commission, confronted with a severe crisis in the American steel industry, failed to overcome ideological and legal barriers to successful cooperation. Where the perception of vulnerability and crisis approaches levels considered "normal" in the small European states, corporatism has become part of America's political repertoire.

But short of a general crisis engulfing all of American society—a crisis like the Great Depression or World War II—corporatism faces substantial difficulties at the national level. In many ways corporatism is antithetical to the core of American politics. Distrust of administrative discretion has encouraged a litigational style of politics and an emphasis on procedural fairness that is at odds with the requirements of corporatist bargaining. Furthermore, American society is relatively unorganized: peak associations that can claim broad social support are rare. For example, corporatism in America would have to include organized labor, yet the proportion of workers organized by American trade unions is only between one-half and one-third of corresponding numbers in the small European states—and the American proportion is declining. Social movements such as the civil rights movement or the women's movement effect political changes on their own in America. In the small European states they are typically captured by existing groups or political parties. In the well-organized societies of the small European states corporatism is inclusionary. Transplanted to America, corporatism tends toward exclusion.

In the case of the small European states, the interaction of national and global factors to force a flexible policy of adaptation is not new. Reflecting on the 1930s, Carol Major Wright concluded in 1939: "If it is not likely that a small country can effectively 'take arms against a sea of troubles,' it is equally clear that efforts at isolation from world market changes are costly and indeed ruinous . . . The little countries must emulate David who rejected the hampering armour that Saul pressed upon him and relied on his mobility and quick adaptability."[52] The insistence on the need for adaptability that Wright derived from the experience of the 1930s is confirmed by the 1970s and 1980s, but the prescription for a certain type of government intervention is not. Today the air resounds with calls for "positive" rather than "negative" adjustment, for policies that accelerate rather than slow the shift of factors of production from "declining" to "growth" sectors. The international bureaucrats who first coined these phrases in the mid-1970s hoped to elevate to a programmatic level the political necessity for a rapid restructuring of domestic economies. How else could one avoid a dangerous relapse into another round of protectionism, 1930s-style? The capacity to maneuver abroad and adapt at home requires a mobility of the factors of production that among the successful developing countries frequently coincides with authoritarianism and political repression.[53] This is an unlikely choice for the small European states. During the last half-century all the advanced industrial states have witnessed vast transformations in the character of their economy and politics. Calls for "positive adjustment" are surrounded by the same air of unreality as policy prescriptions derived from the venerable distinction between market and plan: through excessive repetition they soon acquire the unenviable status of platitudes. Issued often with little understanding of the capacities of political structures and the pressures acting upon them, these exhortations represent the Peter Pan approach to public policy: one closes one's eyes and wishes really hard.

The distinctive strategy by which the small European states adjust to change derives from corporatist domestic structures that have their historical origin in the 1930s and 1940s. Crisis conditions can create domestic structures that combine democratic practices with political efficacy and economic efficiency. In the past decades the large industrial states have moved uneasily part of the way toward the conditions of economic openness and vulnerability long characteristic of the small European states. For optimists among us, this is cause for cheer: it represents movement toward an essential condition if this decade is to deliver the promises rather than the horrors of the 1930s.

The adjustment strategy of the small European states is summed up by the story of the snake, the frog, and the owl. Fearful of being devoured by the snake, the frog asks the owl how he might survive. The owl's response is brief and cryptic: learn how to fly. None of the small European states has learned to soar like the eagle. What they have learned to cultivate is an amazing capacity to jump. Although they appear to land on their stomachs, in fact they always land on their feet and retain the ability to jump again and again in different directions, correcting their course as they go along. In a world of great uncertainty and high-risk choices, this is an intelligent response. Frogs can escape snakes, and the small corporatist states can continue to prosper—not because they have found a solution to the problem of change but because they have found a way to live with change.

Notes

CHAPTER 1. *Introduction*

1. "The Reindustrialization of America," *Business Week,* special issue, 30 June 1980; Barry Bluestone an Bennett Harrison, *The Deindustrialization of America: Plant Closings, Community Abandonment, and the Dismantling of Basic Industry* (New York: Basic, 1982).

2. These figures are calculated in constant U.S. dollars at the exchange rate and price level of 1975. See Organization for Economic Co-operation and Development (OECD), *National Accounts: Main Aggregates,*vol. 1: *1953–1982* (Paris, 1984), p. 86.

3. See, for example, C. Fred Bergsten, "The United States and the World Economy," in J. Michael Finger and Thomas D. Willett, eds., "The Internationalization of the American Economy," *Annals of the American Academy of Political and Social Science* 460 (March 1982), 5.

4. Chalmers Johnson, *MITI and the Japanese Miracle: The Growth of Industrial Policy, 1925–1975* (Stanford: Stanford University Press, 1982).

5. For example, Philip H. Trezise and Yukio Suzuki, "Politics, Government, and Economic Growth in Japan," in Hugh Patrick and Henry Rosovsky, eds., *Asia's New Giant: How the Japanese Economy Works* (Washington, D.C.: Brookings, 1976), pp. 753–811; Trezise, "Industrial Policy in Japan," in Margaret E. Dewar, ed., *Industry Vitalization: Toward a National Industrial Policy* (New York: Pergamon, 1982), pp. 177–95; and George C. Eads, "Industrial Strategies for High Technology," unpublished paper, University of Maryland, February 1983. See also Manhattan Institute for Policy Research, "Industrial Policy, Part 2: Is a New Deal the Answer?" *Manhattan Report on Economic Policy* 3, 2 (1983).

6. Robert Kuttner, *The Economic Illusion: False Choices between Prosperity and Social Justice* (Boston: Houghton Mifflin, 1984). See also Howard D. Samuel and Brian Turner, "An Industrial Policy for the United States?" *Transatlantic Perspectives* 5 (July 1981), 14–17.

7. For example, Melvyn B. Krauss, *The New Protectionism: The Welfare State and International Trade* (New York: New York University Press, 1978); Bruce R.

Scott, "Can Industry Survive the Welfare State?" *Harvard Business Review,* September–October 1982, 70–84.

8. See William Greider, "The Education of David Stockman," *Atlantic Monthly,* December 1981, 27–54.

9. Robert Reich, *The Next American Frontier* (New York: Times, 1983), p. 232.

10. There is very little in English on the political economies of the small European states. A textbook-style survey is Earl H. Fry and Gregory A. Raymond, eds., *The Other Western Europe: A Political Analysis of the Smaller Democracies* (Santa Barbara: ABC-Clio, 1980). A recent useful compendium of small-states theory is Otmar Höll, ed., *Small States in Europe and Dependence* (Vienna: Braumüller, 1983); see also Michael Handel, *Weak States in the International System* (London: Cass, 1981). The experience of the Scandinavian countries is treated in depth in Gösta Esping-Andersen, *The Social Democratic Road to Power* (Princeton: Princeton University Press, forthcoming). On the Low Countries see Arend Lijphart, *The Politics of Accommodation: Pluralism and Democracy in the Netherlands* (Berkeley: University of California Press, 1968); Lijphart, ed., *Conflict and Coexistence in Belgium: The Dynamics of a Culturally Divided Society* (Berkeley: University of California, Institute of International Studies, 1981); and a special issue of *Acta Politica* 19 (January 1984). I have written in detail on Austria and Switzerland in *Corporatism and Change: Austria, Switzerland, and the Politics of Industry* (Ithaca: Cornell University Press, 1984).

11. Margret Sieber, *Dimensionen kleinstaatlicher Auslandabhängigkeit,* University of Zurich, Kleine Studien zur Politischen Wissenschaft, nos. 206–7 (1981), 155, 165.

12. Stephen D. Krasner, "United States Commercial and Monetary Policy: Unraveling the Paradox of External Strength and Internal Weakness," in Peter J. Katzenstein, ed., *Between Power and Plenty: Foreign Economic Policies of Advanced Industrial States* (Madison: University of Wisconsin Press, 1978), p. 52.

13. My thinking on this point has been influenced in particular by Charles E. Lindblom, *Politics and Markets: The World's Political-Economic Systems* (New York: Basic, 1977); Robert B. Kvavik, *Interest Groups in Norwegian Politics* (Oslo: Universitetsforlaget, 1976), pp. 19–22; and Wolfgang Streeck and Philippe C. Schmitter, "Community, Market, State—and Associations? The Prospective Contribution of Interest Governance to Social Order," *European University Institute Working Papers,* no. 94 (March 1984).

14. Some of the best recent studies of industrial policy include John Zysman, *Governments, Markets, and Growth: Financial Systems and the Politics of Industrial Change* (Ithaca: Cornell University Press, 1983); Ira C. Magaziner and Robert Reich, *Minding America's Business: The Decline and Rise of the American Economy* (New York: Harcourt Brace Jovanovich, 1982); a special issue of *Journal of Public Policy* 3 (February 1983) on industrial policies of OECD countries, edited by Wyn Grant and David McKay; William Diebold, *Industrial Policy as an International Issue* (New York: McGraw-Hill, 1980); F. Gerard Adams and Lawrence Klein, eds., *Industrial Policies for Growth and Competitiveness: An Economic Perspective* (Lexington, Mass.: Lexington, 1983); Susan B. Strange and Roger Tooze, eds., *The International Politics of Surplus Capacity: Competition for Market Shares in the World Recession* (London: Allen & Unwin, 1981); Grant, *The Political Economy of Industrial Policy* (London: But-

terworths, 1982); and Johnson, *MITI and the Japanese Miracle*. On America specifically see Reich, *Next American Frontier*, and Zysman and Laura Tyson, eds., *American Industry in International Competition: Government Policies and Corporate Strategies* (Ithaca: Cornell University Press, 1983).

15. I am indebted to Robert Keohane, Charles Sabel, David Vogel, and John Zysman for pressing me to think systematically about the issue of success and failure.

16. The main studies of corporatism include Philippe C. Schmitter and Gerhard Lehmbruch, eds., *Trends toward Corporatist Intermediation* (Beverly Hills: Sage, 1979); Suzanne D. Berger, ed., *Organizing Interests in Western Europe* (Cambridge: Cambridge University Press, 1981) Lehmbruch and Schmitter, eds., *Patterns of Corporatist Policy-Making* (Beverly Hills: Sage, 1982); and Francis G. Castles, ed., *The Impact of Parties* (Beverly Hills: Sage, 1982). See also Ulrich von Alemann and Rolf G. Heinze, "Neo-Korporatismus: Zur neuen Diskussion eines alten Begriffs," *Zeitschrift für Parlamentsfragen* 10 (December 1979), 469–87.

17. See Heinrich August Winkler, ed., *Organisierter Kapitalismus* (Göttingen: Vandenhoeck & Ruprecht, 1974).

18. I am indebted to a long conversation with Gabriel Almond for this idea. See also his article "Corporatism, Pluralism, and Professional Memory," *World Politics* 35 (January 1983), 245–60.

19. Peter Lange, "The Conjunctural Conditions for Consensual Wage Regulation: An Initial Examination of Some Hypotheses" (paper prepared for presentation at the Annual Meeting of the American Political Science Association, New York, September 1981), p. 2

20. Stein Rokkan, "Norway: Numerical Democracy and Corporate Pluralism," in Robert A. Dahl, ed., *Political Oppositions in Western Democracies* (New Haven: Yale University Press, 1966), pp. 70–115.

21. Arend Lijphart, "Consociational Democracy," *World Politics* 21 (October 1968), 217. See also Val R. Lorwin, "Segmented Pluralism: Ideological Cleavages and Political Cohesion in the Smaller European Democracies," in Kenneth D. McRae, ed., *Consociational Democracy: Political Accommodation in Segmented Societies* (Toronto: McClelland & Stewart, 1974), pp. 42–44.

22. Johan P. Olsen, "Integrated Organizational Participation in Government," in Paul C. Nystrom and William H. Starbuck, eds., *Handbook of Organizational Design*, vol. 2 (Oxford: Oxford University Press, 1981), p. 502.

23. The Austrian case is accounted for by the explanation offered below in chapter 4.

24. See McRae, *Consociational Democracy;* Martin O. Heisler, ed., *Politics in Europe: Structures and Processes in some Postindustrial Democracies* (New York: McKay, 1974); and Arend Lijphart, *Democracy in Plural Societies: A Comparative Exploration* (New Haven: Yale University Press, 1977). See also Jeffrey Obler, Jürg Steiner, and Guido Diericx, *Decision-Making in Smaller Democracies: The Consociational "Burden"* (Beverly Hills: Sage, 1977); Dahl, *Political Oppositions in Western Democracies;* Gerhard Lehmbruch, *Proporzdemokratie: Politisches System und politische Kultur in der Schweiz und in Österreich* (Tübingen: Mohr, 1967); Eric A. Nordlinger, *Conflict Regulation in Divided Societies* (Cambridge, Mass.: Harvard University Center for International Affairs, 1972); Brian Barry, "Political Accommodation and Consociational Democracy," *British Journal of*

Political Science 5 (October 1975), 490–500; and Hans Daalder, "The Consociational Democracy Theme," *World Politics* 26 (July 1974), 604–22.

25. Cf. Jürg Steiner, "Major und Proporz," *Politische Vierteljahresschrift* 11 (March 1970), 142–44.

26. Lijphart, *Democracy in Plural Societies,* p. 111.

27. Andrew Shonfield, *In Defence of the Mixed Economy* (Oxford: Oxford University Press, 1984); Gerhard Lehmbruch, "European Neo-Corporatism: An Export Article?" Woodrow Wilson Center *Colloquium Paper* (Washington, D.C., 26 April 1982), p. 33; J. E. Keman and D. Braun, "Social Democracy, Corporatism and the Capitalist State" (paper presented at the ECPR workshop "Modern Theories of State and Society," Lancaster, England, 29 March–4 April 1981), p. 25; and Manfred G. Schmidt, "Economic Crisis, Politics, and Rates of Unemployment in Capitalist Democracies in the Seventies" (paper prepared for the ECPR workshop "Unemployment and Selective Labour Market Policies in Advanced Industrial Societies," Lancaster, England, 29 March–4 April 1981), p. 10.

28. See T. J. Pempel and Keiichi Tsunekawa, "Corporatism without Labor? The Japanese Anomaly," in Schmitter and Lehmbruch, *Trends toward Corporatist Intermediation,* pp. 231–70; Peter J. Katzenstein, "State Strength through Market Competition: Japan's Industrial Strategy," unpublished paper, Cornell University, March 1980.

29. Richard Behrendt, *Die Schweiz und der Imperialismus: Die Volkswirtschaft des hochkapitalistischen Kleinstaates im Zeitalter des politischen und ökonomischen Nationalismus* (Zurich: Rascher, 1932), pp. 12–15.

30. Harry Eckstein, *Division and Cohesion in Democracy: A Study of Norway* (Princeton: Princeton University Press, 1966), p. 3.

31. Sarah Hogg, "A Small House in Order," *Economist,* 15 March 1980, survey, p. 3.

32. Niels Amstrup, "The Perennial Problem of Small States: A Survey of Research Efforts," *Cooperation and Conflict* 3/1976, 176. The late Andrew Shonfield was clearly aware of the importance of the corporatist strain in the evolution of modern capitalism. See *The Use of Public Power* (Oxford: Oxford University Press, 1982), and *In Defence of the Mixed Economy.* Both works are incomplete and have been published posthumously.

CHAPTER 2. *Flexible Adjustment in the Small European States*

1. Cf. George A. Duncan, "The Small States and International Economic Equilibrium," *Economia Internazionale* 3 (November 1950), 939.

2. Gardner C. Patterson, *Discrimination in International Trade: The Policy Issues, 1945–1965* (Princeton: Princeton University Press, 1966), pp. 332–33.

3. Andrew Shonfield, "International Economic Relations of the Western World: An Overall View," in Shonfield, ed., *International Economic Relations of the Western World, 1959–1971,* vol. 1: *Politics and Trade* (London: Oxford University Press, 1976), p. 97.

4. Alice Bourneuf, *Norway, the Planned Revival* (Cambridge: Harvard University Press, 1958), p. 205. See also Günter Zenk, *Konzentrationspolitik in Schweden* (Tübingen: Mohr, 1971), pp. 9, 106; Zenk, *Konzentrationspolitik in*

Dänemark, Norwegen, und Finnland (Tübingen: Mohr, 1971), p. 100; and Anthony Scaperlanda, *Prospects for Eliminating Non-tariff Distortions* (Leyden: Sijthoff, 1973), p. 110.

5. General Agreement on Tariffs and Trade (GATT), *Basic Instruments and Selected Documents,* Supplement 19 (March 1973), pp. 120–30; U.S. Congress, Senate, Committee on Finance, Subcommittee on International Trade, *The GATT Balance of Payments Safeguard Provision: Article XII,* Executive Branch GATT Study no. 7, June 1973, pp. 116–18.

6. U.S. Congress, Joint Economic Committee, *Trade Restraints in the Western Community: With Tariff Comparisons and Selected Statistical Tables Pertinent to Foreign Economic Policy,* 87th Cong. 1st sess. (Washington, D.C., 1961), pp. 11–12.

7. U.S. Congress, Senate, Committee on Finance, Subcommittee on International Trade, *GATT Provisions on Relief from Injurious Imports,* Executive Branch GATT Study no. 8, June 1973, pp. 128–29.

8. Excluded for this computation are restrictions on certain items that have been justified traditionally under GATT articles XX and XXI. See U.S. Congress, Senate, Committee on Finance, Subcommittee on International Trade, *The Quantitative Restrictions in the Major Trading Countries,* Executive Branch GATT Study no. 6, June 1973, appendix.

9. Computed from GATT, *Basic Instruments and Selected Documents,* Supplements 18 (April 1972)–24 (June 1978). Two hundred thirty-seven of the 294 cases were pending in the United States.

10. Shonfield, "International Economic Relations of the Western World," p. 97.

11. Österreichisches Institut für Wirtschaftsforschung, *Monatsberichte* 27 (February 1954), Supplement 24, 8–12.

12. Niclaus G. Krul, *La politique conjoncturelle en Belgique, aux Pays-Bas et en Suisse, 1950–1960* (Geneva: Droz, 1964), pp. 97–98. Data cover only Switzerland, the Netherlands, Belgium, West Germany, and France.

13. Hans Mayrzedt, *Multilaterale Wirschaftsdiplomatie zwischen westlichen Industriestaaten als Instrument zur Stärkung der multilateralen und liberalen Handelspolitik* (Bern: Lang, 1979), p. 376.

14. Wilbur F. Monroe, *International Trade Policy in Transition* (Lexington: Heath, 1975), p. 23. Since the European Economic Community counted free-trade-oriented Netherlands and Belgium among its members, the difference between the small European states and the large industrial states was probably greater.

15. These figures are calculated from the Contracting Parties to the GATT, *Basic Documentation for Tariff Study,* 3 vols. (Geneva: GATT, July 1970).

16. U.S. Congress, Senate, Committee on Finance, Subcommittee on International Trade, *An Economic Analysis of the Effects of the Tokyo Round of Multilateral Trade Negotiations in the United States and Other Major Industrialized Countries,* MTN Studies no. 5 (Washington, D.C., 1979), pp. 44, 64.

17. E. H. Preeg, *Traders and Diplomats: An Analysis of the Kennedy Round of Negotiations under the GATT* (Washington, D.C.: Brookings, 1970), pp. 65–67, 125–26; John W. Evans, *The Kennedy Round in American Trade Policy: The Twilight of GATT?* (Cambridge: Harvard University Press, 1971), p. 222; and William R. Cline, *Trade Negotiations in the Tokyo Round: A Quantitative Assessment* (Washington, D.C.: Brookings, 1978), pp. 74, 121, 142.

18. "A Note on Recent Developments and Problems of Export-Credit Guarantees (with Special Reference to Western Europe)," *UN Economic Bulletin for Europe* 12, 2 (1960), 53.

19. *Die Schweiz im Zeichen des harten Franken* (Zurich: Schweizerische Kreditanstalt, 1978), pp. 12–13.

20. *Botschaft des Bundesrates an die Bundesversammlung über einen Beitrag an die schweizerische Zentrale für Handelsförderung* (Bern, 26 February 1975), p. 11. Norway is excluded from this comparison.

21. Population figures are given in Peer Hull Kristensen and Jørn Levinsen, *The Small Country Squeeze* (Roskilde, Denmark: Institute of Economics, Politics and Administration, 1978), p. 71. I have computed the export trade figures from United Nations, *Yearbook of International Trade Statistics 1976*, vol. 1.

22. Organization for Economic Co-operation and Development (OECD), *Export Cartels: Report of the Committee of Experts on Restrictive Business Practices* (Paris, 1974), pp. 8, 24.

23. Scaperlanda, *Prospects for Eliminating Non-Tariff Distortions;* Cline, *Trade Negotiations in the Tokyo Round,* pp. 192–94.

24. Robert Baldwin, *Nontariff Distortions of International Trade* (Washington, D.C.: Brookings, 1970), pp. 60, 70.

25. Ibid., p. 77; Melvyn Krauss, *The New Protectionism: The Welfare State and International Trade* (New York: New York University Press, 1978), pp. 52–53.

26. Committee on Finance, *Economic Analysis of the Effects of the Tokyo Round,* p.. 81. The amounts are $5 billion for the large industrial states and $0.8 billion for the small European states. This is a ratio of 6:1 as compared to a ratio of 3:1 in the export trade of large and small states. These data suggest, but do not prove, that trade restrictions were more widespread among the large industrial states.

27. Ingo Walter, "Nontariff Protection among Industrial Countries: Some Preliminary Evidence," *Economia Internazionale* 25, 2 (1972), 350; Gerd Junne and Salua Nour, *Internationale Abhängigkeiten, Fremdbestimmung und Ausbeutung als Regelfall internationaler Beziehungen* (Frankfurt: Fischer Athenäum, 1974), pp. 73–74; and Mayrzedt, *Multilaterale Wirtschaftsdiplomatie,* pp. 392–93.

28. U.S. Congress, House, Committee on Ways and Means, *Briefing Material Prepared for Use of the Committee on Ways and Means in Connection with Hearings on the Subject of Foreign Trade and Tariffs,* 93d Cong. 1st sess. (May 1972), pp. 54–150; UNCTAD, Trade and Development Board, Committee on Manufactures, *Liberalization of Non-Tariff Barriers, Including Quantitative Restrictions, Applied in Developed Market Economy Countries to Products of Particular Export Interest to Developing Countries: Report by the UNCTAD Secretariat,* TD/B/C.2/115/Rev.1 (Geneva, 1974), p. 8; and Mayrzedt, *Multilaterale Wirtschaftsdiplomatie,* pp. 524–25.

29. Patterson, *Discrimination in International Trade,* p. 303.

30. Shonfield, "International Economic Relations of the World," p. 98.

31. Mancur Olson, *The Rise and Decline of Nations: Economic Growth, Stagflation and Social Rigidities* (New Haven: Yale University Press, 1982), pp. 61–66, 132–36.

32. OECD, *The Research System: Comparative Survey of the Organization and Financing of Fundamental Research,* vol. 2 (Paris 1973), p. 104; Kristensen and Levinsen, *Small Country Squeeze,* pp. 92, 196–209.

33. Kristensen and Levinsen, *Small Country Squeeze*, pp. 156, 178; Yoram Ben-Porath, "Some Implications of Economic Size and Level of Investment in R and D," *Economic Development and Cultural Change* 21 (October 1972), 100; and Stevan Dedijer, "The Future of Research Policies," in Lawrence W. Bass and Bruce S. Old, eds., *Formulation of Research Policies: Collected Papers from an International Symposium* (Washington, D.C.: American Academy for the Advancement of Science, 1967), pp. 156–58.

34. Kristensen and Levinsen, *Small Country Squeeze*, p. 171.

35. OECD, *The Research System*, 2:103–4.

36. Ibid., pp. 101–3.

37. Kristensen and Levinsen, *Small Country Squeeze*, pp. 185, 188.

38. Ibid., p. 188.

39. Ibid., pp. 164–65, 179, 210–29; OECD, *The Research System*, 2: 33; and Joseph Ben-David, *Fundamental Research and the Universities: Some Comments on International Differences* (Paris: OECD, 1968), p. 26.

40. Oliver Long of Switzerland was the director general of the GATT between 1968 and 1980. He was succeeded by his compatriot, Arthur Dunkel. The managing director of the International Monetary Fund was Camille Gutt of Belgium (1947–50), Ivar Roth of Sweden (1951–56), Per Jacobsson of Sweden (1957–63), and H. Johannes Witteven of the Netherlands (1974–77). The secretary general of the OECD was Thorkil Kristensen of Denmark (1961–68) and since 1969 Emile van Lennerp of the Netherlands.

41. Stephen D. Krasner, *Structural Conflict: The Third World against Global Liberalism* (Berkeley: University of California Press, forthcoming), manuscript chapter 6, p. 45.

42. Jeffrey A. Hart, *The New International Economic Order* (New York: St. Martin's, 1983), pp. 103–23; J. Stephen Hoadley, "Small States as Aid Donors," *International Organization* 34 (Winter 1980), 121–38.

43. Jeanne Kirk Laux, "Small States and Inter-European Relations: An Analysis of the Group of Nine," *Journal of Peace Research* 9 (1971), 147–48. This article summarizes the results of a doctoral dissertation with the same title which was submitted to the University of London in 1972. See also Mario Hirsch, "Influence without Power: Small States in European Politics," *World Today* 34 (March 1976), 116–17.

44. Kristensen and Levinsen, *Small Country Squeeze*, pp. 207, 197; Peter Wiles, "The Importance of Country Size, A Question but Not a Subject," unpublished paper, March 1978, pp. 6–7; Amry Vandenbosch, "Small States in International Politics," *Journal of Politics* 26 (May 1964), 301.

45. V. V. Sveics, *Small Nation Survival: Political Defense in Unequal Conflicts* (New York: Exposition, 1969), pp. 261–62; Gustav Däniker, *Strategie des Kleinstaats: Politische-militärische Möglichkeiten schweizerischer Selbstbehauptung im Atomzeitalter* (Frauenfeld: Huber, 1966), pp. 53–54; Edward E. Azaar, *Probe for Peace: Small State Hostilities* (Minneapolis: Burgess, 1973), pp. 31–32; and Antonin Snejdarek, "Small Countries and European Security," *Adelphi Paper* no. 33 (March 1967), 41.

46. Laux, "Small States and Inter-European Relations"; Annette Baker Fox, "The Small States of Western Europe in the United Nations," *International Organization* 19 (Summer 1965), 775, 783; and Gunnar Heckscher, *The Role of Small Nations: Today and Tomorrow* (London: Athlone, 1966).

47. Fox, "Small States of Western Europe," p. 783; Annette Baker Fox, "Intervention and the Small State," *Journal of International Affairs* 22 (1968), 247–56.

48. Fox, "Small States of Western Europe," pp. 784–85.

49. Annette B. Fox, "Small States in the International System, 1919–1969," *International Affairs* 24, 4 (1969), 764.

50. Fox, "Small States of Western Europe," p. 782.

51. Robert L. Rothstein, *Alliances and Small Powers* (New York: Columbia University Press, 1968), pp. 30–45, 60–64, 116–27, 170–78, 242–45.

52. Ibid., p. 244; David Vital, *The Inequality of States: A Study of Small Powers in International Relations* (Oxford: Clarendon, 1967).

53. Richard Blackhurst, Nicolas Marian, and Jan Tumlir, *Trade Liberalization, Protectionism and Interdependence*, GATT Studies in International Trade no. 5 (Geneva, 1977), p. 41.

54. Svlatopuk Tikal, "Soviet Economists and Their Works on Social-Economic Problems of Small Countries," *Politicka Ekonomie* 22, 5 (1974), 469–72; J. I. Judanow, "Die kleinen Industrieländer Westeuropas im System des gegenwärtigen Kapitalismus," *IPW-Berichte*, 11/1973, 14–22; and Béla Kádár, *Small Countries in World Economy* (Budapest: Hungarian Academy of Sciences, Center of Afro-Asian Research, 1970).

55. See Assar Lindbeck, *Swedish Economic Policy* (Berkeley: University of California Press, 1973), pp. 58, 72–73, 97–104; Harold G. Jones, *Planning and Productivity in Sweden* (London: Croom Helm, 1976), pp. 16–17, 151–62; Andrew Shonfield, *Modern Capitalism: The Changing Balance of Public and Private Power* (London: Oxford University Press, 1965), pp. 201–3; Martin Schnitzer, *The Swedish Investment Reserve: A Device for Economic Stabilization?* (Washington, D.C.: American Enterprise Institute, 1967); Holger Heide, *Die langfristige Wirtschaftsplanung in Schweden* (Tübingen: Mohr, 1965), pp. 130–31; and Jutta Grohmann, *Finanzpolitik und Konjunktur in Schweden seit 1933* (Frankfurt: Knapp, 1968), pp. 72–177.

56. Jones, *Planning and Productivity*, pp. 159–60.

57. Schnitzer, *Swedish Investment Reserve*, p. 22.

58. "Measures Employed by OECD Governments to Influence Industrial Investment," *OECD Observer* no. 19 (December 1965), 42–45; Hans Schmid, *Die staatliche Beschaffungspolitik: Ein Beitrag zu den Einkaufsverfahren der öffentlichen Hand* (Bern: Haupt, 1972), p. 120.

59. OECD, *Selected Industrial Policy Instruments: Objectives and Scope* (Paris, 1978), pp. 14–15; Theodore Geiger, *Welfare and Efficiency: Their Interactions in Western Europe and Implications for International Economic Relations* (Washington, D.C.: National Planning Association, 1978); Robert H. Haveman, "The Dutch Social Employment Program," in John L. Palmer, ed., *Creating Jobs: Public Employment Programs and Wage Subsidies* (Washington, D.C.: Brookings, 1978), p. 243; Cornelius Weststrate, *Economic Policy in Practice: Netherlands, 1950–1957* (Leiden: Stenfert Kroese, 1959), pp. 203–7; and M. Gardner Clark, "The Swiss Experience with Foreign Workers: Lessons for the United States," *Industrial and Labor Relations Review* 36 (July 1983), 606–23.

60. Lindbeck, *Swedish Economic Policy*, pp. 77–78, 104–7, 156–57; Schnitzer, *Swedish Investment Reserve*, p. 27.

61. Eric Einhorn and John Logue, *Welfare States in Hard Times: Denmark and Sweden in the 1970s* (Kent: Popular, 1980), pp. 20–27; OECD, *Selected Industrial Policy Instruments*, pp. 128–29; and Jones, *Planning and Productivity*, p. 40.

62. Kenneth Hanf, Benny Hjern, and David O. Porter, *Networks of Implementation and Administration for Manpower Policies at the Local Level in the Federal Republic of Germany and Sweden* (Berlin: International Institute of Management, dp/77–16, 1977), p. 25.

63. Jones, *Planning and Productivity*, p. 40.

64. Nils Elvander, "Collective Bargaining and Incomes Policy in the Nordic Countries: A Comparative Analysis," *British Journal of Industrial Relations* 12 (November 1974), 418. See also Klaus Armingeon, "Determining the Level of Wages: The Role of Parties and Trade Unions," in Francis G. Castles, ed., *The Impact of Parties: Politics and Policies in Democratic Capitalist States* (Beverly Hills: Sage, 1982), pp. 21–96; Robert J. Flanagan, David W. Soskice, and Lloyd Ulman, *Unionism, Economic Stabilization and Incomes Policies: European Experience* (Washington, D.C.: Brookings, 1983); and Gary W. Marks, "Neocorporatism, Incomes Policy, and Socialist Participation in Government" (paper prepared for presentation at the Comparative Socialist Studies Committee in conjunction with the Annual Meeting of the American Political Science Association, Chicago, September 1983).

65. Murray Edelman and R. W. Fleming, *The Politics of Wage-Price Decisions: A Four-Country Analysis* (Urbana: University of Illinois Press, 1965), p. 4.

66. Bram Peper, "The Netherlands: From Ordered Harmonic to a Bargaining Relationship," in Solomon Barkin, ed., *Worker Militancy and Its Consequences, 1965–1975* (New York: Praeger, 1975), p. 148.

67. Anne E. Millons, *Twenty-one Years of Wages and Wage Policy in the Netherlands, 1945–1966* (Ithaca: Cornell University Press, 1968), pp. 287–88.

68. Ibid., p. 61.

69. Steven B. Wolinetz, "Wage Regulation in the Netherlands: The Rise and Fall of the Postwar Social Contract" (paper prepared for presentation at the Council for European Studies Conference of Europeanists, Washington, D.C., 13–15 October 1983).

70. Elvander, "Collective Bargaining," pp. 425–31; Nils Elvander, "The Role of the State in the Settlement of Labor Disputes in the Nordic Countries: A Comparative Analysis," *European Journal of Political Research* 2 (December 1974), 363–83.

71. Sergio Lugaresi, (Neocorporatism between Change and Stability: The Case of Sweden) *Il Mulino,* no. 6 (November–December 1983), 857–87.

72. *Wall Street Journal,* 13 April 1984, p. 37.

73. Don S. Schwerin, "Norwegian and Danish Incomes Policy and European Monetary Integration," unpublished paper, Oakland University, n.d.; Scherwin, "Corporate Incomes Policy: Norway's Second-Best Institutions," unpublished paper, Oakland University, n.d.

74. Lloyd Ulman and Robert Flanagan, *Wage Restraint: A Study of Incomes Policies in Western Europe* (Berkeley: University of California Press, 1971), p. 202.

75. Gerhard Lehmbruch, "European Neo-Corporatism: An Export Article?" Woodrow Wilson Center *Colloquium Paper* (Washington, D.C., 26 April 1982), pp. 8–11, 14–15, 23; Robert W. Russell, "Can Incomes Policies Work?" in Kristen R. Monroe, ed., *The Political Process and Economic Change* (New York: Agathon, 1983), pp. 108–40.

76. Quoted in Harry Bernstein and Joanne Bernstein, *Industrial Democracy in 12 Nations,* U.S. Department of Labor, Bureau of International Affairs, Monograph no. 2 (Washington, D.C., 1979), p. iv.

77. Efén Córdova, "A Comparative View of Collective Bargaining in Industrialized Countries," *International Labour Review* 117 (July–August 1978), 429, 436–37.

78. Ibid., pp. 437–38. See also Michele Salvati and Giorgio Brosio, "The Rise of Market Politics: Industrial Relations in the Seventies," *Daedalus*, Spring 1979, 63.

79. Quoted in Ann Romanis Braun, "The Role of Incomes Policy in Industrial Countries since World War II," *IMF Staff Papers* 22 (March 1975), 28.

80. John D. Stephens, *The Transition from Capitalism to Socialism* (London: Macmillan, 1979), p. 20. See also Manfred G. Schmidt, "The Growth of the Tax State: The Industrial Democracies, 1950–1978," in Charles L. Taylor, ed., *Why Governments Grow: Measuring Public Sector Size* (Beverly Hills: Sage, 1983), pp. 261–85.

81. OECD, *Public Expenditure Trends* (Paris, 1978), p. 12.

82. David R. Cameron, "On the Limits of the Public Economy" (paper prepared for delivery at the Annual Meeting of the American Political Science Association, New York, September 1981), Table 3.

83. Stephens, *Transition from Capitalism to Socialism*, pp. 96, 118.

84. OECD, *Public Expenditure on Income Maintenance Programmes* (Paris, 1976), pp. 7, 20, 35.

85. OECD, *Public Expenditure Trends*, pp. 14–15, 20–21, 25.

86. Ibid., pp. 14–15.

87. Henry Aron, "Social Security: International Comparisons," in Otto Eckstein, ed., *Studies in the Economics of Income Maintenance* (Washington, D.C.: Brookings, 1967), p. 47; Harold L. Wilensky, *The "New Corporatism": Centralization and the Welfare State* (Beverly Hills: Sage, 1976), p. 11. The data are not comparable over time.

88. Warren G. Nutter, *Growth of Government in the West* (Washington, D.C.: American Enterprise Institute, 1978), p. 6.

89. Ibid., p. 12.

90. OECD, *Public Expenditure Trends*, p. 12. This may be due partly to the sharp contraction of the Swiss gross domestic product in the mid-1970s.

91. OECD, *Public Expenditure Trends*, p. 42.

92. The precise meaning of this term is explored empirically in Douglas A. Hibbs and Henrik Jess Madsen, "Public Reactions to the Growth of Taxation and Government Expenditure," *World Politics* 33 (April 1981), 421–35.

93. Nutter, *Growth of Government in the West* pp. 12, 90.

94. OECD, *The Industrial Policies of 14 Member States* (Paris, 1971), p. 120.

95. Einhorn and Logue, *Welfare States in Hard Times*, p. 27.

96. Douglas A. Hibbs, Jr., "On the Political Economy of Long-Run Trends in Strike Activity," *British Journal of Political Science* 8 (April 1978), 154.

97. Krauss, *New Protectionism*.

98. Lawrence G. Franko, "Current Trends in Protectionism in Industrialized Countries: Focus on Western Europe," in G. K. Helleiner et al., *Protectionism or Industrial Adjustment* (Paris: Atlantic Institute for International Affairs, 1980), p. 31. See also Franko, *European Industrial Policy: Present and Future*, The Conference Board in Europe, European Research Report (n.p., February 1980).

99. Steven Langdon, "Industrial Restructuring in the Dutch Textile Industry" (paper presented to the European Politics Group Conference, Canadian Political Science Association, Ottawa, December 1981); Harald Ettl, "Inter-

nationale Arbeitsteilung in der Textil- und Bekleidungsindustrie und ihre Auswirkungen auf die Beschäftigten," *Informationen über multinationale Konzerne* 4/1980, 1–4.

100. OECD, *Structural Problems of the Textile and Clothing Industry* (Paris, 1977), pp. 8, 29–30; Anders Ericson, "Stagnation, Crisis and Development: Strategies and Development Processes in Swedish Textile and Clothing Firms" (Berlin: International Institute for Management, dp 80–6, 1980).

101. Boston Consulting Group, *A Framework for Swedish Industrial Policy* (Stockholm: Departmentens Offsetcentral, 1979), appendix 5, p. 2; Michael B. Dolan, "European Restructuring and Import Policies for a Textile Industry in Crisis," *International Organization* 37 (Autumn 1983), 588.

102. Patterson, *Discrimination in International Trade,* pp. 127, 129, 131, 135–38, 165–66; Irving B. Kravis, *Domestic Interests and International Obligations: Safeguards in International Trade Organizations* (Philadelphia: University of Pennsylvania Press, 1963), pp. 91–92.

103. Committee on Finance, *Quantitative Restrictions in the Major Trading Countries,* appendix.

104. Milan Lasser, "Handelspolitische Probleme im Textilbereich" (speech delivered at the Generalversammlung des IVT, 2 May 1978), pp.6, 8–11.

105. Robert Black, Stephen Blank, and Elizabeth C. Hansen, *Multinationals in Contention: Responses at Governmental and International Levels* (New York: Conference Board, 1978), pp. 6–7, 36–41; OECD, *Adjustment for Trade: Studies on Industrial Adjustment Problems and Policies* (Paris, 1975); and Scaperlanda, *Prospects for Eliminating Non-Tariff Distortions,* p. 25.

106. On Norway see *Nationalbudget und Wirtschaftspolitik* (Hannover: Verlag für Literatur und Zeitgeschehen, 1962); Petter Jakob Bjerve, "Trends in Quantitative Economic Planning in Norway," in Leif Johansen and Harald Hallaråker, eds., *Economic Planning in Norway: Methods and Models* (Oslo: Universitetsforlaget, 1970), pp. 4, 22; Fritz C. Holte, "A Model for Estimating the Consequences of an Income Settlement," in ibid., p. 68; E. S. Kirschen et al., *Economic Policy in Our Time* (Amsterdam: North Holland, 1964), 2: 174–75; and Per Kleppe, *Main Aspects of Economic Policy in Norway since the War* (Oslo: Oslo University Press, 1966), p. 3. On Sweden see Erik Lundberg, *Business Cycles and Economic Policy* (Cambridge: Harvard University Press, 1957); Jutta Grohman, *Finanzpolitik und Konjunktur in Schweden* (Frankfurt: Knapp, 1968), pp. 211–12; *Nationalbudget und Wirtschaftspolitik,* pp. 89–90; and Heide, *Langfristige Wirtschaftsplanung in Schweden,* pp. 3–5, 30.

107. Jack Barbash, *Trade Unions and National Economic Policy* (Baltimore: Johns Hopkins Press, 1972), p. 7. The difference between Sweden and France is also discussed in Lindbeck, *Swedish Economic Policy,* pp. 168–69.

108. Shonfield, *Modern Capitalism,* p. 204. In this quotation Shonfield refers only to Sweden.

109. Weststrate, *Economic Policy in Practice,* pp. 1, 210; Hildegard Graebner, *Die langfristige Planung in Norwegen, Schweden und den Niederlanden* (Cologne: Deutsches Industrieinstitut, 1965), pp. 85, 96.

110. James G. Abert, *Economic Policy and Planning in the Netherlands, 1950–1965* (New Haven: Yale University Press: 1969), p. 129.

111. Abert, *Economic Policy and Planning,* pp. 117–18; Graebner, *Langfristige Planung,* pp. 95–96; and Marita Estor, *Der sozial-ökonomische Rat der niederländischen Wirtschaft* (Berlin: Duncker & Humblot, 1965), p. 121.

112. Kleppe, *Main Aspects of Economic Policy in Norway*, pp. 3–4; Johansen and Hallaråker, *Economic Planning in Norway*, pp. 10, 13; and "Longer-Term Plans in Western Europe," *Economic Bulletin for Europe* 14 (November 1963), 84–85.

113. Bourneuf, *Norway, the Planned Revival*, p. 200; Kleppe, *Main Aspects of Economic Policy*, p. 7; Johansen and Hallaråker, *Economic Planning in Norway*, p. 25; Graebner, *Langfristige Planung*, p. 43; and John Zysman, *Governments, Markets, and Growth: Financial Systems and the Politics of Industrial Change* (Ithaca: Cornell University Press, 1983).

114. Bourneuf, *Norway, the Planned Revival*, pp. 203, 206; Graebner, *Langfristige Planung*, pp. 33–34; and Johansen and Hallaråker, *Economic Planning in Norway*, pp. 6–7.

115. Graebner, *Langfristige Planung*, pp. 118–19, 123; "Long-term Plans in Western Europe," pp. 82–84.

116. René Capreau, *Ziele und Instrumente der belgischen Wirtschaftspolitik* (Tübingen: Mohr, 1967), pp. 53, 58–66; Christian Franck, "Die ordnungspolitische Neugestaltung in Belgien: Einflussgrössen und Lösungsversuche" (Ph.D. diss., University of Cologne, 1966), pp. 16–17, 95.

117. Graebner, *Langfristige Planung*, pp. 19, 95–96; Erhard Fürst, "Die holländische Planung—Vorbild für Österreich?" *Quartalshefte*, 1/1969, 95–98; and Bjvere, "Trends in Quantitative Economic Planning," pp. 18–19.

118. Barbarsh, *Trade Unions*, p. 5.

119. Raymond Vernon, "Enterprise and Government in Western Europe," in Vernon, ed., *Big Business and the State: Changing Relations in Western Europe* (Cambridge: Harvard University Press, 1974), p. 10.

120. Kristensen and Levinsen, *Small Country Squeeze*, pp. 43–46, 165–66, 261–63; Carmi, "Science and Technology Policy in Small States: First Report," unpublished manuscript, Jerusalem Group for National Planning, 1975, pp. 10–11; K. Pavitt and S. Wald, *The Conditions for Success in Technological Innovation* (Paris: OECD, 1971), p. 122; and Bela Balassa, " 'Revealed' Comparative Advantage Revisited: An Analysis of Relative Export Shares of the Industrial Countries, 1953–1971," *Manchester School of Economic and Social Studies* 45 (December 1977), 331–36.

121. OECD, *Policies for the Stimulation of Industrial Innovation: Analytical Report*, vol. 1 (Paris, 1978), pp. 16, 48, 127–37; OECD, Science Resources Unit, *Science Resources Newsletter* no. 2 (Spring 1977), 11.

122. Kristensen and Levinsen, *Small Country Squeeze*, pp. 40–42, 182–83, 289; OECD, *The Research System*, 2: 118.

123. World Bank, *World Bank Tables, 1976* (Baltimore: Johns Hopkins University Press, 1976), p. 523. The vocational enrollment rate as a percentage of total secondary enrollment is about twice as large in the small European states as in the larger countries. On the other hand, the number of students enrolled in higher education is greater in the large countries than in the seven small states. See Peter Flora, *Quantitative Historical Sociology*, HIWED Report no. 2 (Cologne, 1975), Table 10.

124. OECD *The Research System*, 2: 117; "A New Challenge for Small Countries: The Reorientation of Research Systems," *OECD Observer* no. 64 (June 1973), 31–34; and Kristensen and Levinsen, *Small Country Squeeze*, pp. 156–64.

125. OECD, *The Research System*, 2: 157.

126. Kristensen and Levinsen, *Small Country Squeeze*, p. 115.

127. OECD, *The Research System*, 2: 7, 24, 27; Kristensen and Levinsen, *Small Country Squeeze*, p. 115.

128. OECD, *The Research System*, 2: 7.

129. Göran Ohlin, "Sweden," in Vernon, *Big Business and the State*, pp. 126–27.

130. Boston Consulting Group, *Framework for Swedish Industrial Policy*.

131. Norges Offentlige Utredninger, *Employment and Working Conditions in the 1980s: Perspectives on the Significance of the Technological and Economic Development for Employment and Working Conditions* (Oslo: Universitetsforlaget, 1980), p. 75.

132. Alan Whiting, "Overseas Experience in the Use of Industrial Subsidies," in Whiting, ed., *The Economics of Industrial Subsidies* (London: HMSO for the Department of Industry, 1976), p. 47.

133. OECD, *The Case for Positive Adjustment Policies: A Compendium of OECD Documents, 1978–79* (Paris, 1979), pp. 19, 30, 32, 74.

134. Volker Bornschier and Peter Heintz, eds., *Compendium of Data for World-System Analysis: A Sourcebook of Data Based on the Study of MNCs, Economic Policy and National Development* (Zurich: University of Zurich, Institute of Sociology, March 1979), author's calculations.

135. Richard Blackhurst, Nicholas Marian, and Jan Tumlir, *Adjustment, Trade and Growth in Developed and Developing Countries* (Geneva: GATT, 1978), p. 89, author's calculations. See also Franko, "Current Trends in Protectionism," p. 39.

136. Peter J. Katzenstein, *Corporatism and Change: Austria, Switzerland, and the Politics of Industry* (Ithaca: Cornell University Press, 1984), pp. 162–238.

137. Assar Lindbeck, "Stabilization Policy in Open Economies with Endogenous Politicians," *American Economic Review: Papers and Proceedings of the 86th Annual Meeting of the American Economic Association, Dallas, Texas, December 28–30*, May 1975: 1–19.

138. OECD, *The Aims and Instruments of Industrial Policy: A Comparative Study* (Paris, 1975), p. 13; OECD, *The Industrial Policies of 14 Member Countries*, pp. 259–61, 263–65; OECD, *Reviews of National Science Policy: Netherlands* (Paris, 1973), pp. 121–23; and L. B. M. Mennes, "Adjustment of the Industrial Structure of Developed Economies, in particular the Netherlands" (paper prepared for the International Symposium on Maritime Research and European Shipping and Shipbuilding, Rotterdam, 29–31 March 1978).

139. OECD, *Adjustment for Trade*, pp. 172, 179; Netherlands Scientific Council for Government Policy, *Industry in the Netherlands: Its Place and Future*, Reports to the Government no. 18 (English ed., 1982); and H. W. de Jong and Robert Jan Spierenburg, "The Netherlands: Maintenance of Employment as a Primary Objective," in Brian Hindley, ed., *State Investment Companies in Western Europe: Picking Winners or Backing Losers?* (New York: St. Martin's, 1983), pp. 59–95.

140. OECD, *Adjustment for Trade*, p. 179.

141. Scaperlanda, *Prospects for Eliminating Non-Tariff Distortions*, pp. 119–23; Nicolas Jequier, "Compuers," in Vernon, *Big Business and the State*, pp. 201, 203.

142. Boston Consulting Group, *Framework for Swedish Industrial Policy*, p. 51.

143. OECD, *Industrial Policies of 14 Member Countries*, p. 300; Vernon, "En-

terprise and Government in Western Europe," p. 6; Gunnar Eliasson and Bengt-Christer Ysander, "Sweden: Problems of Maintaining Efficiency under Political Pressure," in Hindley, *State Investment Companies,* pp. 156–91; and Office of the Under Secretary of State for Economic Affairs, "Sweden: Industrial Policy in a Small Industrialized Nation," unpublished paper, Washington, D.C., July 1980.

144. U.S. Congress, Joint Economic Committee, *Monetary Policy, Selective Credit Policy, and Industrial Policy in France, Britain, West Germany, and Sweden: A Staff Study* (Washington, D.C., 26 June 1981), p. 179.

145. Boston Consulting Group, *Framework for Swedish Industrial Policy,* Appendix 13, p. 7.

146. OECD, *Aims and Instruments,* p. 43; Jones, *Planning and Productivity,* pp. 176–79.

147. Boston Consulting Group, *Framework for Swedish Industrial Policy,* Appendix 7, pp. 23, 26, and Appendix 13, p. 4.

148. Ohlin, "Sweden," pp. 134–35, 139, 126–45.

149. OECD, *Policies for Promoting Industrial Adaptation* (Paris, 1976), p. 24; *Monetary Policy,* pp. 4, 170–71.

150. Boston Consulting Group, *Framework for Swedish Industrial Policy,* p. iii, and Appendix 13, p. 56.

151. OECD, *Industrial Policies of Member Countries,* pp. 127–37.

152. Norges Offentlige Utredninger, *Employment and Working Conditions,* p. 76.

153. OECD, *Aims and Instruments,* p. 13; OECD, *Industrial Policies of Member Countries,* pp. 52, 65; and Scaperlanda, *Eliminating Non-Tariff Distortions,* pp. 143–45.

154. Robert Senelle, *The Political and Economic Structure of Belgium* (Brussels: Ministry of Foreign Affairs and External Trade, 1966), p. 129; OECD, *Industrial Policies of Member Countries,* p. 59; OECD, *Promoting Industrial Adaptation,* p. 30; J. J. Boddewyn, "The Belgian Economic Expansion Law of 1970," in Ezra N. Suleiman and Steven J. Warnecke, eds., *Industrial Policies in Western Europe* (New York: Praeger, 1975), pp. 51–54; Stuart Holland, "Europe's New Public Enterprises," in Vernon, *Big Business and the State,"* pp. 37–38; and Paul De Grauwe and Greet van de Velde, "Belgium: Politics and the Protection of Failing Companies," in Hindley, *State Investment Companies,* pp. 96–124.

155. Boddewyn, "Belgian Economic Expansion," p. 54.

156. *Wall Street Journal,* 14 October 1981, pp. 1, 16.

157. At this point an analysis of the adjustment strategies of the small European states converges with that provided by Zysman's *Governments, Markets, and Growth.* In Zysman's terminology West Germany and the small European states have both followed a strategy of "negotiated adjustment."

158. OECD, *Industrial Policies of Member Countries,* pp. 245, 247–56.

159. These two terms are used respectively by Ohlin, "Sweden," p. 127, and Salvati and Brosio, "Rise of Market Politics," p. 60.

160. OECD, *Adjustment for Trade,* p. 215; OECD, *Aims and Instruments,* p. 18; and Graebner, *Langfristige Planung.*

161. *Neue Zürcher Zeitung,* 7 September 1966, and 9 December 1973; "Umrisse und Aspekte der Industriepolitik," *Mitteilungsblatt für Konjunkturfragen* 29, 1 (1973), 3–14.

162. Egon Tuchtfeldt, ed., *Schweizerische Wirtschaftspolitik zwischen Gestern*

und Morgen: Festgabe zum 65. Geburtstag von Hugo Sieber (Bern: Haupt, 1976). See also Francesco Kneschaurek, "Neue Probleme der Stabilitätspolitik im Zeichen der kommenden Entwicklung," *Schweizer Zeitschrift für Volkswirtschaft und Statistik* 115, 3 (1979), 253–72. Developments in the 1970s are described in OECD, *Economic Survey: Switzerland* (Paris, 1979), pp. 44–47; and Heinz Hollenstein and Rudolf Loertscher, *Die Struktur- und Regionalpolitik des Bundes: Kritische Würdigung und Skizze einer Neuorientierung* (Diessenhofen: Rüegger, 1980).

163. Interview, Zurich, June 1981.

164. Gerhard Winterberger, *Die Schweiz im internationalen Wettbewerb* (Zurich: Schweizerischer Handels- und Industrie-Verein, 1978), p. 14. See also OECD, *Industrial Policies of Member Countries*, pp. 321–48.

165. D. Maillat, C. Jeanrenaud, and J. P. Widmer, "Transfert d'emplois vers les pays qui disposent d'un surplus de main-d'oeuvre comme alternative aux migrations internationales; le cas de la Suisse," *World Employment Programme, Working Paper, Migration for Employment Project*, 2 pts. (Geneva: International Labor Office, 1976 and 1977). The authors have summarized their main findings in "Reactions of Swiss Employers to the Immigration Freeze," *International Labour Review* 117, 6 (November–December 1978), 733–45. See also their "Le comportement de l'entrepreneur face à la pénurie de main-d'oeuvre: résultats d'une enquête par questionnaire," *Documents d'Economie Appliquée* (Neuchatel University, n.d.); and Schweizerischer Handels- und Industrie-Verein, "Mittlere und kleinere Fabrikationsunternehmen (PME): Enquête" (Zurich: SHIV, 1977), no. 1, p. 2, and no. 5, p. 19.

166. Silvio Borner, ed., *Produktionsverlagerung und industrieller Strukturwandel* (Bern: Haupt, 1980); Hilmar Stetter, *Schweizer Fabriken: Ab in die 3. Welt? Produktionsverlagerung der schweizer Grossindustrie* (Basle: Z-Verlag, 1980); and Philippe Queyrance and Bruno Simma, *A Survey of Industrial Redeployment Opportunities in Switzerland for the United Nations Industrial Development Organization (UNIDO)* (Zurich: Industrial Consulting & Management Engineering Co., 1976).

167. The company is criticized by Ditmar Wenty, "Hoffmann-LaRoche: Der weltgrösste Pharmakonzern," *Informationen über multinationale Konzerne* 1/1980, 4–10.

168. Gottfried Berweger, *Investition und Legitimation: Privatinvestitionen in Entwicklungsländern als Teil der schweizerischen Legitimationsproblematik* (Diessenhofen: Rüegger, 1977), p. 196.

169. *Die Schweiz im Zeichen des harten Franken* (Zurich: Schweizerische Kreditanstalt, 1978), p. 17; Fritz Leutwiler, *Die Schweiz als internationaler Finanzplatz: Wachstum in Grenzen* (Zurich: Schweizerischer Handels- und Industrie-Verein, 1977), p. 26; and F. Kneschaurek, "Die internationale Wettbewerbsfähigkeit der Schweiz," *Mitteilungsblatt des Delegierten für Konjunkturfragen* 32 (July 1976), 22.

170. *Die Schweiz im Zeichen des harten Franken*, p. 16; Leutwiler, *Schweiz als Finanzplatz*, p. 21; and Bernhard Wehrli, "Wege der schweizerischen Wirtschaftsordnung," *Schweizer Monatshefte* 49, 9 (1969), 811, 813.

171. Herbert Ammann, Werner Fassbind, and Peter C. Meyer, "Multinationale Konzerne der Schweiz und Auswirkungen auf die Arbeiterklasse in der Schweiz" (Zurich: University of Zurich, Institute for Sociology, 1975), p. 55; Jonathan Steinberg, *Why Switzerland?* (Cambridge: Cambridge Univer-

sity Press, 1976), p. 141; and Jürg Niehans, "Benefits of Multinational Firms for a Small Parent Economy: The Case of Switzerland," in Tamir Agmon and Charles P. Kindleberger, eds., *Multinationals from Small Countries* (Cambridge: MIT Press, 1977), pp. 22–23.

172. P. de Weck, *Outlook for the Swiss Economy* (Zurich: Union Bank of Switzerland, March 1977), p. 10.

173. Ferdinand Lacina, "Development and Problems of Austrian Industry," in Kurt Steiner, ed., *Modern Austria* (Palo Alto: SPOSS, 1981), pp. 155, 171. Hans Wehsely, "Industriepolitik in den siebziger Jahren—Rückblick und Ausblick," *Österreichische Zeitschrift für Politikwissenschaft*, 1/1981, 27–38; Wolfgang C. Müller, "Economic Success without an Industrial Strategy: Austria in the 1970's," *Journal of Public Policy* 3 (February 1983), 119–30; OECD, *Policies for the Stimulation of Industrial Innovation: Country Reports,* vol. 2-2 (Paris, 1978), pp. 20–30; Vereinigung Österreichischer Industrieller, *Mittelfristiges Industrieprogramm* (Vienna, 1974), pp. 55–57; "Austrian Industrial Development," *Financial Times,* 29 August 1975, pp. 9–11; *Neue Technologien und Produkte für Österreichs Wirtschaft* (Vienna: Zentralsparkasse und Kommerzialbank, 1979), p. 43; and Ronald Müller, "Strukturwandel in Österreichs Industrie," *Österreich-Bericht* 86/1984, p. 2.

174. Eduard März, "Austrian Investment Policy in the Post War Period," *Zeitschrift für Nationalökonomie* 23, 1–2 (1964), 163–88; Franz Nemschak, *Längerfristiges Wirtschaftswachstum und Wirtschaftsplanung in Österreich,*" Vorträge und Aufsätze," 23 (Vienna: Österreichisches Institut für Wirtschaftsforschung, 1965); Othmar Peham, "Walter Eucken und seine Auswirkungen auf die Wirtschaftspolitik, insbesondere in der Ära Kamitz in Österreich," (Diplom, Vienna, Hochschule für Welthandel, 1975); and Herbert Reisenhofer et al., "Kommentar zum Johnstone Bericht 1952," unpublished manuscript, Vienna, 1952.

175. Egon Matzner, *Modell Österreich: Skizzen für ein Wirtschafts- und Gesellschaftskonzept* (Vienna: Europa, 1967). Friedrich Placek, "Bankenkonzerne: Machtkonzentration oder Strukturpolitik?" *Wirtschaftspolitische Blätter* 2 (March–April 1976), 102–13, contains data for the years 1969–76.

176. OECD, *The Industrial Policy of Austria* (Paris, 1971), pp. 67–79; Ferdinand Lacina, *The Development of the Austrian Public Sector since World War II,* University of Texas, Institute of Latin American Studies, Office of Public Sector Studies, Technical Paper Series no. 7 (Austin, 1977), p. 17; and *ÖIAG Journal* 2/1978, 3.

177. Margit Scherb, "International Factors Determining Austrian Industrial Structure" (paper prepared for the Conference on Small States and Dependence, Austrian Institute for International Affairs, Laxenburg, 10–12 June 1981).

178. Quoted in *News from Austria* 1/1980 (7 January 1980), p. 2.

179. "The Austrian Lesson in Economic Harmony," *Euromoney,* May 1979, Supplement, 30–31.

180. *News from Austria* 24/1980 (14 October 1980), p. 3, and 28/1980 (25 November 1980), p. 2. The programmatic demands of Austria's business community are summarized in Vereinigung Österreichischer Industrieller, *Programm '80* (Vienna, n.d.), pp. 47–84.

181. Beirat für Wirtschafts- und Sozialfragen, *Vorschläge zur Industriepolitik II* (Vienna: Ueberreuter, 1978), pp. 33–47.

182. Quoted in "Austrian Industrial Development," *Financial Times*, 29 August 1975, pp. 9–11. See also Michaela Dorfwirth and Jörg Schram, "Bürgschaften und Garantien der öffentlichen Hand als Instrument der Investitionsfinanzierung," *Quartalshefte* 1/1968, 15–18; OECD, *Aims and Instruments of Industrial Policy*, pp. 45, 89; and Manfred Drennig, "Staatliche Wachstumspolitik in Österreich," *Quartalshefte* 4/1966, 19–28.

183. Quoted in *Kurier*, 23 May 1976. See also Oskar Grünwald, "Industrieadministration in Österreich," *IBE-Bulletin*, 21–22 August 1976, pp. 11–15.

184. Oskar Grünwald, "Austrian Industrial Structure and Industrial Policy," in Sven W. Arndt, ed., *The Political Economy of Austria* (Washington, D.C.: American Enterprise Institute, 1982), p. 139. The dollar figure quoted represents 10 billion schillings at the 1974 exchange rate of 18.693 schillings per dollar; see OECD, *National Accounts: Main Aggregates*, vol. 1: *1952–1981* (Paris, 1983), p. 102.

185. Grünwald, "Austria's Industrial Structure," p. 140.

186. Wilhelm Hankel, *Prosperity admidst Crisis: Austria's Economic Policy and the Energy Crunch* (Boulder: Westview, 1981), p. 32.

187. Gunther Tichy, "Wie wirkt das österreichische System der Investitionsförderung?" *Quartalshefte*, special issue, 1/1980, 20–21.

188. Vereinigung Österreichischer Industrieller, *Zur Wirtschaftspolitik*, 2d ed. (Vienna, 1975), p. 20.

189. Lacina, *Development of the Austrian Public Sector*, p. 20.

190. Karl Socher, "Die öffentlichen Unternehmen im österreichischen Banken- und Versicherungssystem," in Wilhelm Weber, ed., *Die Verstaatlichung in Österreich* (Berlin: Duncker & Humblot, 1964), pp. 452–53.

191. Quoted in "Austrian Lesson in Harmony," p. 12.

192. *World Business Weekly*, 29 June 1981, p. 51.

193. *Der Spiegel*, 24 September 1979, pp. 82–83.

194. Sarah Hogg, "A Small House in Order," *Economist*, 15 March 1980, Survey, p. 22. See also Christof Gaspari and Enrique H. Prat de la Riba, "Die Problemlösungskapazität des österreichischen Wirtschaftssystems," *Wirtschaftspolitische Blätter* 22, 6 (1975), 37–40, and *Die Presse*, 11 December 1981.

195. OECD, *Economic Surveys: Austria* (Paris, 1967), p. 12.

196. Felix Butschek, "The Economic Structure," in Steiner, *Modern Austria*, p. 151.

197. John Gerard Ruggie, "International Regimes, Transactions, and Change: Embedded Liberalism in the Postwar Economic Order," in Stephen D. Krasner, ed., *International Regimes* (Ithaca: Cornell University Press, 1983), pp. 195–232.

198. Alasdair I. Macbean, *Export Instability and Economic Development* (London: Allen & Unwin, 1966); Joseph D. Coppock, *International Economic Instability: The Experience after World War II* (New York: McGraw-Hill, 1962); Coppock, *International Trade Instability* (Farnborough: Saxon, 1977); and Odin Knudsen and Andrew Parnes, *Trade Instability and Economic Development* (Lexington, Mass.: Heath, 1975).

199. Coppock, *International Economic Instability*, p. 105.

200. Andrew Boyd, "How the Storm Changed the Signs," *Economist*, 28 January 1978, p. 24. See also Charles P. Kindleberger, *Multinational Excursions* (Cambridge: MIT Press, 1984), pp. 105–6.

CHAPTER 3. *Democratic Corporatism and Its Variants*

1. James N. Rosenau, *The Study of Political Adaptation* (London: Pinter, 1981), pp. 102–4.
2. Except when noted, "small European states" in this analysis will refer only to the seven states. At times they will be compared to five large industrial states: the United States, Britain, West Germany, France, and Japan.
3. Some of the literature on the subject is reviewed in Fritz Breuss, *Komparative Vorteile im österreichischen Aussenhandel* (Vienna: Österreichische Akademie der Wissenschaften, 1975), pp. 58–59; Antoine Basile, *Commerce extérieur et développement de la petite nation: Essai sur les contraintes de l'exiguïté économique* (Geneva: Droz, 1972).
4. United Nations, Department of Economic and Social Affairs, *A Study of Industrial Growth* (New York, 1963), pp. 9, 13–14. Foreign trade is not included in this study.
5. United Nations, Economic Commission for Europe, *Structure and Change in European Industry* (New York, 1977), p. 27. Foreign trade is included in this study.
6. UNCTAD, *Restructuring of World Industry: New Dimensions for Trade Cooperation* (New York, 1978), p. 6; see also pp. 5, 8–9. "Comparative Analysis of Economic Structures by Means of Input-Output Tables," *UN Economic Bulletin for Europe* 23, 1 (1971), 3, 17, 21.
7. UN, *Study of Industrial Growth*, pp. 9–12; UN, *Structure and Change in European Industry*, pp. 13–14. See also United Nations Industrial Development Organization, *World Industry since 1960: Progress and Prospect. Special Issue of the Industrial Development Survey for the Third General Conference on UNIDO* (New York, 1979), pp. 43–49, 331–365; Bela Balassa, "'Revealed' Comparative Advantage Revisited: An Analysis of Relative Export Shares of the Industrial Countries, 1953–1971," *Manchester School of Economic and Social Studies* 45 (December 1977), 337. Another statistical study showed that industries with large economies of scale (such as textiles, paper, printing, rubber, chemicals, petroleum products, metals, machinery, and transport equipment) become more important in the process of industrialization. Statistically speaking, their contribution to total manufacturing output increases from 40% to almost 60% per capita as income levels increase from $300 to $600. See Hollis B. Chenery, "Patterns of Industrial Growth," *American Economic Review* 50 (September 1960), 646.
8. Ibid., p. 643; Hollis B. Chenery and Lance Taylor, "Development Patterns: Among Countries and over Time," *Review of Economics and Statistics* 50 (November 1968), 399, 412–13.
9. Béla Kádár, *Small Countries in World Economy* (Budapest: Hungarian Academy of Sciences, Center for Afro-Asian Research, 1970), pp. 11, 15, Table 5.
10. Alfred Maizels, *Industrial Growth and World Trade* (Cambridge: Cambridge University Press, 1963), pp. 266–67 and 135–36. The sample of countries included in Maizels's analysis differs from the group of states analyzed here.
11. Peter J. Lloyd, *International Trade Problems of Small Nations* (Durham: Duke University Press, 1968), p. 37. In the 1950s the difference between the small European states and the large industrial states in the value added in

industrial output was considerably smaller in the consumer than in the producer goods industry. See UN, *Study of Industrial Growth*, pp. 7, 12.

12. "Comparative Analysis of Economic Structures," pp. 19, 41–42. The comparison is between the Netherlands, Belgium, and Norway on the one hand and Britain, France, and West Germany on the other.

13. L. B. M. Mennes, "Adjustment of the Industrial Structure of Developed Economies, in particular the Netherlands" (paper prepared for the International Symposium on Maritime Research and European Shipping and Shipbuilding, Rotterdam, 29–31 March 1978), p. 3.

14. Boston Consulting Group, *A Framework for Swedish Industrial Policy* (Stockholm: Departementens Offsetcentral, 1979), Appendix 9, p. 1.

15. Simon Kuznets, "Economic Growth of Small Nations," in E. A. G. Robinson, ed., *Economic Consequences of the Size of Nations: Proceedings of a Conference Held by the International Economic Association* (London: Macmillan, 1960), pp. 14–32; Lloyd, *International Trade Problems*, pp. 28–29, 33–34; Nadim G. Khalaf, *Economic Implications of the Size of Nations: With Special Reference to Lebanon* (Leiden: Brill, 1971), pp. 99–122; Khalaf, "Country Size and Trade Concentration," *Journal of Development Studies* 11 (October 1974), 81–85; Raimo Väyrnen, "The Position of Small Powers in the West European Network of Economic Relations," *European Journal of Political Research* 2 (June 1974), 153; D. H. Macgregor, "Trade of Large and Small Countries," *Economic Journal* 35 (December 1925), 642–45; Maizels, *Industrial Growth and World Trade*, p. 721; and Breuss, *Komparative Vorteile*, p. 60.

16. Raoul Gross and Michael Keating, "An Empirical Analysis of Competition in Export and Domestic Markets," *Occasional Studies, OECD Economic Outlook*, December 1970, 15.

17. Hans Genberg, *World Inflation and the Small Open Economy* (Stockholm: Swedish Industrial Publications, 1975); B. L. Scarfe, "A Model of the Inflation Cycle in a Small Open Economy," *Oxford Economic Papers* 25 (July 1973), 192–203; Martin F. J. Prachowny, *Small Open Economies: Their Structure and Policy Environment* (Lexington: Heath, 1975); Heinrich Otruba, "Inflation in Small Countries," *Wirtschaftspolitische Blätter* 22, 2 (1975), 119–25; Odd Aukrust, "Inflation in the Open Economy: A Norwegian Model," in Lawrence B. Krause and Walter S. Salant, eds., *Worldwide Inflation: Theory and Recent Experience* (Washington, D.C.: Brookings, 1977), pp. 107–53.

18. Organization for Economic Co-operation and Development (OECD), *Towards Full Employment and Price Stability (The MacCracken Report)* (Paris, 1977), p. 60, for example, calculates the external price influence in 1972–74 at 10.6% for the small European states and at 6.0% for the five larger countries.

19. UN, *Structure and Change in European Industry*, pp. 25–26. The sample of large countries excludes the United States and Japan but includes Italy. See also UN, *World Industry since 1960*, p. 48.

20. M. Carmi, "The Economics of Small Developed States," unpublished paper, Jerusalem, 1975, pp. 11–12; Fritz Breuss, "Die Makrostruktur der österreichishen Wirtschaft im Vergleich mit den europäischen Wirtschaftspartnern," in *Der Kleinstaat in der europäischen wirtschaftlichen Zusammenarbeit aus der Sicht Ungarns und Österreichs* (Vienna: Geschichte und Politik, 1975), pp. 62–63. See also Carmi, "Economics of Small Developed States," pp. 32–

33; Peer Hull Kristensen and Jørn Levinsen, *The Small Country Squeeze* (Roskilde, Denmark: Institute of Economics, Politics and Administration, 1978), pp. 112, 117.

21. "Comparative Analysis of Economic Structures," pp. 19, 43.

22. Kádár, *Small Countries in World Economy*, pp. 11, 15, Table 5; UN, *Study of Industrial Growth*, pp. 9, 13–14.

23. Beirat für Wirtschafts- und Sozialfragen, *Vorschläge zur Industriepolitik* (Vienna: Ueberreuter, 1970), p. 31; Helmut Kramer, *Industrielle Strukturprobleme Österreichs* (Vienna: Signum, 1980), p. 52.

24. Balassa, " 'Revealed' Comparative Advantage," p. 337.

25. See also Dieter Senghaas, *Weltwirtschaftsordnung und Entwicklungspolitik: Plädoyer für Dissoziation* (Frankfurt: Suhrkamp, 1977), pp. 34–35.

26. Chenery, "Industrial Growth," p. 639.

27. For 1954 see Michael Michaely, *Concentration in International Trade* (Amsterdam: North Holland, 1962), pp. 11–12, 19–20. For 1964 see Lloyd, *Trade Problems of Small Nations*, p. 33 and Appendix 2. See also Kristensen and Levinsen, *Small Country Squeeze*, p. 117; Kuznets, "Economic Growth of Small Nations," p. 22; Simon Kuznets, *Six Lectures on Economic Growth* (New York: Free, 1961), p. 95; Niclaus G. Krul, *La politique conjoncturelle en Belgique, aux Pays-Bas et en Suisse, 1950–1960* (Geneva: Droz, 1964), p. 92; and Guy F. Erb and Salvatore Schiavo-Campo, "Export Instability, Level of Development and Economic Size of Less Developed Countries," Oxford University Institute of Economics and Statistics *Bulletin* 31 (1969), 263–83. Due to differences in the sample of small states, time periods, and methods of computation, a number of null findings have been reported in the economics literature. See Värynen, "Position of Small Powers," pp. 160–61; Lloyd, *Trade Problems of Small Nations*, pp. 28–29, 33–34; and Khalaf, *Economic Implications*, pp. 93, 98.

28. Albert O. Hirschman, *National Power and the Structure of Foreign Trade* (Berkeley: University of California Press, 1945), pp. 85, 101–5, 109–14. Interestingly this was not true for the small European states, because their trade was more diversified than that of the Eastern European countries.

29. Kádár, *Small Countries in World Economy*, pp. 10–11, 23.

30. Kristensen and Levinsen, *Small Country Squeeze*, p. 114. Switzerland and Austria are not included in the figures for the small European states. Since they differ along a number of dimensions measuring the relative modernity of their industrial structures, their exclusion from these figures probably does not bias the findings.

31. *World Development Report, 1979* (Washington, D.C.: World Bank, August 1979), Table 15, p. 155. Switzerland has been excluded from the calculations.

32. OECD, *Balance of Payments of OECD Countries, 1960–1977* (Paris, 1979), author's calculations.

33. Donald B. Keesing, "Population and Industrial Development: Some Evidence from Trade Patterns," *American Economic Review* 58, 3 (Part I) (June 1968), 454–55.

34. Kristensen and Levinsen, *Small Country Squeeze*, p. 108.

35. Krul, *Politique conjoncturelle*, pp. 113–14; Committee on Invisible Exports, *World Invisible Trade* (London, August 1978), pp. 32–33.

36. Per Kleppe, *Main Aspects of Economic Policy in Norway since the War* (Oslo: Oslo University Press, 1966), p. 12; Kádár, *Small Countries in World Economy*,

p. 12; Committee on Invisible Exports, *World Invisible Trade*, p. 14; and James A. Storing, *Norwegian Democracy* (Boston: Houghton Mifflin, 1963), p. 3.

37. Committee on Invisible Exports, *World Invisible Trade*, pp. 6–7.

38. Richard Blackhurst, Nicolas Marian, and Jan Tumlir, *Trade Liberalization, Protectionism and Interdependence* (Geneva: GATT, 1977), p. 62, note 10; Shmuel N. Eisenstadt, "Sociological Characteristics and Problems of Small States: A Research Note," *Jerusalem Journal of International Relations* 2 (Winter 1976–77), 39; and Levinsen and Kristensen, *Small Country Squeeze*, pp. 127, 135.

39. Committee on Invisible Exports, *World Invisible Trade*, pp. 15, 30, 32; author's calculations.

40. Ibid., p. 3; Committee on Invisible Exports, *World Invisible Trade* (London, 1969), p. 1; and Blackhurst, Marian, and Tumlir, *Trade Liberalization*, p. 62, note 10.

41. Compared to the flow of foreign direct investment into the large advanced industrial states, it increased from 11% in 1960 to 35% a decade later before declining to 17% in 1978–80. OECD, *Policy Perspectives for International Trade and Economic Relations: Report by the High Level Group on Trade and Related Problems to the Secretary-General of the OECD* (Paris, 1972), p. 158; United Nations, *Transnational Corporations in World Development: Third Survey*, Sales no. E.83.II.A. 14 (New York, 1983), p. 19. See also Volker Bornschier, *Wachstum, Konzentration und Multinationalisierung von Industrieunternehmen* (Frauenfeld: Huber, 1976), pp. 562–64.

42. UN, *Transnational Corporations: A Re-Examination*, pp. 263–64.

43. Between 1960 and 1977 the basic balance of trade tended to be positive for the small European states and negative for the large industrial countries.

44. Béla Kádar, "Adjustment Patterns and Policies in Small Countries," in István Dobozi, Clare Keller, and Harriet Matejka, eds., *Small Countries and International Structural Adjustment* (Geneva: Graduate Institute of International Studies, 1982), p. 96.

45. Margret Sieber, *Dimensionen kleinstaatlicher Auslandsabhängigkeit*, Kleine Studien zur Politischen Wissenschaft, nos. 206–7 (Zurich: University of Zurich, Forschungsstelle für Politische Wissenschaft, 1981), pp. 155, 165; Boston Consulting Group, *Framework for Swedish Industrial Policy*, Appendix 2, p. 2. See also OECD, *Economic Surveys: Switzerland* (Paris, April 1978), p. 35; Charles Lipson, "The Transformation of Trade: The Sources and Effects of Regime Change," in Stephen D. Krasner, ed., *International Regimes* (Ithaca: Cornell University Press, 1983), p. 239.

46. Glenn Fong, "Export Dependence versus the New Protectionism: Constraints on Trade Policy in the Industrial World" (Ph.D. diss., Cornell University, 1983), pp. 303–4. Switzerland and Belgium are missing in this calculation.

47. In addition to the books listed in footnote 16 of chapter 1, see John Goldthorpe, ed., *Order and Conflict in Contemporary Capitalism: Studies in the Political Economy of Western European Nations* (Oxford: Clarendon, 1984). Both the *Journal für Sozialforschung* 23, 4 (1983), and the *International Political Science Review* 4, 2 (1983), have published special issues devoted to the question of corporatism. See also Philippe C. Schmitter, "Democratic Theory and Neo-Corporatist Practice," *Social Research* 50 (Winter 1983), 885–928; Wolfgang

Streeck and Schmitter, "Community, Market, State—and Associations? The Prospective Contribution of Interest Governance to Social Order," *European University Institute Working Papers* no. 94 (March 1984).

48. Douglas A. Hibbs, Jr., "On the Political Economy of Long-Run Trends in Strike Activity," *British Journal of Political Science* 8 (April 1978), 162. Cross-national aggregate statistics lend further support to this conclusion. The ratio between the average population for the small European state and large countries in 1975 was 1:12.6. But it is 1:17.6 for deaths from political violence (1948–77) 1:18.7 for riots (1948–77); and 1:23.6 for protest demonstrations (1948–77). See Charles Lewis Taylor and David A. Jodice, eds., *World Handbook of Political and Social Indicators*, vol. 1: *Cross National Attributes and Rates of Change*, 3d ed. (New Haven: Yale University Press, 1983), pp. 91–94, and vol. 2: *Political Protest and Government Change*, pp. 22–25, 33–36, 48–51.

49. Harold L. Wilensky, "Political Legitimacy and Consensus: Missing Variables in the Assessment of Social Policy," in Shimon E. Spiro and Ephraim Yuchtman-Yaar, eds., *Evaluating the Welfare State: Social and Political Perspectives* (New York: Academic, 1983), pp. 63–64.

50. Arend Lijphart, "Consociational Democracy," in Kenneth D. McRae, ed., *Consociational Democracy: Political Accommodation in Segmented Societies* (Toronto: McClelland & Stewart, 1974), pp. 88–89.

51. Val R. Lorwin, "Belgium: Religion, Class, and Language in National Politics," in Robert A. Dahl, ed., *Political Opposition in Western Democracies* (New Haven: Yale University Press, 1966), p. 178.

52. See in particular Phillipe C. Schmitter, "Still the Century of Corporatism," in Schmitter and Gerhard Lehmbruch, eds., *Trends toward Corporatist Intermediation* (Berverly Hills: Sage, 1979), pp. 7–52.

53. Robert A. Dahl and Edward R. Tufte, *Size and Democracy* (Stanford: Stanford University Press, 1973), p. 40. See also Jane J. Mansbridge, *Beyond Adversary Democracy* (New York: Basic, 1980), pp. 278–89; Margret Sieber, *Die Abhängigkeit der Schweiz von ihrer internationalen Umwelt: Konzepte und Indikatoren* (Frauenfeld: Huber, 1981), pp. 372–74.

54. Peter Wiles, "The Importance of Country Size," unpublished paper, n.p., n.d., pp. 9–10.

55. Hans Geser and François Höpflinger, "Problems of Structural Differentiation in Small Societies: A Sociological Contribution to the Theory of Small States and Federalism," *Bulletin of the Sociological Institute of the University of Zurich* 31 (July 1975), 59, 87, 64.

56. Eisenstadt, "Sociological Characteristics and Problems of Small States," p. 40; Gabriel Sheffer, "Public Mood, Policy Making Elites and Surprise Attacks on Some Small States," unpublished paper, Cornell University, 1975, pp. 17–28; and Peter Lange, *Union Democracy and Liberal Corporatism: Exit, Voice and Wage Regulation in Postwar Europe*, Cornell University, Western Societies Program, Occasional Paper no. 16 (Ithaca, 1983).

57. See for example for Norway, Storing, *Norwegian Democracy*, p. 125; for Austria and Switzerland, Peter J. Katzenstein, *Corporatism and Change: Austria, Switzerland and the Politics of Industry* (Ithaca: Cornell University Press, 1984), pp. 72, 112; and for Sweden, Dankwart A. Rustow, *The Politics of Compromise: A Study of Parties and Cabinet Government in Sweden* (New York: Greenwood, 1969), pp. 151–52.

58. Ulf Torgersen, "Political Institutions," in Natalie Rogoff Ramsøy, ed.,

Norwegian Society (Oslo: Universitetsforlaget, 1974), p. 197.

59. Johan P. Olsen, "Integrated Organizational Participation in Government," in Paul C. Nystrom and William H. Starbuck, eds., *Handbook of Organizational Design*, vol. 2: *Remodeling Organizations and Their Environments* (Oxford: Oxford University Press, 1981), pp. 509–11.

60. John P. Windmuller, "Concentration Trends in Union Structure: An International Comparison," *Industrial and Labor Relations Review* 35 (October 1981), 43–57; John D. Stephens, *The Transition from Capitalism to Socialism* (London: Macmillan, 1979) p. 118. Due to the exodus of foreign workers, the unionization rate of the Swiss work force has increased sharply in the 1970s and was by 1980 about 38% rather than the 27% reported by Stephens who relied on estimates from the early 1970s.

61. Stephens, *Transition from Capitalism to Socialism*, pp. 91–93, 110, 118–19. Japan is not included in this study.

62. Werner Melis, "Aufgaben und Bedeutung der Handelskammern im Ausland," in Johannes Koren and Manfred Ebner, eds., *Österreich auf einem Weg: Handelskammern und Sozialpartnerschaft im Wandel der Zeiten* (Graz: Stocker, 1974), pp. 11–26. See also Vorort des Schweizerischen Handels- und Industrie-Vereins, "Der Aufbau der europäischen Industrie-Spitzenverbände (Stand: Ende 1975)—Ergebnisse einer Umfrage," Zurich, May 1977.

63. Stephens, *Transition from Capitalism to Socialism*, p. 117.

64. Anne Romanis, "Cost Inflation and Incomes Policies in Industrial Countries," *IMF Staff Papers* 14 (March 1967), 196.

65. Gerhard Lehmbruch, "Liberal Corporatism and Party Government," in Schmitter and Lehmbruch, *Trends toward Corporatist Intermediation*, pp. 147–84.

66. Roland Czada and Gerhard Lehmbruch, "Economic Policies and Societal Consensus Mobilization: 'Sectoral Tripartism' vs. 'Corporatist' Integration" (paper prepared for the workshop on Interest Representation in Mixed Polities, European Consortium for Political Research, Lancaster, 29 March–4 April, 1981), pp. 4–5; Lehmbruch, "European Neo-Corporatism: An Export Article?" Woodrow Wilson Center, *Colloquium Paper* (Washington, D.C., April 1982), pp. 12–19.

67. Richard Rose, "Understanding Big Government," manuscript chapter 3, p. 12. Japan, Norway, and Sweden are not included in this comparison.

68. Philippe C. Schmitter, "Interest Intermediation and Regime Governability in Contemporary Western Europe and North America," in Suzanne Berger, ed., *Organizing Interests in Western Europe: Pluralism, Corporatism and the Transformation of Politics* (Cambridge: Cambridge University Press, 1981), especially pp. 304–5, 307.

69. Manfred G. Schmidt, "The Role of Parties in Shaping Macroeconomic Policy," in Francis G. Castles, ed., *The Impact of Parties: Politics and Policies in Democratic Capitalist States* (Beverly Hills: Sage, 1982), pp. 97–176; J. E. Keman and O. Braun, "Social Democracy, Corporatism and the Capitalist State: Economic Crisis, Parliamentary Politics and Policy-Formation in 18 Capitalist Democracies" (paper presented at the ECPR workshop "Modern Theories of State and Society," Lancaster, England, March–April 1981), p. 25; Lehmbruch, "European Neo-Corporatism: An Export Article?" p. 33; Gerhard Lehmbruch, "Introduction: Neo-Corporatism in Comparative Perspective," in Lehmbruch and Philippe C. Schmitter, eds., *Patterns of Corporatist*

Policy-Making (Beverly Hills: Sage, 1982), pp. 16–22; and Lehmbruch, "Concertation and the Structure of Corporatist Networks," in Goldthorpe, *Order and Conflict in Contemporary Capitalism.*

70. Harold L. Wilensky, *The "New Corporatism," Centralization and the Welfare State* (Beverly Hills: Sage, 1976); Wilensky, "Leftism, Catholicism, and Democratic Corporatism: The Role of Political Parties in Recent Welfare State Development," in Peter J. Flora and Arnold J. Heidenheimer, eds., *The Development of Welfare States in Europe and America* (New Brunswick: Transaction, 1981), pp. 345–82; Castles, *Impact of Parties;* Stephens, *Transition from Capitalism to Socialism;* and David R. Cameron, "Social Democracy, Corporatism, and Labor Quiescence: The Representation of Economic Interest in Advanced Capitalist Society" (paper presented at the Conference on Representation and the State: Problems of Governability and Legitimacy in Western European Democracies, Stanford University, October 1982).

71. Robert H. Salisbury, "Why No Corporatism in America?" in Schmitter and Lehmbruch, *Trends toward Corporatist Intermediation,* pp. 213–30; Graham K. Wilson, "Why Is There No Corporatism in the United States?" in Lehmbruch and Schmitter, *Patterns of Corporatist Policy-Making,* pp. 219–36.

72. Andrew Shonfield, *In Defence of the Mixed Economy* (Oxford: Oxford University Press, 1984).

73. T. J. Pempel and Keiichi Tsunekawa, "Corporatism without Labor? The Japanese Anomaly," in Schmitter and Lehmbruch, *Trends toward Corporatist Intermediation,* pp. 231–70.

74. Peter J. Katzenstein, "Problem or Model? West Germany in the 1980s," *World Politics* 32 (July 1980), 577–98.

75. Peter Lange, "The Conjunctural Condition for Consensual Wage Regulation: An Initial Examination of Some Hypotheses" (paper prepared for presentation at the Annual Meeting of the American Political Science Association, New York, September 1981), p. 66.

76. Kristensen and Levinsen, *Small Country Squeeze,* p. 132.

77. Kuznets, "Economic Growth," pp. 28–30; Kuznets, *Six Lectures,* pp. 98–99.

78. Kádár, *Small Countries in World Economy,* pp. 9, 14.

79. David Vital, *The Inequality of States: A Study of Small Powers in International Relations* (Oxford: Clarendon, 1967), pp. 190–91; Lange, "Conjunctural Condition for Consensual Wage Regulation," pp. 62, 64.

80. Arend Lijphart, "Consociational Democracy," *World Politics* 21 (October 1968), 217; Lijphart, *The Politics of Accommodation: Pluralism and Democracy in the Netherlands* (Berkeley: University of California Press, 1968).

81. Gerhard Lehmbruch, "Konkordanzdemokratien im internationalen System: Ein Paradigma für die Analyse von internen und externen Bedingungen politischer Systeme," *Politische Vierteljahresschrift* 10 (1969), special issue no. 1: 149–54.

82. Lehmbruch, "European Neo-Corporatism," p. 17.

83. Lange, "Conjunctural Condition for Consensual Wage Regulation," pp. 62, 64.

84. Lloyd Ulman and Robert J. Flanagan, *Wage Restraint: A Study of Incomes Policies of Western Europe* (Berkeley: University of California Press, 1971), pp. 219, 222–23.

85. Robert B. Kvavik, *Interest Groups in Norwegian Politics* (Oslo: Univer-

sitetsforlaget, 1976), pp. 26–27, 156–58.

86. Jane Kramer, "A Reporter in Zurich," *New Yorker,* 15 December 1980, p. 134.

87. Lehmbruch, "Introduction: Neo-Corporatism in Comparative Perspective," p. 25.

88. Michael Shalev, "Class Politics and the Western Welfare State," in Spiro and Yuchtman-Yaar, *Evaluating the Welfare State,* pp. 27–33; Shalev, "The Social Democratic Model and Beyond: Two 'Generations' of Comparative Research on the Welfare State," *Comparative Social Research* 6 (1983), 319–23. See also Gregory M. Luebbert, Harold L. Wilensky, Susan Reed Hahn, and Adrienne M. Jamieson, "Comparative Social Policy: Theories, Methods, Findings" (paper prepared for a joint Wissenschaftszentrum Berlin/Stanford University conference on Cross-national Policy Research, Berlin, 18–21 December 1983); Leo Panitch, "Trade Unions and the Capitalist State," *New Left Review* no. 125 (January–February 1981), 21–43; and Jonas Pontusson, "Behind and Beyond Social Democracy in Sweden," *New Left Review* no. 143 (January–February 1984), 69–96.

89. Francis G. Castles, *The Social Democratic Image of Society: A Study of the Achievements and Origins of Scandinavian Social Democracy in Comparative Perspective* (London: Routledge & Kegan Paul, 1978), p. 131. See also Pontusson, "Behind and Beyond Social Democracy," p. 90.

90. Wilensky, "Leftism, Catholicism, and Democratic Corporatism," p. 359 and *passim.*

91. Gösta Esping-Andersen and Walter Korpi, "From Poor Relief to Institutional Welfare States: The Development of Scandinavian Social Policy," unpublished paper, Swedish Institute for Social Research, September 1981, Table 1.

92. David R. Cameron, "The Expansion of the Public Economy: A Comparative Analysis," *American Political Science Review* 72 (December 1978), 1253.

93. Shalev, "Class Politics and the Welfare State," p. 40.

94. Ibid., p. 37. See also Shalev, "Social Democratic Model," pp. 338–39.

95. Stephens, *Transition from Capitalism to Socialism,* p. 124.

96. Gerhard Lehmbruch, "Interorganisatorische Verflechtungen im Neokorporatismus," in J. W. Falter, C. Fenner, and M. T. Greven, eds., *Politische Willensbildung und Interessenvermittlung* (Opladen: Westdeutscher Verlag, forthcoming), manuscript pp. 11–12. On Switzerland see also T. Michael Clarke, "Is Switzerland an Economic Success? An Empirical Evaluation of the Theories of Mancur Olson and Jean-Christian Lambelet" (Geneva: Graduate Institute of International Studies, Center for Empirical Research in International Relations [1983]); Jean Christian Lambelet, "Switzerland's Economy: World Dependence versus Domestic Stability," in Dobozi, Keller, and Matejka, *Small Countries and International Structural Adjustment,* pp. 147–62; and Leonardo Parri, "Svizzera: Ancora un caso di neocorporativismo," *Stato e Mercato* 10 (April 1984), 97–130.

97. Steven B. Wolinetz, "Wage Regulation in the Netherlands: The Rise and Fall of the Postwar Social Contract" (paper prepared for presentation at the Council for European Studies Conference of Europeanists, Washington, D.C., 13–15 October 1983), p. 48.

98. Erwin Zimmermann, "Entwicklungstendenzen des Korporatismus und die Industriepolitik in den Niederlanden," in University of Constance *Diskus-*

sionsbeitrag 1/1983, 107–31. On the 1970s see also Norbert Lepszy, *Regierung, Parteien und Gewerkschaften in den Niederlanden: Entwicklung und Strukturen* (Dusseldorf: Droste, 1979); Ilja Scholten, "Does Consociationalism Exist? A Critique of the Dutch Experience," in Richard Rose, ed., *Electoral Participation: A Comparative Analysis* (Beverly Hills: Sage, 1980), pp. 329–54; and Ronald A. Kieve, "Pillars of Sand: A Marxist Critique of Consociational Democracy in the Netherlands, *Comparative Politics* 13 (April 1981), 313–37.

99. M. C. P. M. Van Schendelen, "Crisis of the Dutch Welfare State," *Contemporary Crises* 7 (1983), 227.

100. Shalev, "Social Democratic Model," pp. 324–25, 327, 331, 334–35.

101. See for example Castles, *Social Democratic Image of Society*, pp. 112–13, 131–42; Francis G. Castles, "How Does Politics Matter? Structure or Agency in the Determination of Public Policy Outcomes," *European Journal of Political Research* 9 (June 1981), 127–28.

102. Castles, "How Does Politics Matter?" p. 126. See also his "The Impact of Parties on Public Expenditure," in Castles, *Impact of Parties*, pp. 21–96.

103. Shalev, "Class Politics," pp. 45–46.

104. Stein Rokkan, *Citizens, Elections, Parties: Approaches to the Comparative Study of the Processes of Development* (Oslo: Universitetsforlaget, 1970), p. 89.

105. Ronald Rogowski, "Some Possible Effects of Trade and War on Representative Institutions and Party Systems: Evidence from the OECD States between 1955 and 1980," unpublished paper, Center for Advanced Study, Stanford, Calif., 1984, pp. 40–41.

106. Kaare Strom, "Party Goals and Government Performance in Parliamentary Democracies" (paper prepared for delivery at the 1983 Annual Meeting of the American Political Science Association, Chicago, 1–4 September 1983), p. 8. This paper builds on his "Minority Government and Majority Rule" (Ph.D. diss., Stanford University, 1983). See also Hans Daalder, "Cabinets and Party Systems in Ten Smaller European Democracies," *Acta Politica* 6 (1971), 282–303.

107. *New York Times*, 10 January 1984, p. A3.

108. Hans Daalder, "The Netherlands: Opposition in a Segmented Society," in Dahl, *Political Oppositions*, p. 219.

109. Nils Stjernquist, "Sweden: Stability or Deadlock?" in Dahl, *Political Oppositions*, pp. 133, 136.

110. Katzenstein, *Corporatism and Change*.

111. Kaare Strom, "Minority Government and Majority Rule," unpublished paper, Stanford University, January 1982, p. 36.

112. G. Bingham Powell, Jr., *Contemporary Democracies: Participation, Stability, and Violence* (Cambridge: Harvard University Press, 1982), pp. 14, 81, 90, 91.

113. Gösta Esping-Andersen, "Fifty Years of Social Democratic Rule: Single Party Dominance in Sweden" (paper prepared for presentation at Cornell University, April 1984), p. 9.

114. Cameron, "Expansion of the Public Economy," pp. 1253–54. See also Castles, "How Does Politics Matter?" pp. 119–32.

115. Rudolf Klein, "Public Expenditures in an Inflationary World," paper delivered at a Brookings Institution conference on inflation, Washington, D.C., 1978, p. 46.

116. Cameron, "Expansion of the Public Economy." See also Michael Wal-

lerstein, "The Structure of Labor Federations, the Growth of Welfare Expenditures, and International Openness," unpublished manuscript, University of Chicago, January 1983.

117. Schmidt, "Role of Parties." See also Manfred G. Schmidt, "The Welfare State and the Economy in Periods of Economic Crisis: A Comparative Study of Twenty-Three OECD Nations," *European Journal of Political Research* 11 (March 1983), 1–26; Schmidt, "Arbeitslosigkeit und Vollbeschäftigungspolitik: Ein internationaler Vergleich," *Leviathan* 11, 4 (1983), 451–72.

118. Shalev, "Class Politics and the Welfare State," p. 46.

119. Shalev, "Social Democratic Model," pp. 317, 325–26, 332–33, 335–36, 340. These distinctions are being developed by Gösta Esping-Anderson and Walter Korpi; see their "The State as a System of Stratification: Class Mobilization and the Manufacturing of Solidaristic Policies" (paper prepared for the Third Annual Council for European Studies Conference, Washington, D.C., April 1982).

120. Bornschier, *Wachstum, Konzentration und Multinationalisierung*, pp. 457, 497.

121. Kristensen and Levinsen, *Small Country Squeeze*, p. 176; Lawrence G. Franko, *The European Multinationals: A Renewed Challenge to American and British Big Business* (Stamford: Greylock 1976).

122. Bornschier, *Wachstum, Konzentration und Multinationalisierung*, p. 342; United Nations, *Transnational Corporations in World Development: A Re-Examination* (New York, 1978), p. 212.

123. United Nations, *Multinational Corporations in World Development* (New York, 1973), p. 127. See also UN, *Transnational Corporations: A Re-Examination*, p. 138.

124. UN, *Transnational Corporations: A Re-Examination*, p. 238.

125. Bornschier, *Wachstum, Konzentration und Multinationalisierung*, p. 342, and UN, *Transnational Corporations: A Re-Examination*, p. 212.

126. United Nations, *Transnational Corporations in World Development: Third Survey* (1983), pp. 19, 285–90.

127. Bornschier, *Wachstum, Konzentration und Multinationalisierung*, pp. 471, 474; *Information über multinationale Konzerne* 1/1980, 17.

128. Seev Hirsch, *Location of Industry and International Competitiveness* (Oxford: Clarendon, 1967), pp. 127–29.

129. UN, *Transnational Corporations: A Re-Examination*, p. 163.

130. Theodore Geiger, *Welfare and Efficiency: Their Interactions in Western Europe and Implications for International Economic Relations* (Washington, D.C.: National Planning Association, 1978), p. 94.

131. UN, *Transnational Corporations: A Re-Examination*, p. 179.

132. Ibid., p. 26; OECD, *The Industrial Policies of 14 Member Countries* (Paris, 1971), p. 306; and C. Fred Bergsten, Thomas Horst, and Theodore H. Moran, *American Multinational Corporations and American Interests* (Washington, D.C.: Brookings, 1978), pp. 38–40, 112–13.

133. Sune Carlson, "Company Policies for International Expansion: The Swedish Experience," in Tamir Agmon and Charles P. Kindleberger, eds., *Multinationals from Small Countries* (Cambridge: MIT Press, 1977), p. 68; *Economist*, 10–16 December 1983, p. 74.

134. UN, *Transnational Corporations: A Re-Examination*, pp. 215–17.

135. Ibid., p. 48.

136. Krul, *Politique conjoncturelle*, pp. 113–14.

137. Carlson, "Company Policies," pp. 53–54; UN, *Transnational Corporations: A Re-Examination*, p. 48; European Communities, Statistical Office, *Tableaux entrées-sorties 1965* (Brussels, 1965), p. 69; and Krul, *Politique conjoncturelle*, p. 113.

138. Committee on Invisible Exports, *World Invisible Trade*, pp. 3–4, shows Austria, Denmark, and Norway not among the top twenty exporters of financial services and insurance.

139. OECD, Committee for Scientific and Technological Policy, *Science and Technology in the New Socio-Economic Context* (Paris, 1979), p. 150. See also Science Council of Canada, *Seminar on Science Policies in Small Industrialized Northern Countries, Montebello, Quebec, 27–29 November 1977* (Ottawa: Minister of Supplies and Services, SS31–4/1978).

140. K. Pavitt and S. Wald, *The Conditions for Success in Technological Innovation* (Paris: OECD, 1971), pp. 53, 144–47. See also the different tone in Kristensen and Levinsen, *Small Country Squeeze*, which reflects both views without successfully resolving this intellectual tension. See pp. 115, 238–39, 247–48.

141. Pavitt and Wald, *Conditions of Success*, p. 53. Statistical evidence supporting this view is reported on pp. 144–45 and in Kristensen and Levinsen, *Small Country Squeeze*, pp. 276–77.

142. Kristensen and Levinsen, *Small Country Squeeze*, p. 147.

143. OECD, *Gaps in Technology: Comparisons between Member Countries in Education, Research and Development, Technological Innovation, International Economic Exchanges* (Paris, 1970), p. 198.

144. Balassa, "'Revealed' Comparative Advantage," pp. 334–36. The Netherlands is the sole exception; Switzerland is not included in this sample.

145. Hirsch, *Location of Industry*, pp. v, 32–34, 83–85, 121–27. For the Netherlands see also OECD, *Reviews of National Science Policy: Netherlands* (Paris, 1973).

146. OECD, *The Research System: Comparative Survey of the Organization and Financing of Fundamental Research*, vol. 2 (Paris, 1973), pp. 117, 128–29; Hirsch, *Location of Industry*, pp. 127–29; and Balassa, "'Revealed' Comparative Advantage," p. 333.

147. OECD, *The Research System*, 2:33; Katzenstein, *Corporatism and Change*, pp. 99–101.

148. OECD, *Policies for the Stimulation of Industrial Innovation: Country Reports*, vol. 2–2 (Paris, 1978), p. 132; Steven Langdon, "Industrial Restructuring and the Third World: The Case of Dutch Textile Manufacturing, 1965–1979," unpublished paper, Ottawa, April 1980, p. 5.

149. Anthony Scaperlanda, *Prospects for Eliminating Non-Tariff Distortions* (Leyden: Sijthoff, 1973), p. 127.

150. Felix Streichenberg, *Forschung und volkswirtschaftliches Wachstum unter besonderer Berücksichtigung schweizerischer Verhältnisse* (Bern: Lang, 1968), p. 129.

151. Frederick Seitz, "Summary Comments on Government-Science Relationships," in Lawrence W. Bass and Bruce S. Old, eds., *Formulation of Research Policies: Collected Papers from an International Symposium* (Washington: American Academy for the Advancement of Science, 1967), p. 95.

152. Ibid., p. 95; Scaperlanda, *Prospects for Eliminating Non-Tariff Distortions,* pp. 145–46.

153. Robert Gilpin, "Technological Strategies and National Purpose," *Science,* 31 July 1970, p. 446.

154. OECD, *Policies for Industrial Innovation,* 2-2: 184; Ingemar N. H. Dörfer, "Science and Technology in Sweden," in T. Dixon Long and Christopher Wright, eds., *Science Policies of Industrial Nations* (New York: Praeger, 1975), pp. 178–79.

155. Carlson, "Company Policies," p. 68.

156. OECD, *Policies for Industrial Innovation,* 2-2: 20, 23.

157. Ibid., p. 33; Seitz, "Summary Comments," pp. 95–96.

158. OECD, *Policies for Industrial Innovation,* 2-2: 105–8, 121; Seitz, "Summary Comments," p. 94.

159. The validity and reliability of fiscal indicators are discussed by Ernst-Jürgen Horn, *Technologische Neuerungen und internationale Arbeitsteilung: Die Bundesrepublik Deutschland im internationalen Vergleich* (Tübingen: Mohr, 1976), pp. 56–61.

160. Kristensen and Levinsen, *Small Country Squeeze,* p. 146. For Switzerland the figure is 2.2%, not 1.2%.

161. Horn, *Technologische Neuerungen,* p. 138; B. R. Williams, *Science and Technology in Economic Growth* (New York: Wiley, 1973), p. 7; and Kristensen and Levinsen, *Small Country Squeeze,* p. 146. The residuals reported in a statistical analysis also support this ranking of the small European states' research and development efforts: see Yoram Ben-Porath, "Some Implications of Economic Size and Level of Investment in R and D," *Economic Development and Cultural Change* 21 (October 1972), 99.

162. OECD, *Policies of Industrial Innovation,* 1: 16. See also Balassa, "'Revealed' Comparative Advantage," p. 337.

163. M. Carmi, "Science and Technology Policy in Small States: First Report," unpublished manuscript, Jerusalem Group for National Planning, April 1975, pp. 10–11. Pavitt and Wald, *Conditions for Success,* p. 122, give more disaggregated data supporting the same point.

164. OECD, *Gaps in Technology,* p. 205.

165. C. Freeman and A. Young, *The Research and Development Effort in Western Europe, North America and the Soviet Union: An Experimental International Comparison of Research Expenditures and Manpower in 1962* (Paris: OECD, 1965), p. 75; Kristensen and Levinsen, *Small Country Squeeze,* pp. 281–82.

166. The ratios are 3.6 as compared to 1.2. See Christof Gaspari and Hans Millendorfer, *Prognosen für Österreich: Fakten und Formeln der Entwicklung* (Vienna: Geschichte und Politik, 1973), p. 86.

167. OECD, *The Research System,* 2: 31; Kristensen and Levinsen, *Small Country Squeeze,* pp. 183–84; and OECD, *Gaps in Technology,* p. 63.

168. Gerard Curzon, *Multilateral Commercial Diplomacy: The General Agreement on Tariffs and Trade and Its Impact on National Commercial Policies and Techniques* (London: Joseph, 1965), p. 161. See also Hans Mayrzedt, *Multilaterale Wirtschaftsdiplomatie zwischen westlichen Industiestaaten als Instrument zur Stärkung der multilateralen und liberalen Handelspolitik* (Bern: Lang, 1979), pp. 325, 380.

169. U.S. Congress, Joint Economic Committee, *Trade Restraints in the Western Community: With Tariff Comparisons and Selected Statistical Tables Pertinent to Foreign Economic Policy* (Washington, D.C., 1961), pp. 11–12.

170. Victoria Curzon, *The Essentials of Economic Integration: Lessons of EFTA Experience* (London: Macmillan, 1974), pp. 68, 70–71, 73.

171. General Agreement on Tariffs and Trade (GATT), *Basic Instruments and Selected Documents*, Supplement 10 (March 1962), p. 114.

172. Ibid., Supplements 18 (April 1972)–24 (June 1978).

173. U.S. Congress, Senate, Committee on Finance, Subcommittee on International Trade, *An Economic Analysis of the Effects of the Tokyo Round of Multilateral Trade Negotiations on the United States and Other Major Industrialized Countries*, MTN Studies no. 5 (Washington, D.C., 1979), p. 48, author's calculations.

174. Curzon, *Multilateral Commercial Diplomacy*, p. 240. Restrictions on trade in cotton textiles are excluded.

175. UNCTAD, Trade and Development Board, Committee on Manufacturers, *International Trade in Textiles and Developing Countries*, TD/B/C.2/174 (Geneva, 1977), p. 2.

176. OECD, *Policy Perspectives for International Trade and Economic Relations* (Paris, 1972), p. 149.

177. The ratio of export promotion (in millions of dollars) over the value of export trade (in billions of dollars) multiplied by 100 is 0.15 for Austria and Denmark and 0.05 for Switzerland, the Netherlands, Belgium, and Sweden. See *Botschaft des Bundesrates an die Bundesversammlung über einen Beitrag an die schweizerische Zentrale für Handelsförderung* (Bern, 1975), p. 11; *United Nations Statistical Yearbook 1972* (New York, 1973).

178. OECD, *Balances of Payments of OECD Countries, 1960–1977* (New York, 1979), p. 48.

179. Österreichisches Institut für Wirtschaftsforschung, *Monatsberichte* 34 (October 1961), 431.

180. Wilbur F. Monroe, *International Trade Policy in Transition* (Lexington: Heath, 1975), p. 23.

181. Calculated from the Contracting Parties to the GATT, *Basic Documentation for Tariff Study*, 3 vols. (Geneva, July 1970).

182. Günter Zenk, *Konzentrationspolitik in Dänemark, Norwegen und Finnland* (Tübingen: Mohr, 1971), p. 95.

183. Günter Zenk, *Konzentrationspolitik in Schweden* (Tübingen: Mohr, 1971), pp. 24–25.

184. Zenk, *Konzentrationspolitik in Dänemark*, pp. 147–48; Zuhayr Mikdashi, "Aluminum," in Raymond Vernon, ed., *Big Business and the State: Changing Relations in Western Europe* (Cambridge: Harvard University Press, 1974), pp. 174–75.

185. Mikdashi, "Aluminum," p. 137; Zenk, *Konzentrationspolitik in Dänemark*, pp. 142–43.

186. Bornschier, *Wachstum, Konzentration und Multinationalisierung*, p. 206. Japan is excluded from this calculation.

187. Christian Franck, "Die ordnungspolitische Neugestaltung in Belgien: Einflussgrössen und Lösungsversuche" (Ph.D. diss., University of Cologne, 1966), p. 33; OECD, *Export Cartels. Report of the Committee of Experts on Restrictive Business Practices* (Paris, 1974), p. 8.

188. OECD, *Industrial Policies of 14 Member Countries*, p. 242.

189. Zenk, *Konzentrationspolitik in Dänemark*, pp. 108, 142, 147.

190. Göran Ohlin, "Sweden," in Vernon, *Big Business and the State*, pp. 139–40; Zenk, *Konzentrationspolitik in Schweden*, pp. 12, 26–36.

191. Jan Olof Edberg and Bengt Ryden, "Large Mergers in Sweden 1962–1976" (Berlin: International Institute of Management, dp/78-14, February 1978).

192. Ohlin, "Sweden," pp. 138–39.

193. OECD, *Industrial Policies of 14 Member Countries*, pp. 315–16.

194. Dörfer, "Science and Technology Policy in Sweden," pp. 179–80; Zenk, *Konzentrationspolitik in Schweden*, p. 110.

195. James G. Abert, *Economic Policy and Planning in the Netherlands, 1950–65* (New Haven: Yale University Press, 1969), p. 122; Hildegard Graebner, *Die langfristige Planung in Norwegen, Schweden und den Niederlanden* (Cologne: Deutsches Industrieinstitut, 1965), pp. 96–97.

196. Graebner, *Langfristige Planung*, p. 84.

197. Ibid., pp. 84–85.

198. Ibid., p. 85; *Nationalbudget und Wirtschaftspolitik* (Hannover: Literatur und Zeitgeschehen, 1962), pp. 19, 21; and OECD, *Reviews of National Science Policy: Netherlands*, p. 272.

199. Cornelius Westrate, *Economic Policy in Practice: The Netherlands, 1950–1957* (Leiden: Kroese, 1959), p. 45; Graebner, *Langfristige Planung*, pp. 86, 114–16.

200. Graebner, *Langfristige Planung*, p. 124.

201. Ibid., p. 12; Leif Johansen and Harald Hallaråker, *Economic Planning in Norway* (Oslo: Universitetsforlaget, 1970), p. 10; and Petter Jakob Bjerve, *Trends in Quantitative Economic Planning in Norway* (Oslo: Statistical Sentralbyra, 1968).

202. *Nationalbudget und Wirtschaftspolitik*, p. 96; Graebner, *Langfristige Planung*, pp. 15–16; Johansen and Hallaråker, *Economic Planning*, pp. 22–24; and Eivind Erichsen, "Economic Planning and Policies in Norway," *Challenge*, January–February 1978, p. 6.

203. *Nationalbudget und Wirtschaftspolitik*, p. 10.

204. Johansen and Hallaråker, *Economic Planning*, p. 4; *Nationalbudget und Wirtschaftspolitik*, pp. 97, 115; and Per Kleppe, *Main Aspects of Economic Policy in Norway since the War* (Oslo: Universitetsforlaget, 1966), pp. 5, 12.

205. Graebner, *Langfristige Planung*, pp. 33, 35.

206. OECD, *Public Expenditure Trends* (Paris, 1978), pp. 14–15.

207. Ibid., p. 18.

208. David Smith, "Public Consumption and Economic Performance," *National Westminster Bank Quarterly Review*, November 1975, pp. 17, 28–29.

209. Ibid., p. 23.

210. The actual figures were 24.3% vs. 13.5%. See OECD, *Public Expenditure Trends*, p. 19.

211. Gross and Keating, "Analysis of Competition in Export and Domestic Markets," pp. 7–8, 11; it is possible that the overvaluation and undervaluation of national currencies in the late 1960s accounts for some of the difference.

212. G. Richard Thoman, *Foreign Investment and Regional Development: The Theory and Practice of Investment Incentives, with a Case Study of Belgium* (New York: Praeger, 1973), pp. 3, 7, 18–19, 32, 52, 164; *Regional Problems and Policies in OECD Countries*, vol. 2 (Paris, 1976), pp. 44–61.

213. UN, *Transnational Corporations: A Re-Examination*, pp. 272–74.

214. Thoman, *Foreign Investment and Regional Development*, pp. 64–66. Monroe, *International Trade Policy*, pp. 49–50, gives a more optimistic appraisal.

215. OECD, *Regional Problems and Policies in OECD Countries*, vol. 1 (Paris, 1976), pp. 91–104; OECD, *Selected Industrial Policy Instruments: Objectives and Scope* (Paris, 1978), pp. 14–15; and Harold G. Jones, *Planning and Productivity in Sweden* (London: Croom Helm, 1976), pp. 202–3.

216. Malcolm MacLennan, Murray Forsyth, and Geoffrey Denton, *Economic Planning and Policies in Britain, France, and Germany* (New York: Praeger, 1968), pp. 286–88.

217. Ohlin, "Sweden," p. 133; OECD, *Industrial Policies of 14 Member Countries*, pp. 301–2.

218. Kenneth Hanf, Benny Hjern, and David O. Porter, *Networks of Implementation and Administration for Manpower Policies at the Local Level in the Federal Republic of Germany and Sweden* (Berlin: International Institute of Management, dp/77-16, 1977), p. 17.

219. Michele Salvati and Giorgo Brosio, "The Rise of Market Policies: Industrial Relation in the Seventies," *Daedalus*, Spring 1979, p. 55; Geiger, *Welfare and Efficiency*, p. 65.

220. UN, *Transnational Corporations: Third Survey*, p. 19.

221. Peter Flora and Jens Alber, "Modernization, Democratization, and the Development of Welfare States in Western Europe," in Flora and Arnold J. Heidenheimer, eds., *The Development of Welfare States in Europe and America* (New Brunswick: Transaction, 1981), p. 55.

222. Wilensky, *"New Corporatism"*, p. 11.

223. Hugh Heclo, *Modern Social Politics in Britain and Sweden: From Relief to Income Maintenance* (New Haven: Yale University Press, 1974); Albert H. Rosenthal, *The Social Programs of Sweden: A Search for Security in a Free Society* (Minneapolis: University of Minnesota Press, 1967); Carl G. Uhr, *Sweden's Social Security System: An Appraisal of Its Economic Impact in the Postwar Period*, Department of Health, Education and Welfare, Social Security Administration, Office of Research and Statistics, Research Report no. 14 (Washington, D.C., 1966), p. 146; and Norman Furniss and Timothy Tilton, *The Case for the Welfare State: From Social Security to Social Equality* (Bloomington: Indiana University Press, 1977), pp. 122–52.

224. Katzenstein, *Corporatism and Change*, pp. 109–12.

225. International Labour Office, *The Cost of Social Security: Eighth International Inquiry, 1967–1971* (Geneva, 1971), pp. 170–71.

226. OECD, *Old Age Pension Schemes* (Paris, 1977), p. 89; Jens Alber, "Social Security (I): Participants in Social Insurance Systems in Western Europe," *Historical Indicators of the Western European Democracies* 4 (Mannheim, July 1976), p. 88; Max Frischknecht, "Der Entwurf zu einem Bundesgesetz über die obligatorische berufliche Vorsorge," *Schweizerische Zeitschrift für Sozialversicherung* 112, 2 (1976), 73–98; and H. P. Tschudi, "Die Entwicklung der schweizerischen Sozialversicherung seit dem zweiten Weltkrieg," *Schweizerische Zeitschrift für Volkswirtschaft und Statistik* 112, 3 (1976), 323.

227. Ernst Heissman, *Blick über die Grenzen: Die betriebliche und staatliche Altersversorgung in 20 Ländern* (Wiesbaden: Arbeit & Alter, 1963), pp. 50, 54; Uhr, *Sweden's Social Security*, p. 146.

228. Ohlin, "Sweden," pp. 132–33.

229. Uhr, *Sweden's Social Security*, p. 68. In Sweden in 1962 only 2% of the 771,000 insured residents were privately covered. For Switzerland see "Cost of Non-Statutory Social Security Schemes," *International Labour Review* 78

(October 1958), 399; Peter J. Katzenstein, *Capitalism in One Country? Switzerland in the International Economy*, Cornell University Western Societies Program, Occasional Papers no. 13 (Ithaca, January 1980), p. 42.

230. OECD, *The Tax/Benefit Position of Selected Income Groups in OECD Member Countries, 1972–76* (Paris, 1978), p. 94. It is not clear how this publication treats cantonal taxation in Switzerland.

231. OECD, *Old Age Pensions*, pp. 63–66; Frederic L. Pryor, *Public Expenditures in Communist and Capitalist Nations* (London: Allen & Unwin, 1968), pp. 130, 150.

232. *Social Security in Ten Industrial Nations* (Zurich: Union Bank of Switzerland, 1977). This comparison is biased in favor of Switzerland because the data in this study are drawn only from the rich canton of Zurich. The per capita income in that canton is about 20% above the Swiss average. See OECD, *Regional Problems and Policies*, 2: 198.

233. Gardner C. Patterson, *Discrimination in International Trade: The Policy Issues, 1945–1965* (Princeton: Princeton University Press, 1966), pp. 352, 371.

234. UN, *Transnational Corporations: A Re-Examination*, p. 27.

235. C. Fred Bergsten, *Toward a New World Trade Policy: The Maidenhead Papers* (Lexington: Heath, 1975), pp. 168–69.

236. *Nachrichten für Aussenhandel* no. 138, 22 July 1974.

237. Katzenstein, *Capitalism in One Country?* pp. 19–20; J. Stephen Hoadley, "Small States as Aid Donors," *International Organization* 34 (Winter 1980), 130.

238. *Nachrichten für Aussenhandel* no. 93, 12 May 1976; Deutsch-Schwedische Handelskammer, *Stockholm Information* no. 10, October 1975; *Neue Zürcher Zeitung*, 16 March 1972 and 28 April 1973; and Hoadley, "Small States," p. 133.

239. Hoadley, "Small States," p. 127.

240. *Neue Zürcher Zeitung*, 9 May 1976 and 12 August 1976; Katzenstein, *Capitalism in One Country?* pp. 18–19.

241. *Die Zeit*, 23 July 1976; *International Herald Tribune*, 6 June 1977; *Süddeutsche Zeitung*, 18 September 1976; *Handelsblatt*, 27 September 1976; *New York Times*, 13 October 1977, p. 1; and Anselm Skuhra, "Austria and the New International Economic Order: A Survey" (paper prepared for the ECPR Joint Session Workshop on the Western Response to the New International Economic Order, Florence, 24–29 March 1980), p. 10.

242. Arthur F. P. Wassenberg, "Neo-Corporatism and the Quest for Control: The Cuckoo Game," in Lehmbruch and Schmitter, *Patterns of Corporatist Policy-Making*, pp. 83–108; Lepszy, *Regierung, Parteien und Gewerkschaften in den Niederlanden;* Kieve, "Pillars of Sand"; Scholten, "Does Consociationalism Exist?"; Erwin Zimmerman, "Entwicklungstendenzen des Korporatismus"; Van Schendelen, "Crisis of the Welfare State," *Acta Politica* 19, 1 (1984); Arend Lijphart, ed., *Conflict and Coexistence in Belgium: The Dynamics of a Culturally Divided Society* (Berkeley: University of California, Institute of International Studies, 1981); and John Fitzmaurice, *The Politics of Belgium: Crisis and Compromise in a Plural Society* (London: Hurst, 1983).

243. Wolinetz, "Wage Regulation in the Netherlands," p. 47.

244. Gösta Esping-Andersen, *The Social Democratic Road to Power* (Princeton: Princeton University Press, forthcoming). This book summarizes and extends the following articles: "Social Class, Social Democracy, and the State: Party Policy and Party Decomposition in Denmark and Sweden," *Comparative*

Politics 11 (October 1978), 42–58; "Comparative Social Policy and Political Conflict in Advanced Welfare States: Denmark and Sweden," *International Journal of Health Services* 9, 2 (1979), 269–93; and "From Welfare State to Democratic Socialism: The Politics of Economic Democracy in Denmark and Sweden," *Political Power and Social Theory* 2 (1981), 111–40. See also the essays in two issues of *Daedalus* (Winter 1984 and Spring 1984) devoted to Scandinavia; Johan P. Olsen, *Organized Democracy: Political Institutions in a Welfare State—The Case of Norway* (Oslo: Universitetsforlaget, 1983); and Henrik J. Madsen, "Social Democracy in Postwar Scandinavia: Macroeconomic Management, Electoral Support, and the Fading Legacy of Prosperity" (Ph.D. diss., Harvard University, 1984).

245. Pontusson, "Beyond and Behind Social Democracy," p. 82.

246. For more detail see Katzenstein, *Corporatism and Change*, especially chaps. 4–6.

247. Franz Schurmann, *The Logic of World Power: An Inquiry into the Origins, Currents and Contradictions of World Politics* (New York: Random, 1974).

248. Irirangi Coates Bloomfield, "Public Policy, Technology, and the Environment: A Comparative Inquiry into Agricultural Policy Approaches and Environmental Outcomes in the United States and Switzerland" (Ph.D. diss., Boston University, 1981), p. 235, note 18.

249. T. J. Pempel, "Japanese Foreign Economic Policy: The Domestic Bases for International Behavior," in Peter J. Katzenstein, ed., *Between Power and Plenty: Foreign Economic Policies of Advanced Industrial States* (Madison: University of Wisconsin Press, 1978), pp. 139–90; Pempel and Keiichi Tsunekawa, "Corporatism without Labor? The Japanese Anomaly," in Schmitter and Lehmbruch, *Trends toward Corporatist Intermediation*, pp. 231–70.

250. Karl-Heinz Nassmacher, *Das österreichische Regierungssystem: Grosse Koalition oder alternierende Regierung?* (Cologne: Westdeutscher, 1968), pp. 158–73.

251. Although it is often left implicit, this taxonomy informs much contemporary writing on corporatism. It is explicit in Stephens, *Transition from Capitalism to Socialism*.

252. Informed by the analysis I have advanced in *Corporatism and Change*, the functional explanation I offer in chapters 2 and 3 thus differs from David Cameron's statistical analysis in "The Expansion of the Public Economy." The historical explanation in chapter 4 below, by contrast, argues that corporatist regimes were a response to economic openness and international vulnerability. The difference between functional and historical analysis as well as correlation and causation is the focus of Dankwart A. Rustow, "Transitions to Democracy: Toward a Dynamic Model," *Comparative Politics* 2 (April 1970), 337–64.

253. Fritz W. Scharpf, "The Political Economy of Inflation and Unemployment in Western Europe: An Outline" (Berlin: International Institute for Management, 1981), p. 46.

CHAPTER 4. *The Historical Origins of Democratic Corporatism*

1. See the references cited above in chapter 1, footnote 16, and in chapter 3, footnote 47.

2. Jens Alber, *Vom Armenhaus zum Wohlfahrtsstaat: Analysen zur Entwicklung der Sozialversicherung in Westeuropa* (Frankfurt: Campus, 1983); Peter Flora et al., *State, Economy, and Society in Western Europe, 1815–1975: A Data Handbook in Two Volumes*, vol. 1: *The Growth of Mass Democracies and Welfare States* (Frankfurt: Campus, 1983); and Seymour Martin Lipset and Stein Rokkan, "Cleavage Structures, Party Systems and Voter Alignments: An Introduction," in Lipset and Rokkan, eds., *Party Systems and Voter Alignments* (New York: Free, 1967), pp. 1–64.

3. Barrington Moore, Jr., *Social Origins of Dictatorship and Democracy: Lord and Peasant in the Making of the Modern World* (Boston: Beacon, 1967).

4. Karl-Gustav Hildebrand, "Economic Policy in Scandinavia during the Inter-War Period," *Scandinavian Economic History Review* 23, 2 (1975), 105. More generally see Ekkart Zimmermann, "The World Economic Crisis of the Thirties in Six European Countries: Causes of Political Instability and Reactions to Crisis: A First Report" (paper prepared for delivery at the European Consortium for Political Research Joint Session of Workshops, University of Salzburg, Austria, 13–18 April 1984).

5. Erik Hansen, "Depression Decade Crisis: Social Democracy and Planisme in Belgium and the Netherlands, 1929–1939," *Journal of Contemporary History* 16 (1981), 301–2.

6. Hansjörg Siegenthaler, "Switzerland in the Twentieth Century: The Economy," in J. Murray Luck, ed., *Modern Switzerland* (Palo Alto: SPOSS, 1978), p. 99; Charbel Ackermann and Walter Steinmann, *Historische Aspekte der Trennung und Verflechtung von Staat und Gesellschaft in der Schweiz: Die Genese der Verschränkung*, Forschungsprojekt Parastaatliche Verwaltung, Projektbericht 14, Institut für Orts-, Regional- und Landesplanung, ETH-Hönggerberg, Zurich, July 1981, p. 63.

7. Hildebrand, "Economic Policy in Scandinavia," pp. 101, 106, 114. See also Tore Hanisch, "The Economic Crisis in Norway in the 1930s: A Tentative Analysis of Its Causes," *Scandinavian Economic History Review* 26, 2 (1978), 145–55.

8. O. Fritiof Ander, *The Building of Modern Sweden: The Reign of Gustav V, 1907–1950.* (Rock Island, Ill.: Augustana Book Concern, 1959); Ingvar Anderson, *A History of Sweden* (London: Weidenfeld & Nicolson, 1956); Kurt Samuelsson, *From Great Power to Welfare State: Three Hundred Years of Swedish Social Development* (London: Allen & Unwin, 1968); Steven Koblik, ed., *Sweden's Development from Poverty to Affluence, 1750–1970* (Minneapolis: University of Minnesota Press, 1975); and A. S. Kan, *Geschichte der skandinavischen Länder* (East Berlin: Deutscher Verlag der Wissenschaften, 1978).

9. Sven Anders Söderpalm, "The Crisis Agreement and the Social Democratic Road to Power," in Koblik, *Sweden's Development*, p. 259.

10. Ibid., p. 267.

11. Ibid., p. 271. See also Samuelsson, *From Great Power to Welfare State*, p. 235.

12. Dankwart A. Rustow, *The Politics of Compromise* (Princeton: Princeton University Press, 1955), pp. 104–5. See also Rustow, "Sweden's Transition to Democracy: Some Notes toward a Genetic Theory," *Scandinavian Political Studies* 6 (1979), 9–26.

13. Peter Alexis Gourevitch, "Breaking with Orthodoxy: The Politics of

Economic Policy Responses to the Depression of the 1930s," *International Organization* 38 (Winter 1984), 117.

14. Stewart Oakley, *A Short History of Denmark* (New York: Praeger, 1972); W. Glyn Jones, *Denmark* (New York: Praeger 1970); Kenneth E. Miller, *Government and Politics in Denmark* (Boston: Houghton Mifflin, 1968); and Palle Svensson, "Support for the Danish Social Democratic Party, 1924–39: Growth and Response," *Scandinavian Political Studies* 9 (1974), 127–46.

15. Ulrich Menzel, *Der Entwicklungsweg Dänemarks (1880–1940): Ein Beitrag zum Konzept autozentrierter Entwicklung,* Projekt Untersuchung zur Grundlegung einer praxisorientierten Theorie autozentrierter Entwicklung, University of Bremen, Forschungsbericht 8, May 1980, pp. 123–24.

16. Gösta Esping-Andersen, *The Social Democratic Road to Power,* manuscript chapter 3, p. 10.

17. Karen Larsen, *A History of Norway* (Princeton: Princeton University Press, 1948); Natalie R. Ramsøy, ed., *Norwegian Society* (London: Hurst, 1974); Esping-Andersen, *Social Democratic Road to Power,* manuscript chapter 3, pp. 15–18; and Edward Bull, *Sozialgeschichte der norwegischen Demokratie* (Stuttgart: Klett, 1969).

18. T. K. Derry, *A History of Modern Norway, 1814–1972* (Oxford: Clarendon, 1973).

19. Cf. Fritz Hodne, *An Economic History of Norway, 1815–1970* (Trondheim: Tapir, 1975), pp. 443–44.

20. Hildebrand, "Economic Policy in Scandinavia," p. 105.

21. Hansen, "Depression Decade Crisis," p. 296.

22. Ibid., p. 299. See also Johan de Vries, "Benelux, 1920–1970," in - Carlo M. Cipolla, ed., *The Fontana Economic History of Europe,* vol. 6, pt. 1: *Contemporary Economies* (Glasgow: Collins, 1976), pp. 1–71; Willem Verkade, *Democratic Parties in the Low Countries and Germany: Origins and Historical Developments* (Leiden: Universitaire pers Leiden, 1965), pp. 86–106; and Val R. Lorwin, "Belgium: Religion, Class, and Language in National Politics," in Robert A. Dahl, ed., *Political Oppositions in Western Democracies* (New Haven: Yale University Press, 1966), pp. 161–65.

23. Hansen, "Depression Decade Crisis," pp. 301–4.

24. Adrien de Meeüs, *History of the Belgians* (New York: Praeger, 1962), p. 360.

25. Lorwin, "Belgium," pp. 162–63.

26. Quoted in Verkade, *Democratic Parties,* p. 105.

27. Hansen, "Depression Decade Crisis," p. 315; Verkade, *Democratic Parties,* pp. 107–21; de Vries, "Benelux"; Hans Daalder, "The Netherlands: Opposition in a Segmented Society," in Dahl, *Political Oppositions,* pp. 211–12; P. W. Klein, "Depression and Policy in the Thirties," *Acta Historiae Neerlandicae* 8 (1975), 123–58; Steven B. Wolinetz, "Wage Regulation in the Netherlands: The Rise and Fall of the Postwar Social Contract" (paper prepared for presentation at the Council of European Studies Conference of Europeanists, Washington, D.C., 13–15 October 1983), pp. 5–12.

28. Quoted in Klein, "Depression and Policy," p. 125. See also Johan de Vries, *The Netherlands Economy in the Twentieth Century: An Examination of the Most Characteristic Features in the Period 1900–1970* (Assen: Van Gorcum, 1978), pp. 86–95.

29. De Vries, *Netherlands Economy*, p. 88.

30. H. Vos, one of the principal authors of the *Plan van de Arbeid*, as quoted in Klein, "Depression and Policy," p. 124.

31. Hansen, "Depression Decade Crisis," p. 308.

32. Verkade, *Democratic Parties*, pp. 120–21.

33. Ackermann and Steinmann, *Historische Aspekte;* Luck, *Modern Switzerland.*

34. Ackermann and Steinmann, *Historische Aspekte*, pp. 63–85.

35. Esping-Andersen, *Social Democratic Road to Power*, manuscript chapter 3, p. 10.

36. Lukas F. Burckhardt, "Industry-Labor Relations: Industrial Peace," in Luck, *Modern Switzerland*, pp. 173–98; Dieter Berwinkel, "Das Friedensabkommen in der schweizer Maschinen- und Metallindustrie und die Möglichkeit seiner Übertragung auf die BRD" (Ph.D. diss., University of Freiburg/ Breisgau, 1962).

37. Michael Shalev, "Lies, Damned Lies, and Strike Statistics: The Measurement of Trends in Industrial Conflict," in Colin Crouch and Alessandro Pizzorno, eds., *The Resurgence of Class Conflict in Western Europe since 1968*, vol. 1: *National Studies* (New York: Holmes & Meier, 1978), p. 15.

38. Harry Eckstein, *Division and Cohesion in Democracy: A Study of Norway* (Princeton: Princeton University Press, 1966), p. 109. On the genesis of this book on Norway, as well as the wider intellectual context in which it should be placed, see Harry Eckstein, *The Natural History of Congruence Theory*, Monograph Series in World Affairs 18, 2 (Denver, 1980), pp. 14–18. See also Stein Rokkan, "Norway: Numerical Democracy and Corporate Pluralism," in Dahl, *Political Oppositions*, p. 73.

39. Palle Lauring, *A History of the Kingdom of Denmark* (Copenhagen: Host, 1960), pp. 248–51.

40. Lorwin, "Belgium," p. 165; on the Dutch case see Arend Lijphart, *The Politics of Accommodation: Pluralism and Democracy in the Netherlands* (Berkeley: University of California Press, 1968), p. 182.

41. Wolinetz, "Wage Regulation in the Netherlands," pp. 6–7; cf. Burckhardt, "Industry-Labor Relations," p. 174.

42. Nils Stjernquist, "Sweden: Stability or Deadlock?" in Dahl, *Political Oppositions*, p. 137; Esping-Andersen, *Social Democratic Road to Power*, manuscript, chapter 3, p. 28.

43. Gourevitch, "Breaking with Orthodoxy"; Charles S. Maier, "Preconditions for Corporatism," in John Goldthorpe, ed., *Order and Conflict in Contemporary Capitalism: Studies in the Political Economy of Western European Nations* (Oxford: Clarendon, 1984); Thomas Ferguson, "From Normalcy to New Deal: Industrial Structure, Party Competition, and American Public Policy in the Great Depression," *International Organization* 38 (Winter 1984), 41–94.

44. Samuel H. Beer, *British Politics in the Collectivist Age* (New York: Random, 1969).

45. Maier, "Preconditions for Corporatism," p. 11.

46. Hodne, *Economic History of Norway*, p. 443. Social expenditure as an approximate percentage of National Income in the early 1930s was 6.4 in Norway, 5.7 in Sweden, and 3.3 in Denmark. The corresponding figures in the late 1930s were, respectively, 6.6, 7.5, and 5.6. See Henrik Jess Madsen, "Social Democracy in Postwar Scandinavia: Macroeconomic Management,

Electoral Support and the Fading Legacy of Prosperity" (Ph.D. diss., Harvard University, 1984), p. 153.

47. De Vries, *Netherlands Economy*, p. 92; Val R. Lorwin, "Segmented Pluralism: Ideological Cleavages and Political Cohesion in the Smaller European Democracies," in Kenneth McRae, ed., *Consociational Democracy: Accommodation in Segmented Societies* (Toronto: McClelland & Stewart, 1974), p. 50.

48. Stein Rokkan, *Citizens, Elections, Parties: Approaches to the Comparative Study of the Processes of Development* (Oslo: Universitetsforlaget, 1970), pp. 76, 80.

49. Lipset and Rokkan, "Cleavage Structures," p. 32, quoting Karl Braunia.

50. Cf. Seymour Martin Lipset, "Political Cleavages in 'Developed' and 'Emerging' Polities," in Erik Allardt and Stein Rokkan, eds., *Mass Politics: Studies in Political Sociology* (New York: Free, 1970), p. 34.

51. For general information see Stein Rokkan and Jean Meyriat, eds., *International Guide to Electoral Statistics*, vol. 1: *National Elections in Western Europe* (The Hague: Mouton, 1969), pp. 47–101, 232–329; Arend Lijphardt, *Democracies: Patterns of Majoritarian and Consensus Government in Twenty-One Countries* (New Haven: Yale University Press, 1984), pp. 150–68; and Rokkan, *Citizens, Elections, Parties*, pp. 147–68.

52. Miller, *Government and Politics in Denmark;* A. H. Hoomann, *Democracy in Denmark* (Washington, D.C.: National Home Library Foundation, 1936); J. H. S. Birch, *Denmark in History* (London: Murray, 1938); and Werner Kath, *Die geschichtliche Entwicklung und gegenwärtige Gestalt des dänischen Regierungssystems* (Bonn: Rohrscheid, 1937).

53. Oakley, *Short History of Denmark*, p. 207; Miller, *Government and Politics in Denmark*, p. 36.

54. Oakley, *Short History of Denmark*, pp. 207–8.

55. Birch, *Denmark in History*, p. 394; Miller, *Government and Politics in Denmark*, p. 39; and Jones, *Denmark*, pp. 119–21.

56. Larsen, *History of Norway*, p. 497. See also Henry Valen and Daniel Katz, *Political Parties in Norway: A Community Study* (Oslo: Norwegian Research Council for Science and the Humanities, 1964), pp. 19–22.

57. Berndt Schiller, "Years of Crisis, 1906–1914," in Koblik, *Sweden's Development*, p. 202. See also Nils Andrén, *Modern Swedish Government* (Stockholm: Almqvist & Wiksell, 1968), p. 59; Rustow, *Politics of Compromise*, pp. 44, 62–63, 70–71, 123–32; and Stjernquist, "Sweden," p. 121.

58. Schiller, "Years of Crisis," p. 218.

59. Ander, *Building of Modern Sweden*, p. 416; Rustow, *Politics of Compromise*, p. 73.

60. Stjernquist, "Sweden," p. 139.

61. Daalder, "The Netherlands"; Verkade, *Democratic Parties;* Rudolf Steininger, *Polarisierung und Integration: Eine vergleichende Untersuchung der strukturellen Versäulung der Gesellschaft in den Niederlanden und in Österreich* (Meisenheim am Glan: Hain, 1975), pp. 133–37; Arend Lijphart, *Democracy in Plural Societies: A Comparative Exploration* (New Haven: Yale University Press, 1977), pp. 52, 131, 187; Jonathan Tumin, "Pathways to Democracy: A Critical Revision of Barrington Moore's Theory of Democratic Emergence and an Application of the Revised Theory to the Case of the Netherlands" (Ph.D. diss., Harvard University, 1978); Norbert Lepszy, *Regierung, Parteien und*

Gewerkschaften in den Niederlanden: Entwicklung und Strukturen (Dusseldorf: Droste, 1979); and Ilja Scholten, "Does Consociationalism Exist? A Critique of the Dutch Experience," in Richard Rose, ed., *Electoral Participation: A Comparative Analysis* (Beverly Hills: Sage, 1980), pp. 329–54.

62. Lijphart, *Politics of Accommodation*, p. 171. Cf. Verkade, *Democratic Parties*, p. 55; Lepszy, *Regierung, Parteien und Gewerkschaften*, p. 55.

63. Lijphart, *Politics of Accommodation*, p. 100. Since 1956 the threshold has been lowered to two-thirds of one percent.

64. Tumin, "Pathways to Democracy," pp. 284–86; Verkade, *Democratic Parties*, p. 55.

65. Daalder, "The Netherlands," p. 207.

66. Hans Heinrich Schälchlin, "Die Auswirkungen des Proportionalwahlverfahrens auf Wählerschaft und Parlament: Unter besonderer Berücksichtigung der schweizerischen Verhältnisse" (Ph.D. diss., University of Zurich, 1946), p. 3; George A. Coddington, Jr., "The Swiss Political System and the Management of Diversity," in Howard R. Penniman, ed., *Switzerland at the Polls: The National Elections of 1979* (Washington, D.C.: American Enterprise Institute, 1979), p. 26.

67. Schälchlin, "Auswirkungen des Proportionalwahlverfahrens," pp. 3, 18–19.

68. Ibid., pp. 4, 19, 42–43, 28, 40.

69. Coddington, "Swiss Political System," p. 29.

70. Lorwin, "Belgium," pp. 154–57; de Meeüs, *History of the Belgians*, pp. 332–34.

71. Lorwin, "Belgium," p. 157.

72. Seymour Martin Lipset, letter to the author, 15 May 1984.

73. Cf. Andrén, *Modern Swedish Government*, pp. 61–62. See also Rustow, *Politics of Compromise*, pp. 208–12, 223–25.

74. Valen and Katz, *Political Parties in Norway*, p. 17; Madsen, "Social Democracy in Postwar Scandinavia," p. 145.

75. Daalder, "The Netherlands," p. 207.

76. Carl Henrik Höjer, *Le régime parlementaire belge de 1918 à 1940* (Uppsala: Almqvist, 1946), pp. 313–15.

77. This is a central question, which Rokkan and Hans Daalder have posed in their comparative studies of smaller democracies. My formulation is indebted to their important studies. See especially Stein Rokkan, "The Structuring of Mass Politics in the Smaller European Democracies: A Developmental Typology," *Comparative Studies in Society and History* 10 (1968); Rokkan, *Citizens, Elections, Parties*.

78. Maier, "Preconditions for Corporatism," p. 35.

79. Michael Hechter and William Brustein, "Regional Modes of Production and Patterns of State Formation in Western Europe," *American Journal of Sociology* 85, 5 (1980), 1061–94.

80. Charles Tilly, letter to the author, 18 April 1984. See also Flora et al., *State, Economy and Society*, pp. 11–26.

81. Hans Daalder, "Cabinets and Party Systems in Ten Smaller European Democracies," *Acta Politica* 6 (1971), 299.

82. Rokkan, *Citizens, Elections, Parties*, p. 128. More generally see Jerome Blum, *The End of the Old Order in Rural Europe* (Princeton: Princeton Univer-

sity Press, 1978); *Handwörterbuch der Staatswissenschaften*, 3d ed., vol. 2 (Jena: Fischer, 1909), pp. 541–627.

83. Benjamin R. Barber, *The Death of Communal Liberty: A History of Freedom in a Swiss Mountain Canton* (Princeton: Princeton University Press, 1974). See also Alan S. Milward and S. B. Saul, *The Economic Development of Continental Europe, 1780–1870* (London: Allen & Unwin, 1973), especially pp. 435–36.

84. Jan de Vries, *The Dutch Rural Economy in the Golden Age, 1500–1700* (New Haven: Yale University Press, 1974), pp. 38, 41.

85. Franklin F. Mendels, *Industrialization and Population Pressure in Eighteenth-Century Flanders* (New York: Arno, 1981).

86. Cf. Hans Daalder, "On Building Consociational Nations: The Cases of the Netherlands and Switzerland," in McRae, *Consociational Democracy*, p. 110.

87. Amanda Tillotson-Becker, "The Art of the State: Agricultural Modernization and Industrialization in Denmark," unpublished paper, University of California, Los Angeles, n.d., p. 5.

88. Seymour Martin Lipset, "Radicalism or Reformism: The Sources of Working-Class Politics," *American Political Science Review* 77 (March 1983), 5.

89. Øywin Østerud, *Agrarian Structure and Peasant Politics in Scandinavia: A Comparative Study of Rural Response to Economic Change* (Oslo: Hestholms, 1978), p. 102.

90. Esping-Andersen, *Social Democratic Road to Power*, manuscript, chapter 2, p. 2. See also Francis G. Castles, *The Social Democratic Image of Society* (London: Routledge & Kegan Paul, 1978), pp. 134–40.

91. Timothy Tilton, "The Social Origins of Liberal Democracy: The Swedish Case," *American Political Science Review* 68 (June 1974), 565.

92. Ibid., p. 565. See also Francis G. Castles, "Barrington Moore's Thesis and Swedish Political Development," *Government and Opposition* 8 (Summer 1973), 318–20. Suzanne Keller, *Beyond the Ruling Class: Strategic Elites in Modern Society* (New York: Random, 1963), notes on p. 229 that Swedish nobility has extended only very rarely beyond four generations.

93. See Stein Rokkan, "Centre-Formation, Nation Building, and Cultural Diversity: Report of a UNESCO Programme," in S. N. Eisenstadt and Stein Rokkan, eds., *Building States and Nations*, vol. 1: *Models and Data Resources* (Beverly Hills: Sage, 1973).

94. Daalder, "On Building Consociational Nations," p. 109; Lorwin, "Segmented Pluralism," p. 44.

95. Tillotson-Becker, "Art of the State," p. 5.

96. Tilton, "Social Origins of Liberal Democracy," p. 566.

97. David Friedman, "A Theory of the Size and Shape of Nations," *Journal of Political Economy* 85 (February 1977), 61–62.

98. Cf. Lipset, "Radicalism or Reformism," p. 1.

99. See Lipset, "Political Cleavages in 'Developed' and 'Emerging' Polities," p. 31; Daalder, "On Building Consociational Nations"; and Esping-Andersen, *Social Democratic Road to Power*.

100. Lipset, "Radicalism or Reformism," p. 9, quoting Walter Galenson, and pp. 5–6; Lijphart, *Politics of Accommodation*, pp. 20–21.

101. Lipset, "Radicalism or Reformism," pp. 8–9.

102. Rokkan, *Citizens, Elections, Parties*, p. 85; Lipset, "Radicalism or Reformism," p. 9; and Daalder, "The Netherlands," p. 295.

103. Lipset, "Radicalism or Reformism," p. 4.

104. Ibid., p. 9; Stjernquist, "Sweden," p. 120.

105. Lipset, "Radicalism or Reformism," p. 6.

106. On the development of this concept see Sidney Tarrow, *Struggling to Reform: Social Movements and Policy Change during Cycles of Protest*, Cornell University, Western Societies Program, Occasional Papers no. 15 (Ithaca, n.d.).

107. Lipset and Rokkan, "Cleavage Structures, Party Systems, and Voter Alignments," p. 20.

108. Esping-Andersen, *Social Democratic Road to Power*, manuscript, chapter 9.

109. Lorwin, "Belgium," pp. 147, 156.

110. Lipset, "Political Cleavages in 'Developed' and 'Emerging' Polities," p. 30.

111. Tumin, "Pathways to Democracy," pp. 239, 263.

112. Daalder, "The Netherlands," p. 208; Erik Hansen, "Workers and Socialists: Relations between the Dutch Trade-Union Movement and Social Democracy, 1894–1914," *European Studies Review* 7 (April 1977), 199–226.

113. Daalder, "The Netherlands," pp. 209–10; Lipset, "Radicalism or Reformism," pp. 9–10.

114. Erich Gruner, "The Political System of Switzerland," in Luck, *Modern Switzerland*, pp. 339–60.

115. Rokkan, "Norway," p. 79.

116. Lipset, "Radicalism and Reformism," p. 9. See also Valen and Katz, *Political Parties in Norway*, pp. 23–25.

117. Stjernquist, "Sweden," p. 120; Lipset, "Radicalism or Reform," p. 9.

118. Miller, *Government and Politics in Denmark*, p. 35; Jones, *Denmark*, pp. 106–7.

119. Rokkan, *Citizens, Elections, Parties*, pp. 114, 116. Rokkan's model was continually refined. Its last published version can be found in Stein Rokkan, "Territories, Nations, Parties: Toward a Geoeconomic-Geopolitical Model for the Explanation of Variations within Western Europe," in Richard L. Merritt and Bruce M. Russett, eds., *From National Development to Global Community: Essays in Honour of Karl W. Deutsch* (London: Allen & Unwin, 1981), pp. 70–96. This model is reviewed in Peter Flora, "Stein Rokkan's Makro-Modell der politischen Entwicklung Europas: Ein Rekonstruktionsversuch," *Kölner Zeitschrift für Soziologie und Sozialpsychologie* 33, 3 (1981), 397–436. A shortened English version of this article can be found in Flora et al., *State, Economy and Society*, pp. 11–26. See also Charles Tilly, "Stein Rokkan's Conceptual Map of Europe," University of Michigan Center for Research on Social Organization, Working Paper no. 229 (Ann Arbor, February 1981).

120. Rokkan, *Citizens, Elections, Parties*, p. 120.

121. Ibid., p. 128.

122. Dieter Senghaas, *Von Europa Lernen: Entwicklungsgeschichtliche Betrachtungen* (Frankfurt: Suhrkamp, 1982).

123. John A. C. Conybeare, "Tariff Protection in Developed and Developing Countries: A Cross-Sectional and Longitudinal Analysis," *International Organization* 37 (Summer 1983), 444–45.

124. League of Nations, Economic and Financial Section, *Tariff Level Indi-*

ces (Geneva, 1927), p. 15. See also *Monatsberichte des österreichischen Instituts für Wirtschaftsforschung* 27 (February 1954), supplement 24, p. 11; K. W. Rothschild, "The Small Nation and World Trade," *Economic Journal* 54 (April 1944), 38.

125. *Monatsberichte des österreichischen Instituts,* pp. 9, 11; Rothschild, "Small Nations and World Trade," p. 38. These estimates are approximate because of statistical difficulties as well as differences in the coverage of nations in different studies.

126. See his University of Bremen monographs from the Projekt Untersuchung zur Grundlegung einer praxisorientierten Theorie autozentrierter Entwicklung: Ulrich Menzel, *Autozentrierte Entwicklung trotz Weltmarktintegration* (August 1981); *Entwicklungsweg Dänemarks; Der Entwicklungsweg Schwedens (1800–1913): Ein Beitrag zum Konzept autozentrierter Entwicklung* (December 1980); *Der Entwicklungsweg der Schweiz (1780–1850); Ein Beitrag zum Konzept autozentrierter Entwicklung* (October 1979). These monographs should soon appear in a book to be published by Suhrkamp. The subsequent discussion is heavily indebted to Menzel's work.

127. Cf. Milward and Saul, *Economic Development, 1780–1870,* p. 463.

128. Menzel, *Entwicklungsweg der Schweiz,* pp. xii–xiii, 73–74, 115–36; Milward and Saul, *Economic Development, 1780–1870,* pp. 454, 463; N. Gardner Clark, "Modernization without Urbanization, or Switzerland as Model of Job Development outside Large Urban Areas," *Schweizerische Zeitschrift für Soziologie* 6, 1 (1979), 1–40.

129. Menzel, *Entwicklungsweg Dänemarks;* Milward and Saul, *Economic Development, 1780–1870,* p. 512; Sven Aage Hansen, *Early Industrialization in Denmark* (Copenhagen: Møller & Landschultz, 1970).

130. Tilton, "Social Origins of Liberal Democracy," pp. 563, 568.

131. Mendels, *Industrialization and Population Pressure;* Peter Kriedte, Hans Medick, and Jürgen Schlumbohm, *Industrialisierung vor der Industrialisierung. Gewerbliche Warenproduktion auf dem Land in der Formationsperiode des Kapitalismus* (Göttingen: Vandenhoeck & Ruprecht, 1977); and Charles Tilly, "Flows of Capital and Forms of Industry in Europe, 1500–1900," *Theory and Society* 12 (March 1983), 123–42.

132. See Charles Tilly, "Did the Cake of Custom Break?" in John M. Merriman, ed., *Consciousness and Class Experience in Nineteenth Century Europe* (New York: Holmes & Meier, 1979), p. 33.

133. I am indebted to Charles Tilly for this idea.

134. Castles, *Social Democratic Image of Society,* pp. 112–13, 131–42; Francis G. Castles, "How Does Politics Matter? Structure or Agency in the Determination of Public Policy Outcomes," *European Journal of Political Research* 9, 2 (1981), 127–28.

135. Francis G. Castles, "The Impact of Parties on Public Expenditure," in Castles, ed., *The Impact of Parties: Politics and Policies in Democratic Capitalist States* (Beverly Hills: Sage, 1982), p. 82.

136. Eckstein, *Division and Cohesion,* p. 127 and see pp. 122, 125–26. See also Sten S. Nilson, "Wahlsoziologische Probleme des National-Sozialismus," *Zeitschrift für die Gesamte Staatswissenschaften* 110 (1954), 302–3.

137. Alan S. Milward and S. B. Saul, *The Development of the Economies of Continental Europe, 1850–1914* (Cambridge: Harvard University Press, 1977),

p. 193. See also Milward and Saul, *Economic Development, 1780– 1870*, p. 452.

138. Milward and Saul, *Development of the Economies, 1850–1914*, pp. 148–49; cf. Lorwin, "Belgium," pp. 148–49.

139. Milward and Saul, *Development of the Economies, 1850–1914*, p. 147.

140. Quoted in Menzel, *Entwicklungsweg der Schweiz*, p. 73, footnote 24.

141. Tilton, "Social Origins of Liberal Democracy," p. 568.

142. Milward and Saul, *Development of the Economies, 1850–1914*, p. 191. See also J. H. Van Stuijvenberg, "A Reconsideration of the Origins of the Agricultural Cooperative," *Acta Historiae Neerlandicae* 13 (1980), 114–32.

143. Menzel, *Entwicklungsweg Dänemarks*, pp. 52–60, 69–77, 84–98; Tillotson-Becker, "Art of the State," pp. 27–28; Peter Manniche, *Living Democracy in Denmark* (Westport: Greenwood, 1970); and Henry R. Haggard, *Rural Denmark and Its Lessons* (London: Longmans, 1911).

144. Peter Manniche, *Denmark: A Social Laboratory* (New York: Oxford University Press, 1939), pp. 11, 70.

145. Eckstein, *Division and Cohesion*, p. 63.

146. Ibid., pp. 38–67; Stein Rokkan and Henry Valen, "Regional Contrasts in Norwegian Politics," in Allardt and Rokkan, *Mass Politics*, especially pp. 192–94; and Rokkan, "Geography, Religion, and Social Class: Crosscutting Cleavages in Norwegian Politics," in Lipset and Rokkan, *Party Systems and Voter Alignments*, pp. 367–446.

147. Eckstein, *Division and Cohesion*, p. 84; see also pp. 122–27, 133–35.

148. Daalder, "The Netherlands," p. 193; Tumin, "Pathways to Democracy."

149. Tumin, "Pathways to Democracy," p. 172.

150. Daalder, "The Netherlands," pp. 216, 218.

151. I am indebted to Martin Shefter for his insights on this subject.

152. Alexander Gerschenkron, *Economic Backwardness in Historical Perspective: A Book of Essays* (Cambridge: Harvard University Press, Belknap Press, 1962), especially pp. 1–30; Gerschenkron, *Continuity in History and Other Essays* (Cambridge: Harvard University Press, Belknap Press, 1968), especially pp. 77–97.

153. Alexander Gerschenkron, *An Economic Spurt that Failed: Four Lectures in Austrian History* (Princeton: Princeton University Press, 1977); Steven Loren Barsby, "An Empirical Examination of the Gerschenkron Hypothesis: Economic Backwardness and the Characteristics of Development" (Ph.D. diss., University of Oregon, 1968). See also Barsby, "Economic Backwardness and the Characteristics of Development," *Journal of Economic History* 29 (September 1969), 449–72.

154. Senghaas, *Von Europa Lernen*, and the works cited in footnote 126 provide the basis for much of the subsequent discussion.

155. Volker Bornschier, *Wachstum, Konzentration und Mutinationalisierung von Industrieunternehmen* (Frauenfeld: Huber, 1976), p. 486. More generally see Menzel, *Entwicklungsweg der Schweiz*.

156. Pierre Lebrun et al., *Essai sur la révolution industrielle en Belgique, 1770–1847* (Brussels: Palais des Academies, 1979); Jan Dhont and Marinette Bruwier, "The Low Countries, 1700–1914," in Carlo M. Cipolla, ed., *The Fontana Economic History of Europe*, vol. 4, pt. 1: *The Emergence of Industrial Societies* (London: Collins, 1973), pp. 329–66.

157. Joel Mokyr, *Industrialization in the Low Countries, 1795–1850* (New Haven: Yale University Press, 1976); Richard T. Griffiths, *Industrial Retardation in the Netherlands, 1830–1850* (The Hague: Nijhoff, 1979); Eric Schiff, *Industrialization without National Patents: The Netherlands, 1869–1912; Switzerland, 1850–1907* (Princeton: Princeton University Press, 1971), pp. 25–27; Mokyr, "Industrialization and Poverty in Ireland and the Netherlands," *Journal of Interdisciplinary History* 10, 3 (1980), 429–58; J. A. de Jonge, "Industrial Growth in the Netherlands, 1850–1914," *Acta Historiae Neerdlandicae* 5 (1971), 158–212; and I. J. Brugmans, "The Economic History of the Netherlands in the 19th and 20th Century," ibid. 2 (1967), 260–98.

158. K.-G. Hildebrand, "Labour and Capital in the Scandinavian Countries in the Nineteenth and Twentieth Centuries," in Peter Mathias and M. M. Postan, eds., *The Cambridge Economic History of Europe*, vol. 7, pt. 1: *The Industrial Economies: Capital, Labour and Enterprise: Britain, France, Germany and Scandinavia* (Cambridge: Cambridge University Press, 1978), pp. 590–628; Lennart Jörberg, "Industrial Development and Foreign Trade in the Nordic Countries, 1870–1914," in Wolfram Fischer, ed., *Beiträge zu Wirtschaftswachstum und Wirtschaftsstruktur im 16. und 19. Jahrhundert* (Berlin: Duncker & Humblot, 1971), pp. 239–260; and Eli F. Heckscher, *An Economic History of Sweden* (Cambridge: Harvard University Press, 1954).

159. Lorwin, "Segmented Pluralism," pp. 42–44.

160. But see Charles de Lannoy, *A History of Swedish Colonial Expansion* (Newark: Department of History and Political Science, University of Delaware, 1938).

161. Paul Bairoch, *Commerce extérieur et développement économique de l'Europe au XIXᵉ siècle* (Paris: Mouton, 1976), p. 101. Bairoch's figures suggest that in 1913 Switzerland's foreign investment was about four times as great as Sweden's, with the Low Countries holding an intermediate position.

162. Bull's article was published in 1922 and has not been translated into English. It is summarized and evaluated critically on the basis of empirical evidence by William M. Lafferty, *Economic Development and the Response of Labor in Scandinavia: A Multi-Level Analysis* (Oslo: Universitetsforlaget, 1971); Lafferty, "Industrialization and Labor Radicalism in Norway: An Ecological Analysis," *Scandinavian Political Studies* 9 (1974), 157–76. See also Walter Galenson, "Scandinavia," in Galenson, ed., *Comparative Labor Movements* (New York: Prentice-Hall, 1952), pp. 104–72.

163. Lipset, "Political Cleavages in 'Developed' and 'Emerging' Polities," p. 30; Michael Shalev and Walter Korpi, "Working Class Mobilization and American Exceptionalism," *Economic and Industrial Democracy* 1 (1980), 36–37.

164. Sein Kuhnle, *Patterns of Social and Political Mobilization: A Historical Analysis of the Nordic Countries* (Beverly Hills: Sage 1975); David Klingman, *Social Change and Public Policy: Norway and Sweden, 1875–1965* (Beverly Hills: Sage, 1976); Sten Sparre Nilson, "Regional Differences in Norway with Special Reference to Labor Radicalism and Cultural Norms," *Scandinavian Political Studies* 10 (1975), 123–38.

165. Daalder, "The Netherlands," pp. 207–8; Lorwin, "Segmented Pluralism," p. 56; Scholten, "Does Consociationalism Exist?" and Ronald A. Kieve, "Pillars of Sand: A Marxist Critique of Consociational Democracy in the Netherlands," *Comparative Politics* 13 (April 1981), 313–37.

166. Lorwin, "Segmented Pluralism," p. 40.

167. Rokkan, *Citizens, Elections, Parties*, p. 135; Lipset, "Political Cleavages in 'Developed' and 'Emerging' Polities," pp. 30–31.

168. Robert A. Dahl and Edward R. Tufte, *Size and Democracy* (Stanford: Stanford University Press, 1973), p. 112.

169. Lijphart, *Democracy in Plural Societies*, pp. 71–81, 104.

170. Denmark's labor movement has a more artisanal character and is less centralized, thus forming a partial exception to this generalization.

171. Rokkan, *Citizens, Elections, Parties*, pp. 132–34; Rokkan, "Structuring of Mass Politics," pp. 187–86 and Rokkan, "Centre-Formation, Nation-Building, and Cultural Diversity," pp. 18–19. See also Bernt Hagtvet and Erik Rudeng, "Scandinavia: Achievements, Dilemmas, Challenges," *Daedalus* 113 (Spring 1984), 228.

172. Immanuel Wallerstein, *The Modern World System: Capitalist Agriculture and the Origins of the European World-Economy in the Sixteenth Century* (New York: Academic, 1974); Perry Anderson, *Lineages of the Absolutist State* (London: NLB, 1974).

173. Daalder, "Cabinets and Party Systems," pp. 299–300.

174. Austria is treated below. The relevant Austrian data for Table 7 are given in footnote 203 below.

175. Moore, *Social Origins of Dictatorship and Democracy*.

176. Sima Lieberman, *The Industrialization of Norway, 1800–1920* (Oslo: Universitetsforlaget, 1970), p. 117. See also Senghaas, *Von Europa Lernen*.

177. Rokkan, "Centre-Formation, Nation-Building, and Cultural Diversity," pp. 20–21; Tumin, "Pathways to Democracy," p. 84.

178. Calculated from Brian R. Mitchell, *European Historical Statistics, 1750–1970* (London: Macmillan, 1975), pp. 19–24, 135. See also James A. Storing, *Norwegian Democracy* (Boston: Houghton Mifflin, 1963), p. 4; Menzel, *Entwicklungsweg Schwedens*, p. 93; and Tilton, "Social Origins of Liberal Democracy," p. 567.

179. Moore, *Social Origins of Dictatorship and Democracy*, p. 418.

180. Jonathan M. Wiener, "Review of Reviews," *History and Theory* 15, 2 (1976), 158–59.

181. Tumin, "Pathways to Democracy"; Castles, "Moore's Thesis and Swedish Development"; and Tilton, "Social Origins of Liberal Democracy."

182. G. J. Renier, *The Dutch Nation* (London: Allen & Unwin, 1944), p. 23.

183. Tumin, "Pathways to Democracy," pp. 143, 228–30, 252.

184. Tilton, "Social Origins of Liberal Democracy," p. 563.

185. Ibid., p. 565; Castles, "Moore's Thesis and Swedish Development," pp. 316–18.

186. Tilton, "Social Origins of Liberal Democracy," pp. 567, 569.

187. Castles, "Moore's Thesis and Swedish Development," p. 328. See also Rustow, *Politics of Compromise*, p. 10.

188. Rustow, quoted in Scholten, "Does Consociationalism Exist?" p. 331.

189. Lijphart, *Politics of Accommodation*, pp. 103–21; Daalder, "The Netherlands."

190. Scholten, "Does Consociationalism Exist?" pp. 331–32.

191. Moore, *Social Origins of Dictatorship and Democracy*, p. xiii.

192. Cf. Robert L. Rothstein, *The Weak in the World of the Strong: The De-*

veloping Countries in the International System (New York: Columbia University Press, 1977).

193. Lipset and Rokkan, "Cleavage Structures, Party Systems, and Voter Alignments," p. 45; Rokkan, *Citizens, Elections, Parties*, pp. 115–17.

194. Rokkan, *Citizens, Elections, Parties*, p. 129.

195. Gary P. Freeman, "Social Security in One Country? Foreign Economic Policies and Domestic Social Programs" (paper prepared for delivery at the 1983 Annual Meeting of the American Political Science Association, Chicago, 1–4 September 1983), p. 6.

196. Lipset, "Radicalism or Reformism," pp. 3–4, 6, 8.

197. N. T. Gross, "The Habsburg Monarchy, 1750–1914," in Cipolla, *Fontana Economic History of Europe*, vol. 4, pt 1, pp. 228–78; David F. Good, "Stagnation and 'Take-off' in Austria, 1873–1913," *Economic History Review* 27 (February 1974), 72–87.

198. League of Nations, *Tariff Levels*, p. 15; Menzel, *Entwicklungsweg Dänemarks*, p. 29.

199. Kurt Steiner, *Politics in Austria* (Boston: Little, Brown, 1972), p. 34; Anton Pelinka, "Die Geschichte des Wahlrechts in der Ersten Republik," in Rodney Stiefbold et al., eds., *Wahlen und Parteien in Österreich: Österreichisches Wahlhandbuch*, vol. 1: *Wahlrecht* (Vienna: Österreichischer Bundesverlag, 1966), pp. 266–70.

200. Daalder, "Cabinets and Party Systems," p. 300.

201. See, for example, McRae, *Consociational Democracy.*

202. Gerschenkron, *A Spurt that Failed.*

203. Had Austria been included in Table 7 it would have ranked in the seven columns thus: 7.0 (21%); 7.0 (82); 7.0 (19); 5.5 (0); 6.5 (.07); 3.0 (0.85); 7.0 (36.0). These figures are derived from the same sources as those in Table 7 except for the first set of figures referring to column 1. The data on the timing of industrialization refer to the western half of the Dual Monarchy in 1890, as reported in Karl Heinz Werner, "Österreichs Industrie- und Aussenhandelspolitik, 1848–1948," in Hans Mayer, ed., *Hundert Jahre österreichische Wirtschaftsentwicklung, 1848–1948* (Vienna: Springer, 1949), p. 369.

204. Ernest Darwin Simon, *The Smaller Democracies* (London: Gollancz, 1939), p. 191.

CHAPTER 5. *Conclusion*

1. Béla Kádár, "Adjustment Patterns and Policies in Small Countries," in István Dobozi, Clare Keller, and Harriet Matejka, eds., *International Structural Adjustment: A Collection of Hungarian and Swiss Views* (Geneva: Graduate Institute of International Studies, 1982), pp. 93–104.

2. International Monetary Fund, *International Financial Statistics*, Supplement Series no. 6 (1983), p. 105.

3. Peer Hull Kristensen and Jørn Levinsen, *The Small Country Squeeze* (Roskilde, Denmark: Institute of Economics, Politics and Administration, 1978). See also *Wall Street Journal*, 14 December 1982, pp. 1 and 17.

4. Kristensen and Levinsen, *Small Country Squeeze*, pp. 37, 47–48, 91–98, 270–73, 316–17.

5. *Der Spiegel,* 3 November 1980, pp. 184–88; *World Business Weekly,* 11 May 1981, p. 11.

6. Andrew Boyd, "How the Storm Changed the Signs," *Economist,* 28 January 1978, Survey, p. 30.

7. "How Sweden's Middle Road Becomes a Dead End," *Forbes,* 27 April 1981, p. 35.

8. Morgan Guaranty, *World Financial Markets,* January 1984, author's calculations.

9. *University of Pennsylvania News,* 20 August 1982 (081682); *Der Österreich-Bericht,* 19 August 1982, p. 1. See also Manfred G. Schmidt, "The Welfare State and the Economy in Periods of Economic Crisis: A Comparative Study of Twenty-Three OECD Nations," *European Journal of Political Research* 11 (March 1983), 1–26; Schmidt, "Arbeitslosigkeit and Vollbeschäftigungspolitik," *Leviathan* 11, 4 (1983), 451–73.

10. Quoted in *Wall Street Journal,* 14 December 1982, p. 17, and 22 September 1983, p. 35. See also *New York Times,* 21 July 1983, p. A8; Bent Rold Andersen, "Rationality and Irrationality of the Nordic Welfare State," *Daedalus,* Winter 1984, pp. 130–34.

11. *New York Times,* 19 January 1984, p. 2; *Der Spiegel,* 16 January 1984, pp. 97–99; and *Economist,* 30 June 1984, pp. 58–59.

12. *New York Times,* 8 December 1983, p. A2, and 3 June 1984, p. 9.

13. M. C. P. M. Van Schendelen, "Crisis of the Dutch Welfare State," *Contemporary Crises* 7(1983), 218.

14. Quoted in *New York Times,* 21 April 1984, p. 31.

15. Arne Ruth, "The Second New Nation: The Mythology of Modern Sweden," *Daedalus,* Spring 1984, p. 56.

16. *New York Times,* 8 December 1983, p. A2.

17. Arthur F. P. Wassenberg, "Neo-Corporatism and the Quest for Control: The Cuckoo Game," in Gerhard Lehmbruch and Philippe C. Schmitter, eds., *Patterns of Corporatist Policy-Making* (Beverly Hills: Sage, 1982), pp. 83–108; Erwin Zimmermann, "Entwicklungstendenzen des Korporatismus und die Industriepolitik in den Niederlanden," in *Neokorporatistische Politik in Westeuropa,* University of Constance, Sozialwissenschaftliche Fakultät, Fachgruppe Politikwissenschaft/Verwaltungswissenschaft, Diskussionsbeitrag 1 (1982), pp. 107–31.

18. Steven B. Wolinetz, "Wage Regulation in the Netherlands: The Rise and Fall of the Postwar Social Contract" (paper prepared for presentation at the Council for European Studies Conference of Europeanists, Washington, D.C., 13–15 October 1983).

19. James R. Kurth, "The Political Consequences of the Product Cycle: Industrial History and Political Outcomes," *International Organization* 33 (Winter 1979), 1–34; Peter Gourevitch, "Breaking with Orthodoxy: The Politics of Economic Policy Responses to the Depression of the 1930s," *International Organization* 38 (Winter 1984), 95–130; and Thomas Ferguson, "From Normalcy to New Deal: Industrial Structure, Party Competition, and American Public Policy in the Great Depression," *International Organization* 38 (Winter 1984), 41–94.

20. Peter J. Katzenstein, *Corporatism and Change: Austria, Switzerland, and the Politics of Industry* (Ithaca: Cornell University Press, 1984), especially chaps. 5 and 6.

21. Charles F. Sabel, "From Austro-Keynesianism to Flexible Specialization: The Political Preconditions of Industrial Redeployment in an *Astgemeinschaft*" (paper delivered at the Österreichische Nationalbank, Vienna, 20 May 1983).

22. *Wall Street Journal*, 6 September 1983, p. 38, and 13 April 1984, p. 37.

23. *New York Times*, 24 January 1984, p. A25.

24. See Peter J. Katzenstein, "Problem or Model? West Germany in the 1980s," *World Politics* 23 (July 1980), 577–98; Katzenstein, "West Germany as Number Two: Reflections on the German Model," in Andrei Markovits, ed., *The Political Economy of West Germany: Modell Deutschland* (New York: Praeger, 1982), pp. 199–215; and Katzenstein, *A Semi-Sovereign State: Policy and Politics in West Germany* (Philadelphia: Temple University Press, forthcoming).

25. Wolfgang Kohte, *Die niederländische Volkswirtschaft heute: Ihre Wandlungen seit der Vorkriegszeit* (Stuttgart: Kohlhammer, 1954); Ludwig Mülhaupt, *Strukturwandlungen und Nachkriegsprobleme der Wirtschaft Schwedens* (Kiel: Institut für Weltwirtschaft, 1952); Gerhard Pfeiffer, *Strukturwandlungen und Nachkriegsprobleme der Wirtschaft der Niederlande* (Kiel: Institut für Weltwirtschaft, 1950); Wolf von Arnim, *Strukturwandlungen und Nachkriegsprobleme der Wirtschaft Dänemarks* (Kiel: Institut für Weltwirtschaft, 1950); Hugo Heeckt, *Strukturwandlungen und Nachkriegsprobleme der Wirtschaft Norwegens* (Kiel: Institut für Weltwirtschaft, 1950); Allan Lyle, *Die Industrialisierung Norwegens* (Jena: Fischer, 1939); Wilhelm Keilhau, *Volkswirtschaftspolitik und weltwirtschaftliche Stellung Norwegens* (Jena: Fischer, 1938); G. M. Verrijn Stuart, *Die Industriepolitik der niederländischen Regierung* (Jena: Fischer, 1936); Jens Samsöe, *Die Industrialisierung Dänemarks* (Jena: Fischer, 1926); and Sven Helander, *Schweden's Stellung in der Weltwirtschaft* (Jena: Fischer, 1922).

26. Marcello de Cecco, "Introduction," in de Cecco, ed., *International Economic Adjustment: Small Countries and the European Monetary System* (Oxford: Blackwell, 1983), p. 3.

27. See for example several contributions in *Österreichische Zeitschrift für Politikwissenschaft*, 1978/3, and Otmar Höll and Helmut Kramer, "Kleinstaaten im Internationalen System: Endbericht," unpublished manuscript, Vienna, 1977. A more sophisticated discussion can be found in Margret Sieber, *Die Abhängigkeit der Schweiz von ihrer internationalen Umwelt: Konzepte und Indikatoren* (Frauenfeld: Huber, 1979), pp. 330–46 and 386, and in Hans Vogel, *Der Kleinstaat in der Weltpolitik: Aspekte der schweizerischen Aussenbeziehungen im internationalen Vergleich* (Frauenfeld: Huber, 1979). A broad range of approaches is contained in Höll, ed., *Small States in Europe and Dependence* (Vienna: Braumüller, 1983).

28. Stephen D. Krasner, *Structural Conflict: The Third World against Global Liberalism* (Berkeley: University of California Press, forthcoming), manuscript, Chapter 2, p. 17.

29. Richard Rose, *Understanding Big Government: The Programme Approach* (Beverly Hills: Sage, 1984), p. 113.

30. Daniel Chirot, "The Corporatist Model and Socialism: Notes on Romanian Development," *Theory and Society* 9, 2 (1980), 378. On the importance of Manoïlescu see also Philippe C. Schmitter, "Still the Century of Corporatism?" in Schmitter and Gerhard Lehmbruch, eds., *Trends toward Corporatist Intermediation* (Beverly Hills: Sage, 1979), pp. 7–52.

31. Helmut Frisch, "Stabilization Policy in Austria, 1970–80," in de Cecco,

International Economic Adjustment, pp. 117–40; René Kästli, "The New Economic Environment in the 1970s: Market and Policy Response in Switzerland," in ibid., pp. 141–59. See also Marian E. Bond, "Exchange Rates, Inflation, and Vicious Circles," *International Monetary Fund Staff Papers* 27 (1980), 679–711; Niels Thygesen, "Exchange-Rate Experiences and Policies of Small Countries: Some European Examples of the 1970s," International Finance Section, Department of Economics, *Essays in International Finance* no. 136, (Princeton, N.J., December 1979); Eduard Hochreiter, "Theoretische und praktische Aspekte der Aussenwährungspolitik kleiner Länder," *Wirtschaftspolitische Blätter* 23, 3 (1976), 21–32; and "Tracking Europe's 'Small' Currencies," *World Business Weekly,* 2 March 1981, pp. 51–52.

32. Rainer E. Gut, "Trends in Foreign Exchange and Finance Markets as Seen from Switzerland," Crédit Suisse *Bulletin* 86 (Autumn 1980), 5–8.

33. Quoted in Paul Lewis, "The Austrian Economy Is a Strauss Waltz," *New York Times,* 22 March 1981, p. F8.

34. Ira C. Magaziner and Robert B. Reich, *Minding America's Business: The Decline and Rise of the American Economy* (New York: Harcourt Brace Jovanovich, 1982), p. 33.

35. Robert B. Reich, *The Next American Frontier* (New York: Times, 1983), pp. 121, 194. The methodology for making this calculation is explained in note 7, p. 296.

36. Jeffrey A. Hart, "Atlantic Riptides: Steel, Automobiles, and Microelectronics in U.S.-European Relations," manuscript (Bloomington, Ind., 1983), Chapter 1, p. 4A. These data are drawn from the World Bank Penetration Data Base.

37. Geoffrey Shepherd and François Duchêne, "Introduction: Industrial Change and Intervention in Western Europe," in Shepherd, Duchêne, and Christopher Saunders, eds., *Europe's Industries: Public and Private Strategies for Change* (Ithaca: Cornell University Press, 1983), pp. 6–7; Glenn R. Fong, "Export Dependence versus the New Protectionism: Constraints on Trade Policy in the Industrial World" (Ph.D. diss., Cornell University, 1983), p. 304.

38. Fritz W. Scharpf, *Economic and Institutional Constraints of Full-Employment Strategies: Sweden, Austria, and West Germany (1973–1982)* (Berlin: Wissenschaftszentrum IIMV/Arbeitsmarktpolitik, IIM/LMP 83–20, 1983), p. 6.

39. L. Tarshis, "The Size of the Economy and its Relation to Stability and Steady Progress," in E. A. G. Robinson, ed., *Economic Consequences of the Size of Nations: Proceedings of a Conference Held by the International Economic Association* (London: Macmillan, 1960), p. 199.

40. *Ithaca Journal,* 28 May 1981.

41. U.S. Congress, Joint Economic Committee, *Austrian Incomes Policy: Lesson for the United States,* 97th Cong., 1st sess., 2 June 1981 (Washington, D.C., 1981).

42. Rainer E. Gut, "Are There Any Swiss Lessons for the U.S.?" Crédit Suisse *Bulletin* 87 (Autumn 1981), 10.

43. Lore Scheer and Fred Praeger, "Austria in the Year 1979: How Austria Weathered the Economic Storm of the Seventies," United Nations University, HSDRGPID-30/UNUP-141 (Tokyo, 1980), p. 23. See also *Wall Street Journal,* 3 January 1984, p. 32.

44. Reich, *Next American Frontier,* p. 277.

45. Melvyn Krauss, "'Europeanizing' the U.S. Economy: The Enduring

Appeal of the Corporatist State," in Chalmers Johnson, ed., *The Industrial Policy Debate* (San Francisco: ICS, 1984), p. 72.

46. Suzanne Berger and Michael Piore, *Dualism and Discontinuity in Industrial Societies* (New York: Cambridge University Press, 1980), pp. 11–12.

47. Andrew Shonfield, *In Defence of the Mixed Economy* (Oxford: Oxford University Press, 1984). See also Shonfield's *The Use of Public Power* (Oxford: Oxford University Press, 1982), p. 104.

48. Robert A. Dahl and Edward R. Tufte, *Size and Democracy* (Stanford: Stanford University Press, 1973); Jane J. Mansbridge, *Beyond Adversary Democracy* (New York: Basic, 1980), pp. 293–98.

49. Mansbridge, *Beyond Adversary Democracy*, p. 293.

50. Theodore J. Lowi, *The End of Liberalism: The Second Republic of the United States*, 2d ed. (New York: Norton, 1979), pp. 127–63.

51. André Jaeggi, "Between Parliamentary Weakness and Bureaucratic Strength: Interest Representation in Swiss Foreign Relations" (paper prepared for the Workshop on Interest Representation in Mixed Polities, European Consortium for Political Research, Lancaster, England, 29 March–4 April 1981), p. 4.

52. Carol Major Wright, *Economic Adaptation to a Changing World Market* (Copenhagen: Munksgaard, 1939), pp. 244, 243.

53. Tony Carty and Alexander McCall Smith, eds., *Power and Manœuverability* (Edinburgh: Q Press, 1978); David B. Yoffie, *Power and Protectionism: Strategies of the Newly Industrializing Countries* (New York: Columbia University Press, 1983).

Index

Abert, James, 61
AFL-CIO, 53; view of industrial policy, 20
Agrarian party: in Norway, 142; in Sweden, 141
Anderson, Perry, *Lineages of the Absolutist State,* 179
Androsch, Hannes, 75
Austria, 60; corporatism, 10, 131–32; democratic development, 186–89; economic policies, 126, 204; economic success, 206; history, 138–39; incomes policy, 92; industrial policy, 27, 29, 69, 70, 74–78, 110, 187; Socialist party, 88–89; strong political parties, 28, 127. *See also* Habsburg Empire

banks, role in industrial policy: Austria, 77, 204; Switzerland, 175, 204; West Germany, 69
Behrendt, Richard, 36
Belgium: cooperative arrangements, 95; economic policy changes, 198; industrialization, 175; industrial policy, 67–78, 110, 118–19; moderate Left in, 163; political compromises, 143–44; PR in, 151, 155; textile and apparel industries, 58
Berger, Suzanne, 207
Bluestone, Barry, 18
Blum, Léon, 148
Boston Consulting Group, report on Swedish industrial policy, 64–67
Bourneuf, Alice, 40
Boyd, Andrew, 79, 195
Braun, O., 93
Brustein, William, 157, 158, 179
Bull, Edward, 177
business community, 125–26; and international politics, 176–77; and labor, 177–78, 180; varying structures, 105–23. *See also* multinationals

Cameron, David R., 97–98
capitalism, contemporary: "dependent," 201–2; economic policies, 23; political forms, 20
Castles, Francis, 97, 99, 168, 179
Cecco, Marcello de, 201
centralization, 33, 89; consequence of, 96; and policy, 90; variations in, 126
Chenery, Hollis, 84
Chirot, Daniel, 203
classes, 97; collaboration among, 136, 140–41; landed aristocracy, 158, 159, 160; peasant, 162–63, 164–65; working, 97, 98–100, 160–61, 163. *See also* labor movements; political groups and organizations
Coddington, George, 155
compromises: historical, 34–36, 141, 143, 147; political, 10, 32, 143–44, 173. *See also* corporatist compromise
consensus, 10, 34, 126–27, 208; strains on, 196
Conservatives, 151; in Denmark, 142, 152–53; in Norway, 143; in Sweden, 103
coordination of conflicting objectives, 33, 91–92; political bargaining, 92–93
Coppock, Joseph, 79
Córdova, Efén, 53
corporatism: definitions, 30; origins, 30, 38; three meanings of, 30–31. *See also* democratic corporatism
corporatist compromise: antecedents, 150; characteristics supporting, 189–90; dangers to, 208–9; in large states,

Library of Congress Cataloging in Publication Data

Katzenstein, Peter J.
  Small states in world markets.

  (Cornell studies in political economy)
  Bibliography: p.
  Includes index.
  1. Industry and state—Europe—Addresses, essays, lectures.
I. Title. II. Series.
HD3616.E8K37 1985   338.94   84-45796
ISBN 0-8014-1729-5 (alk. paper)
ISBN 0-8014-9326-9 (pbk. : alk. paper)